CUTS, PRIVATIZATION & RESISTANCE

To Michael,

Best Wishes
Dave Lowes
April 2013

CUTS, PRIVATIZATION & RESISTANCE

Neoliberalism and the Local State 1974 to 1987

David E Lowes

Merlin Press

First Published in the UK in 2012
by
The Merlin Press
6 Crane Street Chambers
Crane Street
Pontypool
NP4 6ND
Wales

www.merlinpress.co.uk

© David E. Lowes, 2012

ISBN. 978-0-85036-633-4

British Library Cataloguing in Publication Data is available
from the British Library

All rights reserved. No part of this publication may be reproduced, stored
in a retrieval system, or transmitted, in any form
or by any means, electronic, mechanical, photocopying,
recording or otherwise, without the prior permission of the publisher.

Printed in the UK by Imprint Digital, Exeter

CONTENTS

Preface	7
Abbreviations	9
Introduction	13

Part 1: Historical context, 1960-1979

Chapter one: The role of the local state	22
Chapter two: The neoliberal project	40
Chapter three: Labour movement activism	51

Part 2: Retrenchment and retreat, 1979-1984

Chapter four: The conservative agenda	68
Chapter five: The defence of local government	83
Chapter six: Liverpool as enigma	96

Part 3: The primacy parliament, 1983-1987

Chapter seven: The vagaries of rate-capping	112
Chapter eight: The campaign of non-compliance	127

Conclusion	141
Postscript	150
Appendix	151
Bibliography	153
Index	183

This book is dedicated to the men and women who, as local authority councillors in the twentieth century, strove to improve the well-being of working people and, for that reason, fell foul of the judge-invented doctrine of fiduciary duty.

PREFACE

The origins of this book can be found in a doctoral research programme that was completed in 1998. By that time, the struggles it investigated, described and analysed seemed to have receded from the stage of history or at least that is what we were led to believe. Recent developments, however, have given the study a new pertinence and another chance for the lessons of the past to be (re)learned. This applies equally to those who have not had first hand experience of the kind of events now unfolding and to others who, because they do not have to live with the consequences of their actions, are content to ignore the roles they play in the creation of tragedy and farce.

One of the programme's principal research aims was that any subsequent account should be honest and therefore include a clear admission of the author's value system and truth claims. This approach recognizes the reality that all subject matter is open to interpretation – especially if it deals with the way governments choose to affect the prospects and welfare of their citizens - and that even well informed conclusions are likely to be challenged by those who prefer to deal in opinion.

Similarly, spurious assertions about objectivity serve not only as an affirmation of the status quo, but also obscure the fact that an author's values will determine their choice of topic, as well as the methodology that informs their research practice and the presentation of findings. Any examination of socio-economic phenomena will also involve a reciprocal, maybe subconscious interaction between the researcher, their area of interest and the ideological forces pervading the society in which they live. In the case at hand, such factors include the development and influence of the neoliberal perspective, as well as its alternatives.

With this in mind then, let it be absolutely clear that this work is informed by a particular perspective. Stated briefly, it is the prioritization and fulfilment of human need and aspiration over and above doctrinal emphases on markets, profit and enrichment of the few at the expense of the many. Some may call this committed writing, others will consider it biased, but the fact remains that every one of us is influenced by value systems, whether we support or oppose them or even believe ourselves to be immune to them. If you doubt that this is true, you might wish to consider the person who, when disputing the validity of this point and without any sense of irony, remarked: 'I don't buy that'.

Acknowledgements

A debt of gratitude is owed to the many people who, for different reasons, have made this book possible. Most of them were either friends or colleagues in Liverpool NALGO during and after the period it covers. More specifically, I would like to thank the officers and staff of Liverpool NALGO Branch who afforded me unrestricted access to their records.

Ian Cook and Mike Mannin also deserve a special mention for their advice and encouragement in supervising the successful completion of my doctoral thesis and for their friendship and support in the years since. The research process was also assisted by Tony Byrne whose papers from the time were a vital source of original material. Most of all, however, there is only one person who knows how difficult it is to live with someone who does most of their research and writing on a part-time basis. So to Sarah, I say thanks for putting up with it all.

ABBREVIATIONS

The following abbreviations have been used in the text.

AES	Alternative Economic Strategy
AGM	Annual General Meeting
ALA	Association of London Authorities
AMA	Association of Metropolitan Authorities
ASTMS	Association of Scientific, Technical and Managerial Staffs
AUEW	Amalgamated Union of Engineering Workers
BEC	Branch Executive Council
CCLGF	Consultative Council on Local Government Finance
CCSU	Council Central Support Unit
CLP	Constituency Labour Party
CLPD	Campaign for Labour Party Democracy
COHSE	Confederation of Health Service Employees
CPS	Centre for Policy Studies
CPSA	Civil and Public Servants Association
DOE	Department of the Environment
DLO	Direct Labour Organization
DLP	District Labour Party
EETPU	Electrical, Electronic, Telecommunications and Plumbing Union
EZ	Enterprise Zone
FBU	Fire Brigades Union
FIG	Financial Institution Group
GDP	Gross Domestic Product
GLC	Greater London Council
GLLP	Greater London Labour Party
GMBATU	General Municipal Boilermakers and Allied Trades Union
GREA	Grant Related Expenditure Assessments

HFA	Housing Finance Act 1972
HRA	Housing Revenue Account
IEA	Institute of Economic Affairs
ILEA	Inner London Education Authority
IMF	International Monetary Fund
JSSC	Joint Shop Stewards Committee
JTUC	Joint Trade Union Committee
LEA	Local Education Authority
LGCCC	Local Government Campaign Co-ordinating Committee (sub-committee of TUCLGC)
LGCU	Local Government Campaign Unit
LGPLA	Local Government, Planning and Land Act 1980
LPAC	Labour Party Annual Conference
LSE	London School of Economics
MP	Member of Parliament
MPS	Mont Pèlerin Society
MTULMCC	Merseyside Trade Union and Labour Movement Campaign Committee
MTUURC	Merseyside Trade Union and Unemployed Resources Centre
NALGO	National and Local Government Officers Association
NATFHE	National Association of Teachers in Further and Higher Education
NDAM	National Delegate Advisory Meeting (NALGO)
NEC	National Executive Committee/ Council
NHS	National Health Service
NLACC	National Local Authorities Co-ordinating Committee
NLGC	National Local Government Committee (NALGO)
NLGGM	National Local Government Group Meeting (NALGO)
NSC	National Steering Committee Against the Cuts
NUM	National Union of Mineworkers
NUPE	National Union of Public Employees
NUT	National Union of Teachers
OCOF	Our City Out Fight (Liverpool NALGO Bulletin)
PLP	Parliamentary Labour Party
PSBR	Public Sector Borrowing Requirement

QGA	Quasi-Autonomous Governmental Agencies
QUANGO	Quasi-Autonomous Non-Governmental Organization
RCLGM	Rate-Capping Liaison Group Meeting (NALGO)
RPE	Relative Price Effect
RSG	Rate Support Grant
SCPS	Society of Civil and Public Servants
SGM	Special General Meeting
STUC	Scottish Trade Union Congress
TGWU	Transport and General Workers Union
TSG	Transport Supplementary Grant
TUC	Trade Union Congress
TUCLGC	Trade Union Congress: Local Government Committee
UCATT	Union of Construction Allied Trades and Technicians
UDA	Urban Development Area
UDC	Urban Development Corporation

INTRODUCTION

> I pondered ... how men fight and lose the battle, and the thing that they fought for comes about in spite of their defeat, and when it comes turns out not to be what they meant, and other men have to fight for what they meant under another name.
> William Morris, *A Dream of John Ball*, Chapter IV

For the second time in living memory, the well-being of ordinary men, women and children is the target of ruthless reductions in public expenditure and a deliberate degeneration of welfare provision. There are significant similarities between the current programme and its predecessor that ran from the mid-1970s to the mid-1990s, but also important differences. Regardless of what today's politicians might say about 'fairness', both examples involve the specific intention to engender economic privation and social austerity amongst sections of society that are least able to cope. As part of this process, welfare payments are limited to subsistence levels in order to 'make work pay' and the unemployed offered a choice between working for less than a living-wage or having assistance withdrawn.

If accompanying pronouncements are compared to historical antecedents, it is also evident that guarantees to protect the vulnerable amount to little more than modern-day parlance for Poor Law definitions of deserving and undeserving poor. An Act for the Relief of the Poor 1601, for example, included provision:

> for setting to work all such persons married or unmarried, having no means to maintain them, or no ordinary and daily trade of life to get their living by, and also to raise ... competent sums of money, for, and towards the necessary relief of the lame, impotent, old, blind, and such other among them being poor, and not able to work[1]

There is no need to look beyond recent history, however, to uncover the unspoken rule that the only way to deal with capitalist economic crisis – regardless of its causes – is to reduce the living standards of the working population or, in other words, increase the flexibility and reduce the cost of human labour-power. According to some commentators, this approach is also an antidote to levels of public expenditure that have apparently become a barrier to private investment, spending, jobs and therefore economic growth. The fact that such fundamentalist principles are and have been advanced by Conservative Party administrations lacking the legitimacy of an electoral mandate is but another element of continuity; albeit that they are dependent on Liberal support in the most recent example.[2]

Taken at face value, such prescriptions could be mistaken for sensible responses to the spending levels of previous Labour Party administrations. Indeed, they have been portrayed as such in the corporate media, but those accounts do not offer any serious analysis of the reasons for and solutions to the banking crises of 2009; let alone the underlying causes of recurrent capitalist recessions or the legitimacy of proposed remedies. In the modern era that runs from the early 1970s, the International Monetary Fund (IMF) has been a consistent advocate of like-minded approaches. Such solutions it has sought to impose on nations seeking loans to deal with balance of payments problems, include in its structural adjustment programmes, disguise as technical assistance and training, and promote as a panacea to the financial crises that have plagued the 1990s and early twenty-first century and are a consequence of its own policies.[3]

In Britain during the 1980s the strategy to reduce real wages involved an attack on the legal rights and organizational abilities of working people and their trade unions, through confrontation, legislation and unemployment. Just as the General Strike was deliberately orchestrated by a Conservative government in 1926, a series of disputes were prepared for and provoked once the government of the day was confident of its resolve to achieve desired objectives.[4] Acting in its role as employer, the Conservative government elected in 1979 adopted a hands-on approach in what was then the public sector and used the tactic as a precursor to privatization in its drive to undermine unions, pay and working conditions. Examples include the British Steel Corporation (1980), British Rail (1982), the Water Industry (1983) and the National Coal Board (1984-85).

Confrontations were also engineered in the Civil Service (1981) and the National Health Service (NHS) (1983), when the government blocked the involvement of the Advisory, Conciliation and Arbitration Service,[5] and again in 1984 when people working at the government Communication Headquarters in Cheltenham were banned from belonging to a trade union. These experiences, together with other lessons learned from private sector disputes, such as at Messenger Newspapers in 1983, were used to inform no less than six acts of parliament that contained provisions designed to restrict the freedom of trade unions.[6]

In what was effectively a vicious circle, the measures were made more potent by job insecurity associated with levels of unemployment that, in turn, had been made possible by the weakening of workplace organization. Thus, in 1982 the jobless total reached three million and, discounting the statistical manipulation of only recording people claiming unemployment benefit, as opposed to people seeking work, it did not fall below 2 million until 1997.[7]

Perhaps it is too early to tell for sure, but so far there have not been any official announcements of further anti-trade union legislation. There have, however, been uncannily similar calls made by the Conservative mayor of London, Conservative MPs and the Confederation of British Industry (CBI) for the law on strike ballots to be changed. While the mayor suggested that at least 50 per cent of all members should be required to participate in a ballot, the CBI demand that any majority should consist of 40 per cent of balloted members before industrial action is allowed to take place.[8] Despite the fact that Britain already has the most draconian trade union laws in Europe, the CBI went even further and presented ten additional demands that were clearly designed to emasculate the capacity of trade unions to represent the interests of their members.

The justification for this renewed assault is outlined in the report: Keeping the Wheels Turning: Modernising the Legal Framework of Industrial Relations, a significant aspect of which is its allusions to public spending cuts. In particular, the CBI expresses its overriding fear that financial restraint will be resisted by public sector workers who are faced with reductions in their pay and working conditions or with the prospect of losing their jobs altogether. Moreover, the disparity between union densities in the private and public sectors – 14.2 and 56.3 per cent respectively in 2010[9] – is considered to offer a distinct possibility that any such action could be effective. When the situation is viewed in the light of this report and the Institute of Directors repeated calls for an end to national collective bargaining,[10] it seems clear where any renewed attack is likely to be focused and why the present government is hell bent on privatizing and reducing, by any means possible, what remains of the welfare state.

This then is one of two main areas where there are significant differences between the present situation and the period and events that form the focus of this book. Today the trade union movement is, in general terms, much weaker than it was at the end of the 1970s. In 1979, for example, overall trade union membership stood at 13.2 million but by 2010 it had fallen to

6.5 million. Similarly, the Trade Union Congress (TUC) represented 54.5 per cent of the national work-force in 1978 compared to a union density of 26.6 per cent in 2010 which is irrespective of TUC affiliation.[11] One explanation for this disparity is the impact of anti-trade union legislation referred to above, but prior to the 1980s there had also been attempts to limit the ability of trade unions to represent the interests of their members; most notably the 1969 White Paper In Place of Strife and the Industrial Relations Act 1971.

In the 1960s and 1970s, however, trade union representatives and their members had the strength and determination to defeat such attacks. They also engaged in campaigns against redundancies and factory closures, including the occupation of the Upper Clyde Shipyard in 1971 and the Lucas workers' alternative economic plan developed in 1976. There were national strikes by Seamen in 1966, Dock workers 1970 and 1972, Miners 1972 and 1974,[12] and the rebellion against incomes policy toward the end of the 1970s, which culminated in the 'Winter of Discontent'. These and other factors, such as the growth of the activist movement, all contributed to the conclusion that the period was one of 'strong, confident, mobile and innovative trade unionism'.[13]

Understood with the benefit of hindsight, the struggles of the 1970s and 1980s mark the transition from social democratic to neoliberal hegemony in the domestic and global arena. At the international level this is indicated by changes to the outlook, direction and purpose of the Bretton Woods institutions - the IMF and the International Bank for Reconstruction and Development (World Bank) - from a Keynesian to neoliberal perspective. The defining features of the new orthodoxy have been summarized above and will be explored in more detail in Chapter Two. Suffice it to say here, therefore, that by seeking intellectual justification in the neo-classical economic traditions of the nineteenth century, advocates of neoliberalism stand accused of hypostatizing their chosen categories and concepts into laws that they believe to be true regardless of historical conditions.[14]

Of course, this did not stop governments in Britain, New Zealand and the United States all pursuing domestic variants of the same agenda during the 1980s and, partly as a consequence of the provisions of the Treaty of Maastricht 1992, deregulatory aspects of the approach have informed subsequent British government practice. The fact that we are now well and truly ensconced in the neoliberal era is the second significant difference between now and then, but it does not mean that the struggle is over, as resistance in Britain and elsewhere shows. While the terrain of individual battles might differ and the balance of forces is now weighted firmly in favour of the establishment position, it is nevertheless important to recognize parallels and draw attention to similarities. By proceeding in this manner it is possible to demonstrate that the continuing struggle for the core values of the welfare state still centres on the choice between a collectivist and individualist ethos.

In focusing on and exploring one particular aspect of the multifarious contests that accompanied the changes described above, this book offers a unique insight and therefore opportunity to develop the comparative process. Broadly speaking, this involves investigating the principles and practices of campaigns that were mounted against central government attempts to restrict local authority spending and centralize governmental decision-making in Britain during the 1980s. More specifically, it concentrates on local government in England and Wales and on the campaigning role played by Labour Party and trade union activists, leaders, members and officers as constituent sections of the labour movement.

Events are also examined within a specific historical context that begins with the expansion of local service provision and employment in the 1960s, covers retrenchment in the 1970s and early 1980s and concludes with campaigns against the provisions of the Rates Act later in the decade. As has already been mentioned, these developments span and can help illustrate the post-war pinnacle of collectivist welfare state provision and the move from social democratic to neoliberal doctrine. They also help show how factors which exert an influence at the local level can and will find expression in, through and against wider societal processes and that these, in turn, entail both domestic and global dimensions. Any other attempt at explanation should be treated with the utmost care.

This approach is developed and illustrated in the chapters that follow, where the way in which socio-economic developments informed the policy and practices of both government and labour movement are acknowledged and explored. There are, for example, obvious similarities between the approaches that both adopted toward changes in local democratic practice, but the level of uniformity also conceals a hidden dynamic. Namely, the extent to which the forces of dissent and resistance not only find ways to infiltrate and subvert local, regional and national state structures but also develop and utilize the corresponding geographic and functional strata of other organizations such as trade unions.

On one level, the clash of authority between national and local policy was fuelled by the degree of legitimacy that elections gave to alternative programmes and the values that inspired them. Indeed, the objectives of those sections of the labour movement that sought to resist and defeat the imposition of policies that lacked a local mandate were justified by the persistent claim to be defending local democracy. It would, however, be wrong to assume that such conflicts only occurred between the Conservative government and the labour movement. Just as important, if not more so, are the parallel struggles that took place within the Labour Party and trade unions and involved the conflicting aims, interests, tactics and priorities of local, regional and national structures, as well as those of activists, councillors, full-time officers, national and local leaders, members and MPs.

This book offers a fresh perspective by including such factors in the examination and explanation of the campaigns mounted against reductions in local expenditure, service provision and employment in the 1980s. Until now, the overwhelming majority of the sources that address the political activity of trade unions during the period have focused on the national level and, more particularly, on relations with the Labour Party when in government. Similarly, assessments of local Labour councils and their attempts to resist central government policy rarely investigate the relations between local Labour parties, Labour groups and local authority trade unions. Such accounts usually concentrate on the role of councillors and Labour groups rather than the local labour movement in general.[15]

In contrast, this study offers a vivid description of events and shows how people were involved in local campaigns as activists and full-time officers and describes their interaction with the Labour Party, central government and trade union structures at the national level. This includes an exploration of the activities of the National and Local Government Officers Association (NALGO), which reveals the responsive nature of its activist-led structures. At the time NALGO was not affiliated to the Labour Party and this, together with the participation of activists in the development of strategy, provided an added dimension through the consideration of industrial action as an extra-parliamentary means of achieving campaign aims.

To achieve these objectives, the book is divided into three overlapping parts and, including the Introduction and Conclusion, there are ten chapters. The first part consists of three chapters that delimit the historical context within which the campaigns against Conservative government policy and practice developed. In other words, the book begins with an examination of social, economic and ideological conditions that helped shape the environment within which the campaigns are to be placed, understood and explained.

As part of this process, Chapter One considers changing attitudes to the role and functions of local authorities in reference to the expansion of service provision, fluctuating employment levels and changes in the organization, purpose and practice of local democracy during the 1960s and early 1970s. Attention is also afforded to the way these areas were addressed by Labour governments between 1964-70 and 1974-79 and by the TUC during the period; thereby allowing subsequent analogies to be drawn with those elements of the local state that the labour movement sought to defend in the 1980s.

Chapter Two develops the theme of its predecessor, by charting and explaining the rise of neoliberalism at global and national levels. Domestically, for example, it shows how the realization of problems facing the British economy was accompanied by an increasing acceptance of fundamentalist fiscal analysis. Even before it approached the IMF in 1976, such prescriptions had been adopted by the Labour government and similar ideas had been gaining credence within the Conservative Party for several years. In other words, the chapter demonstrates how government policy and practice that materialized in the 1980s had its origins in the earlier conversion from Keynesian to neoliberal doctrine.

The third chapter completes the historical context by summarizing those developments in labour movement composition, outlook and practice that can be understood as having a bearing on later campaigns. More specifically, the expansion of local government trade unions and recovery of Labour Party membership are considered in terms of the growth of activism and the impact that this had on the struggles for democracy and accountability within the broader movement. The chapter and section are then brought to a close with an exploration of the role such factors played in campaigns against the increasingly neoliberal agenda of successive governments in the 1970s.

Part two also consists of three chapters which, when taken as a whole, develop the themes covered by its predecessor and shows how the diverging approaches to the role and funding of local government played out. Of primary concern are the Conservative Party's agenda, how this translated into central government policy and practice and the different responses it elicited from within the labour movement.

In this vein, Chapter Four pays particular attention to the Conservative government's dealings with local government in the areas of finance, deregulation and economic regeneration between 1979 and 1984. For certain local authorities, this meant reduced central funding, privatization, council house sales and a retreat from proactive economic stimulation. More importantly, these policy changes had detrimental implications for those working in local government, vulnerable people who depended on local services and for the practice of local democracy.[16]

Whereas the previous chapter considered local responses to the Conservative government's programme, the next provides the first focused analysis of attempts to build a national campaign of opposition and resistance. This includes coverage of endeavours to agree shared goals, an effective strategy for achieving them and some of the obstacles encountered. As part of this approach and in recognition of the importance attached to the differing leadership styles within the movement, the chapter concludes with an assessment of the alternative perspectives.

By way of contrast, Chapter Six considers the organization, practice and tactics employed in the campaign for more resources by the Liverpool labour movement between November 1983 and July 1984. Particular attention is paid to the impact of socio-economic similarities and differences between Liverpool and elsewhere and their implications for campaigning activity. Most notably, these include the role of activists and the approach of the parliamentary leadership of the Labour Party.

In part three, attention turns to the campaigns against rate-capping and therefore the culmination of opposition and resistance to those aspects of the neoliberal agenda covered thus far. These campaigns exhibit a degree of maturity, co-ordination and organization that is absent from the earlier, more disparate examples. This is partly a reflection of the fact that efforts were now targeted in one direction but also that lessons had been learned. The two chapters in this section therefore focus on a broader scale of operation and reflect the stages of opposing proposed legislation and resisting the provisions of the Rates Act.

Chapter Seven, begins by analyzing the aims and practices of the Conservative government. Attention then turns to the development of labour movement structures in the process of struggle and the respective involvement and positions adopted by parliamentary leaders, councillors, full-time officers and activists. Finally, Chapter Eight explores the campaign of non-compliance by evaluating its stated aims in reference to the practice of the labour movement. Of particular interest here are the conflicting demands and traditions of a party leadership that is wedded to the parliamentary process and those of activists who, in the final analysis, were prepared to use industrial action to defeat central government and overturn legislation.

These and previous findings are drawn together in a concluding chapter that summarizes and appraises the significance of the various tactics, aims and values that were evident throughout the period and also exhibited in the campaigns studied. The lessons learned are also appraised in the light of subsequent policy and practice.

PART ONE
HISTORICAL CONTEXT 1960–1979

These are signs of the times, not to be hidden by purple mantles or black cassocks. They do not signify that tomorrow a miracle will happen. They show that, within the ruling classes themselves, a foreboding is dawning, that the present society is not solid crystal, but an organism capable of change, and is constantly changing.
Karl Marx, *Capital*, Preface to the First German Edition

Chapter One
THE ROLE OF THE LOCAL STATE

> Because the reproduction of class societies is based on the privileged appropriation of socially produced wealth, all such societies must resolve the problem of distributing the surplus social product inequitably and yet legitimately.
> Jurgen Habermas, *Legitimation Crisis*, Part III

The period that extends, roughly speaking, from the end of the Second World War to the 1970s was one in which successive governments sought to facilitate continuous economic growth based on the accumulation of capital. In the immediate aftermath of war, this task was faced with three major challenges: the material reconstruction of industrial and urban infrastructure (housing, factories, offices, ports, road and rail networks etc.); funding the rebuilding programme; and, securing a reliable supply of wage-labour in terms of an adequate number of people and the avoidance of industrial disputes.

To a large extent, the way in which these problems were addressed was conditioned by the experiences of organizing the war-time economy. In short, this meant state intervention to nationalize key industries and resources, including the Bank of England in 1946, and the creation of a system of welfare based on the Report of the Inter-Departmental Committee on Social Insurance and Allied Services published in 1942.

The essential elements of the economic strategy had been formulated by academics recruited to the Economic Section after its creation in 1941 and included demand management, a mixed economy, planning, price and currency stability based on fixed exchange rates and full employment. In much the same way that the Report on Social Insurance and Allied Services has been associated with its author William Beveridge, these features are now inextricably linked with the work of John Maynard Keynes despite his death in 1946. This may be due to the fact that many of the economists who worked for the government during the war were opposed to state intervention before and after their involvement at this level.

All was not plain sailing however, as structural economic weaknesses such as a reliance on exports and the use of profits to fund private sector investment left economic performance vulnerable to price rises and falling profits. The out-workings of such problems became common features of the 1960s and 1970s with the end of the 'long boom' and unrest that was generated in part by the realization that post-war prosperity had not been distributed as evenly as had been believed.

These developments also had a number of consequences for the operation and organization of the local state during the period, ranging from responsibilities for infrastructural renewal and the expansion of welfare provision to administering retrenchment and managing the reaction to it. Of particular interest are the different labour movement responses to events in the periods of growth and contraction and this is best appreciated by exploring changes in service provision, employment and the practice of local democracy.

On one level, the importance of these categories for the labour movement is confirmed by their identification as areas worth defending from Conservative attack in the 1980s. They are also significant because of the underlying complexities and contradictions that they embody and which present problems for anyone attempting to understand the changes that affected the local state in the latter half of the twentieth century. This can be summarized in two questions that are crucial to the understanding of the events that unfolded during this period: to what extent were extensions in welfare provision part of a process designed to minimize the disruption of private sector production, while containing rank-and-file demands for greater access to political power; and, why was this so?

Local Services

From the mid 1960s to the mid 1970s, elected local government acquired new and expanded responsibilities for welfare functions, especially those relating to social care and infrastructure. Many of these are analogous to the demands of the labour movement and actions of Labour governments during the period. They are also identified as worthy of defence by Labour Party National Executive Committee (NEC) statements issued as Local Government Cuts in 1981 and Rate Controls in 1983 and can be summarized on this basis as affecting: schools; nursery provision and children in care or at risk; housing management and maintenance, including rent levels; residential homes, home helps, meals on wheels and other support for elderly, sick, or disabled people; and local infrastructure such as transport; street lighting, road-sweeping, refuse collection and environmental protection.

Before considering the extent to which changes were made as part of socio-economic programmes, it is worth noting that existing responsibilities faced greater demand due to demographic changes. These included an increase in the total population of Britain that affected both ends of the age spectrum. So much so, that by 1980 there were 1.5 million more retired people than there were in 1960 and between 1951 and 1971 the number of school children increased from 5.4 to 9.6 million.[17]

At one end, therefore, improved longevity translated into an increased need for home helps, home nursing and residential accommodation already provided by local authorities and for the specialized care of health problems related to old age. At the other end, the number of young people did not grow as a proportion of the national population, but an overall increase still had implications for the education system and for associated services such as school meals. Similar expansionary pressures were also evident in the fields of local authority care provision and children's homes.

Improvements in the effective provision of social services also had the cyclical effect of increasing life expectancy and this meant that more people became dependent on, or at least users of, the facilities available. Add to this changes in the recognition and categorization of pre-existing needs or, in other words, the broadening of existing definitions and the introduction of new ones and it seems clear why there is a consensual view that providing services to the young, old, ill and disabled became a primary function of elected local government.

Of specific significance here, is the fact that the expansion of responsibilities in these areas were legislated for by Labour governments as: the Children and Young Persons Act 1969; the Local Authority Social Services Act 1970; and, the Chronically Sick and Disabled Persons Act 1970. The Children and Young Persons Act, for example, added to and improved requirements that had been introduced by the Children's Act 1948 and it also enhanced the provisions of subsequent legislation that dealt with the care, maintenance and supervision of neglected children.

The growth of local service provision cannot, however, be explained by assuming causal connections between increased local expenditure and greater national prosperity or in terms of the needs and demands of an affluent society. The simple assumption that as the economy grows basic living needs are met more easily fails to explain why, in 1960, 7.5 million people were living in relative poverty, including three million older people and one in seven children.[18]

Likewise, the belief that welfare services expanded as the tax base grew, conceals a shameful secret that almost half of those who were considered to be living in poverty were also in paid employment. That wages were not enough to maintain an acceptable standard of living relative to the rest of society is an indictment of the social and economic system and one that is reinforced by the fact that thousands of children were placed in local authority care during the 1960s due to sub-standard housing.

If it is to have any credibility, even a summarized account such as this must look beyond external appearances and at least acknowledge the multiplicity of factors that can exert an influence over the use of available resources. Simply equating increases in the general wealth of society with a proportionate spending on welfare falls well short of recognizing that ideological and other factors inform inter-governmental policy and decision-making.

Such influences are evident in the political and administrative objectives that formed part of the post-war settlement between capital and labour and the development of the welfare state based on Keynesian political economy.[19] The fact that much of the pertinent primary legislation was enacted by Labour governments between 1945 and 1951 brings us back, neatly, to the link between the labour movement and those areas of provision identified above as expanding for demographic and other reasons.

The reports of the Labour Party Annual Conference (LPAC) and those of the TUC contain abundant evidence of the labour movement's interest in issues relating to services provided by local government and the welfare state in general. This can be illustrated by referring to two examples, the first of which dates to 1969 and involves both annual meetings approving motions that called for the early implementation of the recommendations made in the Report of the Committee on Local Authority and Allied Personal Social Services (Seebohm Report). Then in 1976 the General Council's report on the Social Contract 1976-77, records that: 'The TUC has always considered the steady growth of public expenditure as part of the social wage and part of the development of a socially just society'.[20]

The advances in welfare provision that were enacted by the Labour governments of 1964-70 are catalogued in the parliamentary reports to the LPAC, but these advances also serve notice of a cleavage that sits at the heart of the labour movement. According to the more radical, rank-and-file tradition, for example, the welfare state and 'social wage'[21] represent forms of socialist practice, redistributing wealth that, although created collectively, has been appropriated privately by employers, be they individuals or corporations. On this basis, demands for more resources made by those who sell their labour power in order to survive are met through a socialized subsidy from capital to labour that is administered by the state.

The alternative perspective is associated with individuals who are more likely to be motivated by a concern to ameliorate the excesses of the market whilst maintaining capital accumulation and profit maximization. This approach is identified with people who seek positions of leadership or see the movement as an opportunity to develop a career for themselves. Devoid of any transformative aspirations, this grouping relied on Keynesian devices to increase demand, generate economic growth and thereby fund welfare services.

Regardless of the original intention, however, local amenities that supported non-working sections of the population, such as schools and day centres, still became part of the income level of working people who would otherwise have had to pay for them or do without. Not entirely coincidentally, such services also had the effect of reducing demands on employers for wage increases to cover the cost of alternative arrangements.[22]

Another aspect of this inconsistency is apparent if education, housing and transport are understood as welfare services that also constitute parts of the local and national infrastructure. In other words, all three areas involve contradictions because they cater for the economic and social needs of people as workers, employers and as private citizens. Creating polytechnics in the 1960s and increasing the school leaving age to 16 in 1972, for example, provided opportunities for people to develop interests and fulfil their potential as human beings.[23] At the same time, such measures had the effect of training the workers of the future; as the Employment and Training Act 1973 demonstrates in its requirement for pupils who came under the auspices of Local Education Authorities (LEA) to be given vocational and training advice.[24]

If improvements to the local welfare state were to be genuine and sustainable, they also had to be accompanied by the building of new facilities and, more often, the renewal of old and dilapidated infrastructure. Given the size of the problems and the significant amount of investment required to redress them, projects acted as stimuli for local economies and formed an integral part of regeneration schemes. Many school buildings, for example, dated from the Victorian era, needed repair or replacement and, because education services accounted for nearly two-thirds of local authority expenditure and almost half of its employment, the scale of the task was daunting. This can be demonstrated by the post-war reconstruction or renovation of enough primary and secondary school buildings to accommodate as many as seven million pupils by 1974.

Similar developments took place in housing, with 9 million homes or nearly half the housing stock of Britain built between the Second World

War and 1978. By this time, local authorities were responsible for around one third of the overall total and consequently developed comprehensive housing management services. The welfare benefits of new and improved accommodation also had the added advantage of providing an economic stimulus and local authorities were therefore encouraged to increase their involvement in urban renewal and public sector construction. The home improvement grants scheme formed part of this process and was revised by the Housing Act 1969 which introduced an obligatory systematic appraisal of local authority housing standards in line with the recommendations of the Parker Morris Committee.

The third area of infrastructural renewal focused on the transport system that people use as workers and consumers to travel to places of employment, shops, leisure and personal development facilities. As part of this category, local government was responsible for building and maintaining 184,000 miles of local roads by 1974 and for overseeing a variety of local rail networks and bus services. In terms of road traffic alone, motorized transport rose from 2.5 million vehicles in 1945 to 18 million by 1977. This involved increased access to and use of private motor cars and a greater number of vehicles transporting freight: from 1.4 million in 1960 to 3.1 million by 1978. Consequential increases in planning, traffic management systems and policing were therefore required, as was the repair and replacement of Victorian sewers and bridges that were unable to cope with the new type and level of traffic.

Each of these functions can be understood as part of a Keynesian macro-economic programme for welfare provision that helped appease the short-term demands of the different and conflicting traditions within the labour movement. This was possible because, at a theoretical level, the two factors of production: capital and labour are interdependent. In other words, the creation of capital cannot take place without human labour power, so by reducing the price and enhancing the value of the latter, say through cheaper housing and better education, the costs of production are minimized and profit margins increased.

This last point explains why the approach was tolerated by corporate interests at least as long as welfare policy acted as an indirect subsidy that helped minimize wage demands, provide an educated workforce and install transport systems that allowed for the efficient movement of workers and products.[25] As is now well known, however, the socio-economic programme was increasingly found wanting, as arrangements over wages and employment levels began to unravel and international developments contributed to recurrent and ever worsening domestic crises.

Employment

Prior to the 1960s, the post-war goal of full employment had, by and large, been achieved through the application of the economic management devices already referred to. Without external interference, however, the fundamentals of the capitalist market mean that if there is a scarcity of labour-power its price will increase as a consequence of competition between employers. This in turn results in falling profit margins, rising inflation and balance of payment problems that occur when the amount of foreign currency generated through exports is no longer enough to cover the quantity of imported commodities. As the 1960s progressed, the consequences of these factors could be seen in the growth of unemployment at a time when welfare provision and public sector employment levels also grew. Although not determinants of each other, these developments were misinterpreted in some quarters as a simplistic dichotomy that depicted public sector expansion as the cause of private sector contraction.[26]

Once again, however, there is more to this than meets the eye. Each sector is made up of several constituent parts and in the case of the public sector this includes local government employment that can exhibit differences in the numbers and type of jobs depending on local circumstances. In order to appreciate the significance of the changes that took place in the amount and form of local authority employment, it is therefore necessary to consider a number of factors. These include the move towards mass, long-term unemployment, the regions affected by private sector contraction, the type of jobs lost and the effectiveness of local regeneration projects in this context. To begin with, though, it is helpful to take a general look at the extent to which local government employment grew in relation to the economy as a whole and as a proportion of the public sector.

Looking at the evidence that is available from a variety of sources, there is a generally held view that the number of people employed in local government almost doubled between the mid 1950s and mid 1970s; from 7 to 12 per cent of the national work-force and from 1.7 to 2.9 million jobs. Nevertheless, a word of caution is needed as the source figures do not always distinguish between elected local authorities and unelected regional bodies such as the electricity, gas, health and water boards. Similar reservations also apply to the classification of local government employment as a proportion of the public sector and to the assertion that it grew from 29 to 41 per cent over the same period.[27]

In spite of these caveats, it seems safe to conclude that there was a significant rise in local government employment in gross terms and as a percentage of national and public sector employment. This was not simply a consequence of the increased service provision described above, but was also due to the fact that education, policing, social work and local care workers deal with people and their problems. The intimacy of such services means that they are relatively labour intensive and offer only limited scope for technological development and the use of capital intensive machinery.

The increase in local government employment also reflects the values and approaches that prevailed at the time of service expansion and improvement. In other words, quality and effectiveness were measured in terms of worker to service-user ratios rather than the impersonal standards of cost, price or value for money. Enhancements to social services and education therefore translated into more home helps, the numbers of which rose from 6,000 in 1949 to 11,000 in 1975 and an increase in teachers from 344,000 in 1961 to 477,000 in 1971. Similar advances in the standards of other personal services were therefore a significant factor that contributed to higher levels of employment.

Curiously, however, the growth in jobs was not accompanied by increased labour costs as 'the relative price effect' (RPE) predicts. Stated briefly, the RPE hypothesizes that labour intensive industries will have to pay similar wages to those paid by firms that can increase productivity and profitability through the use of technology. This is premised on the assumption that pressures of comparability and inflation will encourage workers to demand wage levels that cannot be financed through increased output.

That local government wages and salaries accounted for similar proportions of current expenditure in both 1958 and 1978, was largely due to the use of low paid, part-time women workers. There was, for example, an overall increase in part-time employees of 224.7 per cent in the twenty years after 1952. More importantly though, this expansion masked the rise in part-time female employees from 15 per cent of the local government work-force in 1950 to 33 per cent in 1980; by which time women accounted for 91 per cent of part-time workers.[28]

The ability to fill part-time jobs was made easier by the expansion of welfare service provision at the local state level. In other words, part-time employment in the local community provided a much needed supplement to income, but also allowed unpaid domestic labour to take place as before. Such conjecture should not, however, be allowed to detract from the fact that women were poorly paid for doing arduous work and afforded little in terms of employment rights and working conditions. This is the reality that lay behind the state's capacity to expand service provision without increasing costs.

The nature and location of jobs such as school secretaries, school meals workers, office cleaners, home helps and carers in social service centres are also factors that helped minimize wages. More specifically, the people involved were slowly and reluctantly unionized and difficult to organize for trade union action due to their isolation and emotional attachment to clients.[29] This represents problems, not only in terms of organizing and mobilizing a fragmented work-force but also indicates some of the kinds of jobs that, in the face of mass unemployment, trade unions sought to protect in 1970s and 1980s when they focused on job numbers at the expense of pay and conditions.

As part of this process, the local state came to be viewed by both government and labour movement, as a means of mitigating the rise in unemployment that occurred between 1964 and 1976. In February 1972, for example, the TUC recommended that trades councils create Unemployment Committees to press local authorities to expand full-time and usually male employment through slum clearance, housing improvement schemes and council house building programmes. This move reflects discussions between the General Council and government ministers in December 1971 and appears to be designed to test the Secretary of State for the Environment's claim that the government was encouraging local authorities to use such schemes as means of regenerating local economies.[30]

In this instance, the government and TUC recognized that a local authority's infrastructural responsibilities are carried out through its capital programme and represent a major form of local investment, providing work for the local building industry, contractors and suppliers. To a certain extent, the approach also acknowledges the economic effect a local authority can have, often as the largest employer in a given area and certainly a major consumer of goods and services, such as insurance, new technology, stationery, building supplies, equipment and food for school meals. What it does not indicate is the scale of the problem faced and therefore the perspective in which the resources available to local authorities should be viewed.

As a first step toward an evaluation of this statement, it is useful to note how far regeneration initiatives developed in response to broader trends and priorities. While full employment was the norm, for example, local authority activity remained small-scale. Significant attempts at regeneration were generally focused on assisted areas and designed to support regional industrial policy. Once unemployment began to rise, however, a change in emphasis becomes apparent with local authorities adapting and re-interpreting particular legislative provisions to meet local needs.[31]

Then, with the advent of mass unemployment, came legislation that allowed direct local authority participation in economic regeneration. The Community Land Act 1975 falls within this category and provided the power and finances to acquire land for industrial development and to fund the provision of infrastructure for sale or lease to the private sector. Similarly, the Inner Urban Areas Act 1978 permitted local authorities to spend a greater proportion of funds on the regeneration of urban infrastructure and has been described as recasting the Urban Programme from a concern with welfare to regeneration.[32] Within two years of the 1978 Act, 30 approved authorities had declared 60 improvement areas and all were eligible for central grants of up to 75 per cent of expenditure levels that had been agreed by the Department of the Environment (DOE).

Nevertheless, there was a considerable disparity between the resources available and what, in post-war terms, was an unprecedented rise in unemployment from 260,000 in 1964 to 1.3 million in 1976.[33] To appreciate the complexity of this divergence, however, it is necessary to consider examples of the jobs involved and the importance of geographical location. As might be expected, activity was most evident in those areas affected by the ravages of economic decline, but variations still existed between the problems experienced, the resolve of those seeking solutions and therefore the nature of the alternatives considered.

Viewed on a superficial level, there seems to be an obvious parallel between the unemployment figures described above and the loss of almost two million manufacturing jobs between 1960 and 1980.[34] This observation is given more weight by the fact that mass unemployment was still the net result, even after the growth in local authority employment and attempts at regeneration are factored in. More specifically, the decline of manufacturing, in the aftermath of the oil crisis of 1973 and the ending of fixed exchange rates can be illustrated by referring to examples from the urban areas and authorities that participated in campaigning activity during the 1980s.

These include Manchester, which lost 20 per cent of its manufacturing base between 1966 and 1971, and Wandsworth, where roughly half of the manufacturing labour force disappeared between 1951 and 1971. Similar trends are evident in Sheffield, where the cutlery industry contracted from 30,000 workers in the 1950s to 5,500 by 1977. Sheffield City Council also estimated that between 1971 and 1983: employment in the City's steel industry fell from 45,000 to 18,000; the total number of steel jobs lost between Sheffield and Rotherham amounted to 35,000; and, 110,000 steel jobs had been lost in Britain during the period.[35]

The inadequate scale and effect of regeneration initiatives during the period is also shown by the total numbers of jobs lost and created in these areas. Looking at Manchester again, 35,000 jobs disappeared between 1966 and 1972, while only 11,000 were created. Similarly, in London as a whole, the employment base was reduced by about 500,000 between 1961 and 1974 and although 100,000 office jobs were created during the period, people who lost their jobs in manufacturing did not necessarily have transferable skills that were suited to clerical work.[36]

These facts put into perspective the idea that the increase in local authority jobs was not only a means of expanding local government services, but also a way of absorbing some of the jobs lost to the manufacturing sector. They also reflect the fact that initiatives which focused on small firms were inevitably small-scale, even if they were considered to be dynamic and offer the potential for rapid expansion. In Tyne and Wear, for example, the 35 nursery factory units built and let by the County Council in 1976 produced only 139 posts, while the 147 firms receiving grants and loans produced 967 jobs.[37]

The comparatively small numbers of jobs created indicate the level of resources available but also the type of activity involved in economic regeneration. Although temporary employment will have resulted from the construction or redevelopment of factories and other infrastructure, for example, the overall quality or numbers of jobs created was of secondary importance to the provision of sites and premises.

Likewise, the provision of grants for plant and machinery was primarily concerned with improving profit margins rather than maximizing the employment of people. In the final analysis, the goal of job creation was reduced to authorities and localities competing with each other to attract the same firms to their area. Instead of developing existing businesses and increasing the overall number of jobs, the net effect was that employers and their jobs simply moved between areas; usually to the ones offering the greatest financial incentives to their particular venture.[38]

The limited success of such schemes, especially in comparison to the move toward long-term mass unemployment, is one of the reasons why local authority jobs came to be regarded as so important. In the context of the continuing economic decline that blighted the 1970s and accelerated in the 1980s, local authorities often represented the main source of employment in a given locality. Even increasingly low paid and part-time jobs were worth defending when there was a dearth of employment opportunities in the private sector.

Motions submitted to the LPAC and TUC during the period demonstrate a growing concern at the levels of unemployment and recognize an interrelation between economic growth, employment and welfare provision. Although composites debated in 1964, 1971, 1972 and 1976 all made such a link and show the breadth of feeling, central government attempts to encourage economic revival fell short of their demands and those initiatives that did take place relied on local resolve and determination to pursue projects within a limited remit. In fact, changes to the organization and practice of local government during the period had the effect of exacerbating the problem by making elected councils less accountable and responsive to their constituents.

Legitimation

The inclusion of an element of elected representation gives certain local authorities the appearance of democratic accountability and autonomy in decision-making, but this is only a partial picture of the nature and purpose of government in general. Similarly, the practice of electing councillors varies from broader interpretations of democracy and this difference is reflected in what follows by use of the term 'constitutional local democracy'.[39]

For an elected body to have more than a mere appearance of self-government and independence, it must be able to exercise a degree of autonomy. Far from being an extension of some ancient right of self-government, however, locally elected councils are a nineteenth century innovation introduced in the wake of the Representation of the People Act of 1832. More specifically, the Municipal Corporations Act 1835 abolished closed corporations and replaced them with elected borough councils based on an all male electorate of ratepayers who had lived in the town for three years. Admittedly, there has been a gradual extension of the franchise since then, but some original features have been retained. These include: electing councillors for three years, annual elections for one-third of the council, councillors selecting a mayor for one year and a responsibility for social improvements.

To a certain extent, it is inevitable that the function and purpose of elected local government has changed over time and because of this there is little to gain from a debate about a perceived advance or decline in local democracy. More important are the effects which result from having an electoral process at the local level and how it relates to developments that take place. This is particularly true of the period covered by this and subsequent chapters when, even though local authorities remained politically and economically subordinate, their tasks moved from administration to government. The significance of this shift lies in the fact that it opened up the opportunity for individual councils to act as either an agent of the centre or as an obstacle to it through the independent formulation and practice of policies.[40]

For there to be a substantive governmental element, however, authorities had to be able to raise, collect and spend enough finance to make it possible for them to vary the level and quality of service provision. They were able to do this prior to the 1980s through the rating system and, as has already been noted, the interpretation of legislation. This afforded a degree of political and financial autonomy that gave local Labour groups, such as those in Clay Cross, South Yorkshire and elsewhere, the room to pursue policies that were premised on the validity of local mandates.

The ability to set local rates and levy supplementary amounts during the financial year effectively put spending beyond central control and established a self-reinforcing linkage with the perception of political autonomy. Furthermore, as local authorities operate within a legal framework that is premised on the granting of powers to act, the only thing they have to do is provide minimum standards in specified areas. Activity beyond this remit is ultra vires, but so long as they could raise their own funds and their electorate agreed there was nothing to stop them improving upon the standards set by central government, should they wish to do so.

This combination of revenue-raising powers with the flexibility to vary service provision, gave an appearance of self-government and helps explain why local authorities might be misunderstood as agencies that could be manoeuvred in any direction. The view was reinforced by successful struggles for improvements at the local level and, even if it was not possible for individual councils to secure long-term redistributive gains for working people, short-term advances certainly contributed to the legitimation of the local state and its functions.

When viewed in such a way, limited local autonomy can be understood as both a consequence and a means of dealing with the uneven development of capitalist society. The extent to which this involves giving local groups access to state power and authority is illustrated by the limited voting rights granted in 1835. The authors of that legislation could not have envisaged how far such rights would be extended, but they no doubt understood that in order for their interests to survive and develop, the laws of accumulation required them to broaden access to the state apparatus; even if this included groups that are potentially hostile to it.[41]

In this context, the labour movement can be considered to represent oppositional interests that were able to make limited gains through tax raising powers and policy variation at the local level. Regardless of other failings, advances in welfare and attempts at regeneration should be recognized as providing practical local benefits. Where such interpretations prevailed, as in Sheffield and South Yorkshire, it is possible to appreciate how and why some advocates for labour were motivated to defend as local democracy what others perceive to be repressive institutions.[42]

The significance of local funding needs to be kept in perspective, however, as an uncritical interpretation can overlook the subordinate status of local government or lead to false conclusions about the centralization of decision-making. In some quarters, for example, the allocation of funding during the 1970s was believed to be evidence of greater central control. This thesis was based on the fact that for every pound collected through rates local authorities received two pounds in government grant. In reality, however, the bald statistic that 50 per cent of local services were funded by central grants in 1973-74 does not demonstrate that the centre was able to dictate local policy.[43]

As with the postulated causal connection between increased local expenditure and greater prosperity, it is equally misleading to assume that a reliance on central grants represents a move toward centralization and therefore a reduction in relative autonomy. Whatever the purpose and level of central funding was, it still allowed for local discretion. In fact, the financial dependence of local authorities on central government did not produce demonstrable effects on policy choice in the sub-national system as local authorities were free to accept or ignore government directives.[44] Limits on local government spending, set since the 1960s by the Public Expenditure Survey Committee, were also exceeded on a regular basis using revenue raised from local rates.

The weakness of this centralization thesis can be illustrated by referring to the DOE's 1972 decision to alter the manner in which local transport was financed. In this instance and as part of the Conservative government's flirtation with neoliberalism, the funding system was transferred from a 'specific' to a 'block' grant scheme; a shift designed to reduce central government's detailed project control but increase its strategic control of resources and policy. The move to a block grant meant that authorities had the discretion to devise their own policy and programme, albeit with the proviso of a central veto, and were therefore allowed a degree of autonomy within overall limits. Similarly, detailed control over local authority capital expenditure was relaxed in 1970, with the introduction of an annual block loan sanction. This replaced the previous practice of central government approving individual projects, though direct control was retained in the key areas of education, housing and social services.[45]

In this case, the distinction between strategic and detailed policy control is the crucial issue. Outright centralization would have employed specific grants as stimuli for particular activities and given central government direct control. By 1973, however, the use of specific grants had been restricted to 47 areas and these accounted for 10 per cent of grant payments. The move toward block grant and the absence of any concerted attempt to control local rate levels therefore gave local authorities room for manoeuvre and a perception of local autonomy. Likewise, because Rate Support Grant (RSG) was calculated on the previous year's spending, this meant that local authorities were able to increase next year's level of central funding by spending more.

The subtleties of these processes need to be appreciated if the perception of autonomy and local democracy is to be understood. Local authorities may have used central funding as opposed to rates to pursue projects, but this does not necessarily imply a form of central control. If as some suggest governments in the 1960s and 1970s pursued a deliberate political programme of expanding local spending while minimizing costs to local tax-payers,[46] this was a process of encouragement that compares favourably to the attempts at coercion and control adopted during the 1980s.

There is therefore little to be gained from trying to use financial support as a way of measuring or exploring constraints that the centre was able to impose on localities during this period. An analysis of changes to the organization of local government in the 1970s, on the other hand, offers a much more fruitful line of enquiry. The re-organization that took place in England and Wales, for example, served to shape the organization and practice of constitutional local democracy by restructuring elected and unelected local government and revising the distribution of functions between each level. These changes also addressed issues relating to size, efficiency, councillor calibre and decision-making and had the aim of encouraging more acceptable forms of policy and practice.

In addition to more than 440 elected local authorities in England and Wales after re-organization, there were also 85 unselected quasi-autonomous governmental agencies (QGA) by 1975. More importantly, the creation of QGAs usually involved the transfer of powers from local authorities, such as in the post-war nationalization of gas and electricity supply. This process of transferring local government responsibilities beyond the influence of local electors has a long history that includes: creating the Unemployment Assistance Board in the 1930s; appointing Regional Hospital Boards and Hospital Management Committees in the 1940s; setting up Regional Economic Planning Councils to bypass local structures in the 1960s; and, establishing regional water authorities in the 1970s. Whatever the official reasons for such changes, they effectively put decision-making in the hands of central government, professionals and private sector interests and beyond the reach of the hoi polloi.[47]

The assumption that elected local government is democratic simply because elections are held annually is based on one of two premises: an electoral chain of command theory whereby voters sanction councillors and officers to act on their behalf; or, a belief that popular participation is evidence of democracy in action. Taking the second argument first, the reality is that voter participation in local elections is low in comparison to that of general elections. Between 1973 and 1978, for example, the average turn-out in contested Metropolitan County elections was 39 per cent, while the highest average was 52 per cent in Welsh District elections. These figures are in sharp contrast to an average of 76 per cent for general elections between 1951 and 1987, but both sets of figures are misleading as they are percentages of those who bothered to register to vote.[48]

Even though some individual areas witnessed higher levels of electoral turn-out at particular times, local government was not a thriving example of participatory democracy. Claims to legitimacy based on a universal franchise are equally questionable, especially in the absence of any effective means of voters influencing local decision-making between elections. Perhaps a more accurate depiction would reflect the Burkean view that councillors are representatives who act in the best interests of all their constituents, regardless of whether they voted for them or for anyone at all.

Paradoxically, the argument that local authorities moved from administration to government is at odds with the trend in the 1960s and 1970s for local government to become concerned with the technical needs of service delivery, rather than democratic participation. The parameters of such developments, which included issues relating to the optimum size and efficiency of local authorities and councillor calibre, were informed by the findings of the Committee on the Management of Local Government that ran between 1964 and 1967 and the Royal Commission on Local Government between 1966 and 1969.

The report issued by the Commission equated local authority size with improved democratic practice, technical proficiency and professionalism as opposed to popular participation. Whereas the categories of democracy and efficiency are not mutually exclusive, the creation of bigger authorities with greater powers and control over local policy and finance had the effect of reducing councillor influence, participation and therefore electoral representation. The new local authorities were also criticized for being too big, too political and subject to vested interests.[49]

The terminology used to justify local government reform concealed a real concern to curtail working-class representation on locally elected bodies; especially when the euphemisms of 'efficiency', 'councillor calibre' and 'vested interests' are used. Sometimes, however, this agenda is brought to the fore in rare moments of candour, as was the case in some of the oral evidence given to the Royal Commission on Local Government in London 1959, when the fragmentation of working-class representation on local authorities was advocated.[50]

Similar objectives were also behind those changes to the internal operation of local authorities that had the effect of limiting the opportunities for back-bench councillors to influence the formulation and implementation of policy. The introduction of new management techniques under the guise of: planning, programming or budgeting systems; policy planning; corporate planning; and, corporate management, for example, ensured that detailed policy decisions were made on the advice of officials in committee and then rubber stamped in the council chamber. In other words, the apparent concern with administrative efficiency and the introduction of distinct management techniques had the effect of marginalizing back-bench representation, focusing power on the political leadership and senior officers and therefore reduced accountability and democratic participation.

An analogy can be drawn between this process and the recession of decision-making from parliament into cabinet and civil service, as the franchise was extended in the nineteenth and twentieth centuries. This move is also in keeping with the proposals made in Report of the Committee on the Management of Local Government to introduce cabinet style government into local authorities and the desire to remake local authorities in a corporate image.[51]

To the extent that the reforms were consistent with the parliamentarist idea that councils could be used to implement policy from above they provoked little overt opposition from the labour movement; apart from isolated examples of local resistance such as in the case of the re-organization of London County Council in the 1960s. This positive attitude also found reflection among trade union members who welcomed the chances for re-grading and enhanced career opportunities that often accompanied re-organization.[52]

Where opposition to the creation of the Greater London Council (GLC) in 1963 and the Conservative government's proposals in 1972 came to the surface it reflected fears that the moves would break up the Labour Party's urban power base by merging the existing authorities with the suburbs. Although the Labour Party's opposition was ostensibly motivated by self-interest, the fact that working-class voters formed its core constituency adds weight to the argument that re-organization was designed to restrict the access of such interests to political power.⁵³

The lack of Labour Party opposition can also be understood in terms of a declining commitment to, and interest in, local democracy. The Labour governments of the 1960s, for example, were exponents of 'technocratic collectivism', extolling the virtues of efficiency and professional competence; a view associated with the Fabian traditions of the Party. There should therefore be little surprise that many of the re-organization proposals and the practices which reflect them emanated from the Royal Commission that had been given its remit by a Labour government in 1966 or that its findings were welcomed by the Party. The TUC, on the other hand, though generally in favour of the re-organization proposals, still valued a degree of autonomy for local authorities.⁵⁴

The foregoing discussion should not be mistaken for an attempt to provide a detailed definition or understanding of the nature, purpose or origin of post-war local government in England and Wales. On the contrary, the intention has been to offer a critical synopsis of those areas that the labour movement sought to develop. This has served to demonstrate the complexity of the concepts involved and support the assertion that the ambiguities and contradictions are best understood as the product of a 'historically emerging, changing, and contradictory class relation'.⁵⁵

Regardless of any perception to the contrary, the welfare functions of the local state were premised on a Keynesian political economy that was designed to facilitate capital accumulation and profit maximization. By choosing this business model, the leadership of the labour movement had, in effect, subscribed to a fundamental acceptance of the existing socio-economic arrangements and relations of post-war capitalist society; albeit with an ameliorative element. For evidence of this, there is no need to look further than the willingness to base welfare provision on poorly paid jobs with pitiful employment rights.

Some advances were possible at the local level, where there existed a degree of organization and determination necessary to utilize the opportunities afforded by revenue raising powers and the transient legitimacy bestowed by electoral mandates. On the whole, however, when such developments were achieved measures were taken to first limit any gains and then prevent repetition. Nevertheless, this social democratic incrementalism at national and local levels had the effect of undermining the very processes of accumulation that such concessions had been intended to secure. As a result, the ensuing economic malaise provided the opportunity for fundamentalist prescriptions to be developed and promoted under the slogan: 'there is no alternative.'

Chapter Two
THE NEOLIBERAL PROJECT

> Earlier in the twentieth century some critics called fascism 'capitalism with the gloves off,' meaning that fascism was pure capitalism without democratic rights and organizations. In fact, we know that fascism is vastly more complex than that. Neoliberalism, on the other hand, is indeed 'capitalism with the gloves off.'
> Robert McChesney, *Profit over People*, Introduction

If the preferment of neoliberalism as the modus operandi of international political economy is depicted as a revolutionary calendar, 15 August 1971 would be day one, month one, year zero. On that day the United States government took the unilateral decision to stop overseas central banks and governments converting dollars into gold. In part, this was recognition that the Federal Reserve did not have enough gold bullion to exchange for the number of dollars in circulation. The move was also one of several measures designed to address problems stemming from the US dollar's role as the global reserve currency and the government's military and economic competition with the Soviet Union. Stated briefly, these obligations resulted in the US running simultaneous balance of payments and balance of trade deficits as it attempted to reconcile short-term domestic and long-term international policy objectives.

This decision was significant on a number of levels, but first and foremost it marked the beginning of the end of the regulation of international financial transactions under the Bretton Woods System.[56] Of course, the move was taken with the tacit approval of the other major capitalist economies, but because the United States acted as the mainstay of the system - the dollar was the principal currency used to underwrite trade and Western European economic recovery was funded by the Marshall Plan – this action proved to be a determining factor for the future of international economic policy.

In terms of post-war political economy, these developments also signalled a shift from Keynesian orthodoxy to monetarist and neoliberal hegemony;

confirmation of which was evidenced in 1976 when the articles of the IMF were amended to allow floating exchange rates. As the delay of five years indicates, this was not some kind of spontaneous or damascene conversion, but was the outworking of a longstanding campaign to demonize certain forms of regulation and intervention. Although not necessarily apparent at the time, the enthusiasm with which this new dogma was accepted in Britain was to have devastating implications for sections of its population and for the welfare state.

To really understand what lay behind the events that are to be recounted in subsequent chapters, it is necessary to first trace the history of neoliberal theory. By proceeding in this manner, it is possible to identify the relevance of such thinking to the formulation of Conservative Party policy during the 1970s and its practice in the following decade. Equally important is the fact that the same approach helps to show how and why the participants in the Labour governments 1974–79 were predisposed to accept the elemental conclusions of a regressive ideology.

Resurrecting Liberalism

For the purposes at hand, there is little to be gained from an attempt to narrate the development of liberalism in general. What is necessary here is an understanding of how and why in the first half of the twentieth century attempts were made to reformulate and popularize selected liberal traditions that originated in the eighteenth and nineteenth centuries. That particular project is all the more fascinating due to its complicated lineage and, although supported in Britain, France, Italy and beyond, the main strands of thought are associated with three universities, at least one of which dates back to the nineteenth century.

Whereas the University of Vienna constitutes the latter example, the universities of Freiburg and Chicago are the other main centres for the promulgation of neoliberal ideology. Their overall influence can be traced from the 1930s to the present day and, although there is a degree to which personnel and ideas overlap, this particular diaspora of opinion should not be perceived as a uniform prospectus. The other institution that has exerted an important influence on the movement's development is the Mont Pèlerin Society (MPS). Formed in April 1947 following a conference convened in the eponymous Swiss resort, the MPS has provided a forum through which representatives of the varying strands meet and exchange views on the perceived dangers of state intervention and planning.[57]

Prior to the Second World War, and in view of the diversity of ideas, the faction is more easily defined in general terms by referring to its negative motivations; what it opposed rather than what it advocated or stood for. To this end, the main themes can be identified as opposition to: macro-economic government intervention; remnants of a war economy in 1920s Europe, Keynsian aspects of the New Deal response to economic crisis in the United States during the 1930s (including full employment, a redistribution of income and wealth and social service provision); the command economy of the Soviet Union; and, the practices of National Socialism in Germany.

In addition to these generalities there are a number of common themes which, when considered together, can be proffered as an outline of neoliberal theory. In other words, there are examples of both positive and negative analysis and prescription that are best understood, not as a coherent theory of the state, but as an exposition of: optimal governmental practice, fundamental economic tenets and coercive welfare policy. Rather than survey all recommendations, the focus here is on those ideas that were associated with the institutions identified above and that also had a particular resonance in British governmental policy and practice during the 1980s.

First and foremost among these is a selective distrust of state control, intervention and planning. This is based on the premise that it is impossible for human beings, whether individually or collectively, to comprehend the simultaneous operation and interaction of domestic, international and global economic processes. From this starting point springs an essentially economistic view of the world that sees government intervention as irrational, unless it is designed to promote the free rein of economic forces. This is not good old fashioned laissez faire et laissez passer, however, but a more sophisticated approach that, instead of rejecting state intervention outright, advocates it in a particular form.[58]

According to this interpretation, the primary role of government is the organization of society in ways that allow the competitive mechanisms of the market to reach their hypothetical potential. In the world of ideas then, state intervention is only rational if it is designed to create a legal framework within which a preferred form of market competition can operate and flourish. One conclusion of this process was evident in the 1980s when legislation designed to curtail the rights of trade unions had the effect of making courts the arbiters of economic disputes. This legalistic approach had other significant consequences that include: minimizing the overt role of government in economic management; reducing the democratic control of economic policy and decision-making; legitimizing state intervention as a function of the judicial system; and ultimately making the balancing of revenue and expenditure a government's main function.

The preoccupation with balanced budgets stems from the preference for a fiscal policy in which control of the supply of money is the central weapon for combating inflation and securing price stability. Put another way, reducing inflation is considered to be a prerequisite in the pursuit of stable business cycles, balance of payments and sustained growth. Although this approach originated at the University of Vienna, from the 1950s onwards it has become inextricably linked to the rehabilitation of the Quantitative Theory of Money by academics in Chicago University's economics department.

Under this thesis, government is afforded the role of regulating the amount of money circulating in the economy, but it is tasked with deregulating just about everything else and leaving market mechanisms to resolve economic and social problems. It therefore follows that macroeconomic policy should be left to employers who, according to a strand of thought associated with the Freiburg tendency, represent a safeguard against centralization. This position was also developed to include a preference for small to medium sized firms that, due to their non-proletarian nature were believed to militate against the development of class-conscious workers.

As Chapter Four will make clear, these and other features bear comparison to governmental practice in the 1980s when: interest rates and unemployment were the main tools used in attempts to control inflation; subsidies were withdrawn from large scale manufacturing industry; and, the illusion of property ownership was promoted through owner-occupation and the sale of shares in privatized corporations. Although flirted with and encouraged for those who could afford private insurance, the goal of privatizing collectivist based guarantees of social security against the risks of illness, accident, old age and unemployment proved to be impractical.[59]

The proposition that people should be responsible for making arrangements to protect themselves and their families is founded on an individualistic interpretation of human nature that, perversely, needs to be encouraged. Private insurance is therefore made attractive by providing tax breaks to those who can afford it and for those that cannot state transfer payments are set at the minimum required for human subsistence. This latter contrivance is expected to be resolved in the longer term, however, as hoped for economic growth helps to make insurance affordable.

Although not immediately obvious, there is an inextricable link between privatized welfare provision, the agenda of financial deregulation and the drive towards balanced budgets. Following on from the removal of capital controls and the dismantling of the Bretton Woods System, for example, governments have been deterred from increasing personal and corporate rates of taxation for those who can transfer their assets abroad. Once this revenue raising option has been removed, a balanced budget can only be achieved by reductions in welfare spending and by the privatization of state assets.

The implications for democratic control and accountability are well documented,[60] but for the advocates of the Public Choice sub-strata of neoliberalism - also known as the Economic Theory of Regulation - the curtailment of elected government is only to be welcomed. According to this hypothesis elections allow interest groups to shape laws and legislation for their own benefit, unless, that is, they are checked by a legal constitutional framework. Once again, the nineteenth century is the point of reference and the British state with its limited voting rights is held up as the ideal independent guarantor of individual rights. This role is believed to have been usurped, however, due to the extension of the franchise and ensuing struggle between classes for control and use of the state apparatus for their own benefit.[61]

As a remedy it is proposed that, in line with other neoliberal prescriptions, state activity should be restricted to providing the conditions for private enterprise to produce commodities and services. Above and beyond this primary role, state involvement in the provision of services would only be allowed to take place where it is impossible for individuals to make private arrangements or private investment would be unprofitable. At the root of this dogma is the belief that state intervention will inevitably result in a self-perpetuating bureaucracy that suffocates economic innovation and growth.[62]

The concept of bureaucracy is very precisely defined, however, so that only those bodies which are financed by grant or appropriation are to be counted. Private corporations are therefore excluded from the definition and exonerated from any suspicion of exerting a distorting influence on the state. That evil is attributed to universal suffrage which is believed to encourage vote maximizing strategies that result in imperfect, selfish, group oriented policies. The remedy for wasteful, inefficient, budget maximizing and empire building bureaucrats is therefore the introduction of competition through the privatization of functions and the restriction of budgets.[63]

With the exception of Public Choice advocates the local state is afforded little specific attention by neoliberal theorists in general. Nevertheless, certain common principles are discernable in the approach that the Conservative Party adopted toward local government in the early 1980s. These include a self-help ideology, privatization, a change in the type and direction of economic intervention, reductions in welfare and social service provision, restricted budgets and limited revenue raising powers. Curiously, however, given the consistent distrust of vested interests, this came about due to the successful struggle of a small but dedicated group of advocates.

Conservative Liberalism

Although the main centres of neoliberal thought were situated in continental Europe and North America, it should not be presumed that economic liberalism was alien to Britain. On the contrary, there is an extensive liberal tradition that has its roots in the nineteenth century and, it should not be forgotten, is one that includes both Beveridge and Keynes. This heritage was largely obscured after the Second World War as political parties attempted to disown the ideas that led to and exacerbated the effects of the Depression and blighted the lives of working people in the 1930s.

At the London School of Economics (LSE), on the other hand, pre-war support for neoliberal prescriptions was maintained and developed by the likes of Lionel Robbins, Arnold Plant and von Hayek, who had links to other advocates through the MPS. Due to memories of inter-war privation, the effectiveness of war-time economic planning and the electoral success of parliamentarist social democracy, however, the LSE remained an isolated outpost in Britain; at least as long as mainstream academia, business organizations and governmental decision-makers favoured a corporatist approach.

As a consequence, the case for neoliberalism was only promoted by fringe groups like Aims of Industry and the Institute of Economic Affairs (IEA), established in 1942 and 1955 respectively. With links to the main centres of liberal economic thought in Europe and the United States, the latter organization engaged in a concerted effort to promote its case through the publication of pamphlets and papers like the Hobart series. The IEA was eventually joined in its endeavours by the Centre for Policy Studies (CPS) in 1974 and the Adam Smith Institute 1977. By which time, what was once an eccentric concern had begun to gain credence in the higher echelons of the Conservative Party.

Throughout its history and certainly since its modern inception under Robert Peel, the Party has been home to a variety of interests and ideas including those of the landed aristocracy, laissez faire liberals, social reformers, imperialists, corporatists, authoritarians and paternalists.[64] During the first half of the nineteenth century, however, the issue of free trade underpinned arguments for and against repeal of the Corn Laws and personified the differences between landed interests and economic liberals. Indeed, the Party split over the issue in 1846 and since then the influence and relevance of the latter grouping has waxed and waned according to time and circumstance.

The legacy of these traditions is evident in post-war publications such as the Industrial Charter and The Right Road for Britain which, in spite of embracing full employment and the welfare state, portrayed the role of government as supporting free enterprise, individual liberty and the free market. On the margins, therefore, the prescriptions of the IEA and others found favour not only with mavericks like Enoch Powell, but they also resonated with traditional party concerns about sound finance, efficiency, taxation, thrift and self-reliance; not to mention the perceived inconvenience of state intervention, economic planning and trade union rights.

The emphasis on markets also struck a chord with both liberal and authoritarian strands. For the former, the idea of a free market is equated with individual liberty defined as the absence of constraints, while for the latter it can be viewed as an instrument for imposing social order and discipline. Both factions also share a common antipathy towards the welfare state, full employment and organized labour that are seen as strengthening the position of those seeking employment and therefore distorting markets and economic performance.

For as long as the effects of related policies remained a lived experience, the encumbrance of universal suffrage and general elections meant that such views were confined to a cabal of politicians, academics and journalists. This was still true even when, following a review of the party's programme during its first period of opposition for over a decade, the 1970 general election manifesto exhibited a decidedly neoliberal emphasis when outlining policy objectives for the economy, industry, welfare, health, public finances and trade unions.

The draft of 'A Better Tomorrow', the Party's General Election manifesto, had been discussed at a meeting of the Shadow Cabinet held at the Selsdon Park Hotel in January 1970, and this location was to hold significance for the supporters of the document's neoliberal contents. In particular, their influence is evident in references to facilitating 'private provision in health and welfare', reducing and reforming taxation, pursuing 'a vigorous competition policy', 'creating an economic climate which favours, and rewards, enterprise and efficiency', 'reductions in the weight of government spending' and 'establishing fair, up-to-date rules for industrial relations'.

Once in government, these commitments were translated into reductions in housing subsidy under the Housing Finance Act (HFA), the creation of a special court to rule on industrial disputes by the Industrial Relations Act and the introduction of value added tax and public expenditure cuts. To the dismay of some Conservative MPs, however, within a year of taking office the government had abandoned its pledge to end subsidies to 'lame duck industries', had nationalized Rolls Royce and intervened to provide funds for the Upper Clyde Shipyard. To add insult to injury, the 1972 budget also made provision for £1.2 million tax cuts, regional development grants and increased spending on social policy and education in an attempt to stimulate economic activity.

Though a minority opinion within the Conservative Party, the response of the core wing of neoliberals was to seek and secure a profile that was disproportionate to their numbers and influence.[65] As part of this strategy two subject committees of the Parliamentary Conservative Party were targeted and as a result Nicholas Ridley was elected Chairman of the Finance Committee and John Biffen Chairman of the Industry Committee. Each coup only lasted for a short period in 1972, however, and was followed by the publication of a Memorial to the Prime Minister under the nom de guerre of 'economic radicals'. Ostensibly anonymous, Richard Body MP was identified as an author of the document that pinpointed the supply of money and government borrowing as the cause of high inflation and excoriated the use of voluntary incomes and prices policies.

This critique gained momentum with the founding of the Selsdon Group in September 1973, the election of Rhodes Boyson as a Conservative MP in 1974, the conversion of Keith Joseph to the cause, the founding of the CPS and the election of Margaret Thatcher as leader of the Party in 1975. Thatcher and Joseph were both instrumental in the creation and operation of the CPS, but the development and presentation of the neoliberal prospectus in a coherent form can be traced through the Party's 1970 General Election manifesto, Nicholas Ridley's Selsdon Group Manifesto (1973), the policy document The Right Approach (1976) and the General Election Manifesto (1979).

The broader emphases on using the supply of money to control inflation, removing subsidies from food and housing, reducing public spending and restricting the role of the state had general implications for local government. Alongside these, however, were specific goals for the operation of local authorities. These included the sale of council housing, extending the role of the private sector in providing welfare, education and local infrastructure, reducing the operation of Direct Labour Organizations (DLO) and introducing cash limits on some local authority funding.

Once the Party was elected in May 1979, it began to put these policies into practice, with serious consequence for local authority workers and the services they provided. These and other implications are considered in

Chapter Four, but while the Conservatives were undertaking a wholehearted conversion, the Labour Party was having its own flirtation with certain neoliberal prescriptions.

Labour Accommodation

While the following chapter affords a fuller analysis of the divergent trends within the Labour Party and broader movement, in the present context it is worth understanding how and why a Labour government was willing to adopt aspects of the neoliberal agenda. To begin with, the detail and complexity of the Public Expenditure Survey Committee report dated June 1974 shows the challenge that would have faced the incoming government if it had wished to follow a programme that was diametrically opposed to that of its predecessor. As most of the senior members of the government had held office before, however, it seems unlikely that this would have been either a surprise or an obstacle.

With this in mind, it should be remembered that for the new administration to be put off by the size of the task faced, it would first need to have a specific programme that it intended to implement, or at least an intention to carry out the commitments made in its election manifesto. So as to leave nobody in any doubt about the new government's intentions, however, the Chancellor's Budget statement delivered on 26 March 1974 confirmed that it would not be reversing the reductions announced by the Conservative government in its December White Paper on public expenditure.[66]

The incoming administration also allowed the reorganization of the Treasury to proceed along the lines decided on by its predecessor in October 1973. This was particularly significant since it entailed the creation of a separate Monetary Policy Group and other measures that affirmed the preference for deflationary policy options among senior Treasury officials. These included the elevation of counter-inflation strategy to a central aim of government policy and focused it on the control of the supply of money. Also important was the transfer of responsibilities for the co-ordination of fiscal policy and budget preparation from the National Economy Group and the Policy Co-ordinating Unit to a new Central Unit in 1975.[67]

This overall approach was also being confirmed by Labour ministers even before the White paper 'The Attack on Inflation' was presented to Parliament in July 1975. Joel Barnett, Chief Secretary to the Treasury, for example, had claimed in May that the public sector used more resources than was compatible with productive investment. Similarly, Shirley Williams as Secretary of State for Prices and Consumer Protection had also warned against the 'cancer of inflation' at the NALGO Annual Conference and told a Cabinet meeting on 20 June 1974 that 'The cardinal aim of the government's policy should be to get the rate of inflation down to a single figure ... and the ultimate target must be a zero rate'. At the same meeting she also advocated 'stringent cuts' to the Public Sector Borrowing Requirement (PSBR).[68]

These views were reflected in the subsequent White Paper's acceptance that the control of inflation was a social and economic priority that required reductions in public sector borrowing and spending, the removal of food subsidies and a real terms reduction in wages. The approach was confirmed in successive White papers and by the introduction of cash limits which were estimated to have affected three quarters of central government expenditure, excluding social security. So much so, that in his reply to the debate on Public Expenditure on 9 March 1976, the Shadow Chancellor Geoffrey Howe was moved to remark: 'I congratulate him on having understood and accepted so much of the analysis we have offered him – but unfortunately, the conversion is apparently only skin deep'.[69]

In seeking to explain the Labour government's behaviour, two other factors are worthy of consideration: one of which involves a common misconception, while the other has received less attention. The first example involves the extent to which conditions attached to the credit negotiated with the Group of Ten and the loan from the IMF served to change government policy during the period.

Briefly stated, the countries participating in the General Arrangements to Borrow scheme agreed to sanction a credit of £5.3 billion to the British state on the condition that it was repaid by December, there would be a £3 billion reduction in the PSBR by 1977-78 and money supply targets would be devised. This was in June 1976, but in September application was made to the IMF for help to repay the Group of Ten. When this was finalized in December it also included provisions for public spending to be cut by £1 billion in 1977-78, £1.5 billion the following year and the sale of £500 million worth of shares in British Petroleum.

As has already been noted, Ministers had been extolling the virtues of a deflationary approach prior to its announcement in 'The Attack on Inflation' and the government had also accepted the 'need to keep the growth of the money supply under firm control' before either intervention.[70] Furthermore, the Chancellor of the Exchequer Denis Healey confirmed that the IMF 'have been at pains to point out that they see it as no part of their function to dictate policies to the United Kingdom government' and that in his assessment 'the broad scale of the action they suggest is about right'.

Taken together then, these statements support the view that the IMF was used as convenient cover for the government's favoured approach.[71]

The period was also one in which membership of the European Economic Community had been confirmed in a national referendum in 1975. This is the less often recognized factor which, although it should not be interpreted as a constraint on the options available to government ministers, indicates how they were willing to go along with a financial policy that was in keeping with the long-term goal of European monetary union. In other words, one of the reasons why the alternative approaches were rejected was because of the undesirable ramifications they might have for this particular project.[72]

Some of these options were discussed in Cabinet and are identified toward the end of the next Chapter. Suffice it to say here, therefore, that the approach adopted by the government was at odds with the policies and objectives outlined in Labour's Programme 1973 and those contained in the subsequent 1974 general election manifestos. Even when negotiating with the IMF the threat of import controls and the possible collapse of Sterling were ruled out as bargaining tools.

Perhaps the most plausible explanation for the Cabinet's acceptance of deflationary and therefore neoliberal prescriptions is one of pragmatic drift, but this does not tell the whole story. The real answer lies in the space between the rhetorical pronouncements and decisions of the LPAC, the demands of rank and file members and the reality of repeated attempts when in government to achieve economic growth based on the laws of capital accumulation.[73] This is the real reason why parliamentary leaders were amenable to whatever international policy trend proved to be flavour of the month, but within the labour movement at large they did not always have it all their own way.

Chapter Three
LABOUR MOVEMENT ACTIVISM

The workers of Britain are getting off their knees, getting on their feet and asserting their dignity. Asserting their abilities in a determined and disciplined way that they will have a say in the decision-making of this country.
Jimmy Reid, Speech to a Glasgow demonstration

If the Conservative Party of the 1980s was the product of its experiences in the 1960s and 1970s, the same can surely be said of the labour movement. Neoliberalism might have infected both, but the latter's association with the historical struggle for socialism meant that it was susceptible to societal trends that called in to question authority structures in general and parliamentarist politics in particular. Indeed, the emergence of a new generation of activists with a preference for decentralization, participation and lay control as opposed to bureaucracy and hierarchical decision-making left an indelible mark.

The radicalism expressed by extra-parliamentary movements like the Campaign for Nuclear Disarmament, women's liberation, opposition to the Vietnam War and demands for civil rights in the North of Ireland inevitably found reflection in the labour movement. Of crucial importance was the growing role played by activists in both industrial and party political spheres. The empowerment of ordinary rank and file trade union members through struggles to keep wages in line with spiralling prices was accompanied by the emergence and development of grass-roots tenants associations, community groups and voluntary organizations that sought to organize and campaign around particular issues.

These developments were mirrored by changes in the numbers and background of people who became members. Trade unions, for example, experienced consistent growth, especially in the public sector and local government, whereas the numbers of people belonging to the Labour Party showed dramatic fluctuations. New people also brought new ideas and experience of organization and representation which were reflected in the introduction of shop stewards systems in unions like NALGO and NUPE and extra-parliamentary campaign groups in the Labour Party. Such changes influenced and were affected by the practice of campaigns to oppose and resist the neoliberal agenda of cutting public spending and service provision at the very time that the domestic and international economies were exhibiting the symptoms of impending crisis.[74]

Rank and File Members

Almost as if to spite media pronouncements and protestations about the power and unpopularity of trade unions, overall membership grew at an accelerated rate during the 1970s. Having grown steadily from 8.8 million in 1946 to 10.5 million in 1969, a high point of 13.2 million trade union members was reached in 1979.[75] This growth spurt was all the more striking for those unions which recruited in local government and the public sector and it is these that are the focus here.

NALGO, the predominant representative of clerical employees and NUPE, the main manual union, increased their respective membership totals by 66 per cent and 91 per cent between 1970 and 1977. These figures alone are impressive, but even more marked when compared to a 21 per cent increase for all unions over the same period. They also imply an increase over and above the rise in local government employment from 1.7 million between 1958 and 3 million in 1980.[76]

Although increases in the membership of some unions can be explained in part by an increase in union mergers following the Trade Union (Amalgamations) Act 1964, this does not apply to NALGO. Neither is it enough to assume that membership levels rested on prior arrangements between employers and full-time union officials, a willingness of governments to recognize unions, or because managers were favourably predisposed due to their own membership of a union.

In any case, where prior arrangements did exist they were challenged by the introduction of shop steward systems and an increase in the number and frequency of disputes. A more likely explanation involves the effective working of trade unions based on the representation of members' interests and the successful resolution of disputes to members' advantage. Before considering this further, it is worth noting that equally striking changes affected Labour Party membership over a similar period.

Although it operates in a different milieu to trade unions, Labour Party membership levels are responsive to the effective representation of members' interests and the adoption and implementation of policies. The loss of 150,000 members between 1964 and 1969, for example, is usually attributed to dissatisfaction with the Party's performance in government. Other explanations include the dissolution of trade council links and associated organizational structures, a decline in working-class politics and disillusionment with the political process in general. This last point is also supported by the decline in Conservative Party membership over the same period.[77]

In the early 1970s, however, Labour Party membership did begin to recover or at least stabilize. One factor in this process was that opposition to the Conservative government's neoliberal economic agenda and its Industrial Relations and Housing Finance acts brought trade unionists and people from tenants associations and other interest groups into local Labour parties. These new members included young public sector professionals some with a working-class background, and male public sector manual workers concerned with defending living standards. They also included radical feminists opposed to the patriarchal structure of the Party, trade unions, workplace and society as a whole. Despite their different roots the new recruits were united in their rejection of the old, closed Labour Party apparatus and showed little deference to existing Party and trade union leaders.

Similar developments were evident in local government trade unions with the introduction of new forces into NALGO in the form of people who had been active in student politics in the late 1960s and early 1970s. The changing employment patterns of the 1970s also saw more people seeking clerical posts in local government due to an absence of job opportunities in the manufacturing sector. Meanwhile in manual trade unions the same economic processes resulted in comparable developments whereby former industrial workers found employment in local government.

Many of these new members who came from a manufacturing background also had experience of trade union organization and used their knowledge to help invigorate their new unions. The shop stewards movement that came to the fore during the 1960s, for example, had been characterized by the control of local bargaining and decision-making by rank and file activists and this trend was repeated in local authority unions following the official recognition of the stewards system by employers in 1969.[78]

NUPE, for example, held its first shop stewards elections in 1970 and its system of steward representation was considered to be the norm by 1974 with only 11 per cent of branches without a steward. The same year, NALGO adopted the principle of organizing local branches on the basis of shop stewards and introduced the system two years later in 1976. Even manual unions used to operating stewards systems in the private sector, like the TGWU and UCATT, saw an increase in lay participation and independence.

This decentralization of power was a response to, and reason for, new levels of activism and rank and file militancy at branch level. In the Camden branch of NUPE, for example, the shop stewards organization contributed to an increase in membership and a successful campaign for improved pay and conditions.[79] Elsewhere, the emergence and development of shop steward organizations was associated with dissatisfaction over wages and conditions and as a response to decisions taken by managers acting under economic pressure. Changes in union structures were also assisted by the re-organization of local government, as unions like NALGO that organized on an authority wide basis, had to merge branches, elect new leaders and develop new ways of operating.

Due to formal links and often interchangeable members, the changes that affected local government trade unions were also reflected by a shift in attitudes and organization within the Labour Party. The lifting of the ban on rank and file organizations in the 1960s formed part of this process and allowed activists to set up groups that were committed to developing the Party as a campaigning organization based on extra-parliamentary alliances between local parties, interest groups and trade unions.[80]

Socialist Charter was the first rank and file body to be formed in 1968 and although it was succeeded by the Young Chartists in 1972 and London Labour Briefing, it had the stated aim of stimulating and developing the work of activists in Constituency Labour parties (CLP). Similar groups included the Labour Co-ordinating Committee and the Socialist Campaign for a Labour Victory, both founded in 1978, and the Rank and File Mobilizing Committee set up two years later.

Perhaps the most prominent amongst these new bodies was the Campaign for Labour Party Democracy (CLPD). Formed in 1973 its main goal was to make the Parliamentary Labour Party (PLP) accountable to the Party at large and, as the sovereign body of the Party, endow the annual conference with responsibility for the development of policy and manifesto commitments. An integral aspect of this approach was the rejection of the Burkean view that elected representatives acted on behalf of all constituents, as opposed to the activists who sponsored, voted or worked for their election. Support for this stance gathered pace with the Labour government's decision to impose income restraint on the public sector and its preference for public expenditure cuts as part of its neoliberal strategy for reducing inflation.

At the constituency and district party levels a similar struggle was also taking place to make Labour groups accountable to the wider membership. This was particularly so in authorities like the GLC, Liverpool, Manchester and Sheffield where the leadership of Labour groups were cutting services, raising rents and ruling with a heavy hand. There should be no surprise therefore that those councillors and party activists who fought for internal party democracy and accountability were the same people who were campaigning against cuts and rent increases.

In Liverpool and Manchester, for example, a successful struggle was waged to establish working parties that formulated proposals for discussion and amendment by CLPs and affiliated trade union branches. The outcome of this consultation process formed the basis of each local party's programme, manifesto and therefore policy of the Labour Group. Like the CLPD's view of MPs, councillors were to be held accountable to the local party organization and expected to act in accordance with policy commitments. This approach was buttressed by the introduction of re-selection procedures, as happened in the Greater London Labour Party (GLLP) following the Conservative victory in the GLC elections of 1977.

The re-organization of local government in 1973 also served to assist the process of change at the local level. In the first instance, the amalgamation of authorities into larger units, elections for all new seats and therefore the selection of new candidates contributed to the removal of old cliques and hierarchies. Add to this the abolition of nominated alderman and the fact that the size and working practices of the new authorities made it impractical for the Leader of the Labour Group to be chairperson of the District Labour Party (DLP) and it is clear how the last vestiges of old style boss politics began to disappear.

The growth of the shop steward movement in trade unions and activist led groups in the Labour Party produced parallel challenges to traditional ideas about representation. In this new way of thinking, all elected representatives whether MPs, councillors, shop stewards or branch officers, are regarded as delegates empowered to implement the wishes of their supporters. This approach had serious consequences for the traditional roles of local authorities and other extra-parliamentary organizations, particularly when it brought them into conflict with central government. These and other implications are apparent in the campaigns mounted by Clay Cross and South Yorkshire against specific aspects of the neoliberal agenda and in the broader opposition to public spending cuts in the 1970s.

Early Resistance

The way in which changes in membership and the growth of activism were translated into practice during the 1970s can be traced through labour movement responses to the first national flirtations with neoliberal doctrine. As the previous chapter records, these policy changes involved first Conservative and then Labour administrations that adopted regressive approaches to service provision and public finances.

For the Conservatives this was exemplified in the White Paper 'A Fair deal for Housing'. Published in July 1971, the document outlined the intention to reduce subsidy for local authority housing and assume powers to set local rent levels. These measures were informed by the Party's experimental neoliberal agenda and therefore targeted at Labour councils and their electoral base for reasons of ideology. In particular, this meant that Labour run local authorities would no longer be able to use money from local rates to help reduce the rents paid by council tenants.

On a general level, the move raised important questions about the rights of local authorities to vary policy on the basis of electoral mandates and to use revenue from local rates as they saw fit. As a result, initial opposition was fairly widespread and 74 out of 87 ruling Labour groups voted for non-implementation at a meeting organized by Sheffield Trades Council and the City's Labour Group in May 1972. By the time the Act received royal assent in August, however, the number of dissenters had been reduced to 45, and it stood at 42 when the first rent increase was due under the Act on 1 October.[81]

At the local level, rank and file activity was organized through a variety of bodies. In Sheffield, for example, there was the Co-ordinating Committee for Tenants, Residents and Community Associations, while in Barnsley a Joint National Union of Mineworkers (NUM) and Tenants Co-ordinating Committee organized a campaign from miners' lodges. Elsewhere there was a South Wales Joint Tenants, Residents and Trades Union Committee Against the Rent Act and a Joint Action Committee in Barking.

Along with the production of publicity, the type of action organized by such bodies included marches, demonstrations, pickets, rallies, conferences, meetings, petitions, industrial action and rent strikes. NALGO's 1972 conference, for example, agreed to support its members who refused to co-operate with commissioners introduced by central government to run local authority affairs and official industrial action took place in Corby, Liverpool and Dundee in support of non-implementation.

Nevertheless, attempts to conduct a broad-based campaign of opposition and non-compliance encountered serious obstacles. In the early 1970s, for example, there was a minimal development of activist structures within those sections of the labour movement that were willing to resist the HFA. There were also other restrictions that included the small and fragmented nature of local authorities, their corresponding trade union branches and local parties prior to re-organization. Also important was the burgeoning divide between the demands, expectations and outlook of rank and file members and those whose main aspiration was to attain positions of national and parliamentary leadership.

Thus, by the end of 1973, only Clay Cross and Bedwas and Machen were still refusing to implement the Act. Thirty-two Labour groups had held out until the final months of 1972, but their acquiescence was followed shortly after by Conisborough, Biggleswade, Camden, Merthyr Tydfil, Clydebank, Cumbernauld, Denny, Saltcoats, Whitburn, Alloa, Barrhead, Midlothian and Cowdenbeath. The extent to which each authority was able to maintain resistance depended on local circumstances and the case of Clay Cross is particularly instructive in demonstrating the mechanisms necessary for staging a trenchant campaign of resistance and opposition.

Of paramount importance was the Labour Party's disciplined form of representation that treated councillors as delegates of the local Party. From the 1960s until the dissolution of Clay Cross in the 1970s, the Labour Group met each Friday to decide policy and decisions were then presented as a united front. Councillors were also answerable to monthly meetings of the local Party and those who disagreed with policy were either de-selected or asked to resign.

Along with this well established practice went the longstanding policy commitments of slum clearance and affordable rents based on a subsidy from the rates.Effectively a redistribution of wealth in the locality, these measures formed the basis of the Labour Party's programme and the focal point of elections that were contested by the Residents' Association on a platform of removing the subsidy. In view of the Party's continuing electoral success, there is therefore a convincing case for arguing that it had a clear local mandate.

The Labour Group also established a close working relationship with local trade unions, especially the NUM and NUPE, and five out of eleven councillors were members of the latter. Examples of how this process worked in practice include: the award of a pay increase to manual council workers in 1970, when elsewhere the pay claim resulted in the 'dirty jobs' strike; refusing to hold council meetings during the Post Office workers strike of 1971; circumventing the 1972 national pay freeze by re-negotiating contracts with manual workers; and unanimous support given to the Miners strikes of 1972 and 1974.

The overall approach adopted in Clay Cross is a prime example of elected representatives working to overcome any breach between themselves and their main constituency. This is all the more instructive because it was in sharp contrast to the method preferred by the parliamentary leadership and NEC, both in terms of their attitude to the HFA and to internal party democracy in general. With regard to the Act, for example, the NEC issued statements in January and March 1972, advising Labour groups not to increase rents until they were forced to and then to blame the government. The latter statement argued that a national lead was impracticable because the position of each local authority was different and each had to make decisions according to their own circumstances.[82]

This stance was maintained, in spite of motions passed at successive party conferences in 1972 and 1973 calling for support to be given to local authorities defying the HFA and for retrospective legislation to relieve councillors of any penalties incurred as a result of their defiance. In true parliamentarist fashion, Edward Short, the Deputy Leader of the Labour Party, told the 1973 conference that it would be an offence to encourage councillors to break the law and that the next Labour government would introduce legislation that might be unpopular, but which it would expect to be carried out.

There was, however, a striking inconsistency in the attitude of the PLP and NEC toward the autonomy of local parties. While it was considered to be perfectly acceptable for Labour groups to defy conference decisions and comply with the Act, the same degree of latitude was not extended to local parties that voted to deselect candidates for refusing to follow local policy. Thus, after re-organization in 1974, North East Derbyshire CLP adopted a policy of not raising rents under the HFA and when 11 councillors refused to accept the decision they were barred from the list of prospective candidates. In spite of the wishes of local party members, however, all 11 were reinstated following an inquiry by national officers.

The case of South Yorkshire's transport policy provides further evidence of this inconsistency, but also illustrates a different way of resisting a neoliberal agenda of reducing expenditure and cutting service provision to the vulnerable. In this case, South Yorkshire was not part of a broad-based campaign against an act of parliament, but it was opposed to a particular aspect of central government policy that was interpreted as reducing local autonomy. Like Clay Cross, its transport commitments lay at the centre of the local Labour Party's programme, and each election success was interpreted as a mandate for that programme.

This particular collision course began with local government reorganization when transport provision became the responsibility of the newly created Metropolitan County councils and local fares, previously set at different levels, had to be unified under the new authority. As part of this process, South Yorkshire fares were set at the level of one of the cheaper districts and frozen as a step toward free public transport based on the assumption that prices would be gradually reduced by inflation.[83]

Around the same time the Labour government introduced a new system of allocating central funding for public transport in place of the old method of using RSG and specific grants for particular projects. The new system was based on a Transport Supplementary Grant (TSG) and this took the form of a block allocation that was supposed to reduce central government control. The fact that the TSG was paid at a fixed rate, meant that any excess would have to be met through a local subsidy from the rates and this, in line with its manifesto commitment, is exactly what South Yorkshire did.

Problems began to arise with the publication of the RSG No. 2 Order in 1974 which not only recommended that local authorities should increase fares in line with costs, but also that: 'authorities who have not increased fares of late should consider what additional increases are necessary to cover some of the lost ground.'[84] Although this advice was easily ignored it signalled the growing influence of neoliberal prescriptions on national party leaders; as did the decision to cut TSG as part of the policy to reduce public expenditure. In South Yorkshire's case, this meant that the Labour government sought to impose a cut of £10 million on the transport programme submitted as part of the TSG settlement for 1977-78.

The government's logic was remarkably similar to that used by its Conservative predecessor when justifying the provisions of the HFA. In both cases, the argument rested on the fact that local subsidies meant higher spending and that this increased central expenditure because it attracted more RSG in the following year. From South Yorkshire's point of view, however, there was a mandate for its policy, not only from the local electorate but also from: the 1973 and 1975 party conferences; the precepted authorities of South Yorkshire; and at CLP, city, county and regional levels of the Labour Party.

Unlike the campaign of non-compliance that was designed to make the HFA unworkable, South Yorkshire put its case through official channels in the form of bilateral meetings that involved council officials, civil servants, council leaders and ministers. Discussions also took place through the Association of Metropolitan Authorities (AMA) and, because it was in government at the time, through the internal channels of the Labour

Party.

The technical nature of the solution adopted by South Yorkshire obviated the need for a protracted and high profile campaign and indicates the level of autonomy available to authorities at that time. Thus, as part of its 1978-79 submission for TSG, South Yorkshire declared only a part of its total revenue support for transport and included the remainder of its planned expenditure in the budget as a whole; a device that resembles the creative accountancy techniques that were favoured by the national Labour Party during the 1980s.

The examples of Clay Cross and South Yorkshire provide evidence of the neoliberal agenda that was favoured by governments during the 1970s and of the different types of opposition adopted within the labour movement. They should also be seen as part of a broader programme of public expenditure cuts and in the context of trade union campaigns against reductions in the social wage and welfare provision. This backdrop includes vestiges of dissent in the Labour Party that, although smaller in scale, are still indicative of the cleavages between parliamentarians and rank-and-file members.

National Opposition

In every day usage the word 'cuts' can have a number of meanings. These range from reductions in public expenditure as a whole to the targeting of specific areas. The phrase can also refer to the effects of curtailed expenditure in terms of the levels and standards of services provided. Moreover, cuts themselves can be the product of a deliberate policy intention, the effect of inflation, of under-spending or involve lower than previously planned levels of expenditure for future years. Less obvious is the tactic of redirecting spending from welfare to the support of private corporations.

As was made clear in the previous chapter, the Labour governments of the 1970s accepted the logic of reducing levels of public borrowing and expenditure. In so doing, however, they had to deal with the contradictory, cyclical and potentially self-defeating effect of cuts. This is most clearly expressed as the need to fund the higher cost of welfare payments because cuts generate unemployment due to job losses in the public sector and amongst private employers whose businesses rely on it for orders. This effect is then exacerbated by the fact that income from tax and national insurance contributions also falls when fewer people are working or they are earning less.

Depending on the perspective taken, however, funding mass unemployment can be viewed as a necessary evil that allows wage costs to be reduced in the private sector or as something that facilitates the restructuring of capital by allowing failing firms to close.[85] In either case, it is still necessary to square the circle of reducing or at least limiting overall spending and borrowing levels while making provision for greater welfare spending and falling revenue. As on numerous occasions since, however, the options for achieving this have been premised on a paring back of local government funding.

An early indication of this strategy appeared in December 1974, when the DOE issued Circular 171/74 'Rate Fund Expenditure and Rate Calls 1975-6'. This document advised local authorities to limit service provision and in the following year the Consultative Council for Local Government Finance (CCLGF) was set up and used to persuade local councils that central guidelines were reasonable.[86]

Local government funding was therefore an issue before the involvement of the IMF toward the end of 1976 and the government built on the approach of its predecessor when, earlier that year, it introduced restrictions on funding in the form of cash limits and loan sanctions. Under these mechanisms, central allocations were fixed at price levels assumed to operate for the whole financial year and could not be adjusted for inflation or interest rate rises.

As the period was one of spiralling inflation and high interest rates the effect was to reduce RSG in real terms and restrict the capital spending of English local authorities by £1.3 billion. The full impact meant that local government spending fell as a proportion of both GDP and total government expenditure between 1976 and 1978: from 17 per cent to 13 per cent and from 28 per cent to 24 per cent respectively.[87]

Whatever the figures might be, the outcomes are difficult to quantify in terms of service provision and employment at the level of individual authorities. In part, this is because lower standards of service, repair and maintenance or the use of inferior materials are less apparent than the wholesale slashing of projects. Likewise, employment levels could be cut by not filling vacancies and costs reduced through the switch from full-time to part-time hours. Redundancies did take place, however, in Surrey County, Strathclyde, Tayside and Glasgow, for example and NALGO estimated that there were 50,000 vacant local government posts in 1976.[88]

As their members felt the effects of cuts directly, trade unions were at the forefront of organized opposition. This activity, it is also worth mentioning, extended beyond NALGO, NUPE and unions like GMBATU, TGWU, EETPU and UCATT that recruited in the public and private sectors. The AUEW, for example, took part in campaigning activity, regardless of conference pronouncements by its leader, and other private sector unions participated through the TUC. There is therefore little to be gained from attempts to draw absolute distinctions between private and public sector interests; especially as all workers use public services, households are often made up of public and private sector workers and many people move between private and public employers.

At a general level, the TUC used the Trade Union-Labour Party Liaison Committee and Social Contract negotiations to secure a commitment for the restoration of cuts in education funding announced by the previous Conservative government. Opposition to the government's own plans for cuts in education was also expressed during the 1976-77 social contract discussions and at a meeting with the education secretary held in November 1976. Similarly, members of the economic committee raised their concerns over proposed reductions in the PSBR for 1977-78 and the effect this would have on unemployment when they met with the chancellor and prime minister in July 1976.[89]

Outside the auspices of the TUC, the main source of opposition was focused on the National Steering Committee Against the Cuts (NSC) set up by ASTMS, COHSE, CPSA, NALGO, NATFHE, NUPE, the National Union of Students, NUT and the TUC South East Regional Council. Originally drawn together to plan a lobby of parliament in November 1976, the NSC was re-established on a continuing basis following a meeting of General Secretaries and National Officers of the unions involved.[90]

As part of its activities the NSC organized: meetings between senior full-time officials; regional 'days of action' involving stoppages, demonstrations and lobbies; regional and local joint union committees; a delegate conference; and, the preparation and publication of literature setting out the arguments against cuts. Collaboration also spread beyond this body with national NALGO and NUPE officials holding meetings in 1976 to explore the: possibility of mounting a common approach to the government's policy of cuts; opportunities for practical co-operation; and a joint approach to other unions to muster support for a joint lobby of parliament on the issue of public expenditure cuts.

This reflected NUPE's analysis that it could not fight to defend member interests through wage negotiating machinery alone, but required trade union action on a broad political front, including withdrawal from involvement in wages policy if the government continued with public expenditure cuts. In another example of joint-working the Civil Service unions SCPS and CPSA argued that Britain consumed less of its national product in public spending than comparable nations and rejected the idea that a programme of cuts could solve the problems of inflation and unemployment.[91]

The decision of the NSC to establish Joint Trade Union Committees (JTUC) corresponds in timing and nature to the TUC's Local Government Committee's (TUCLGC) recommendation that joint committees be formed at the local level to combat redundancies and for trade councils to lobby local authorities to resist government cuts. A distinction needs to be drawn, however, between JTUCs that developed in response to local struggles and those that were the product of national edicts. TUC and NSC engendered committees, for example, were geared toward full-time officials as opposed to shop stewards, whereas the involvement of activists in the Local Authority Workers Shop Stewards Combine in Coventry and the Joint Shop Stewards Committee in Liverpool City Council were more likely to be responsive to local events and reflective of local demands.[92]

Local campaigns were organized by the Trades Council in Lancashire and by JTUCs in South Wales, Birmingham, Sheffield, Tyneside, Humberside, Oldham, Bristol, Portsmouth and Southampton. These involved the usual demonstrations and days of action toward the end of 1976 and during early 1977. In Birmingham British Leyland shop stewards supported campaigning activity and in London workers from Greenwich Reinforcements, a British Steel subsidiary, were disciplined for supporting a day of action against public expenditure cuts that had been called jointly by NALGO and NUPE.[93]

Despite attempts to develop a campaign that encouraged mass participation and the utilization of official channels, the absence of a unified national programme of action meant that opposition remained isolated and sporadic. The methods will be familiar to any student of labour movement campaigning activity and included national delegate conferences, such as those called by the National Right to Work Campaign in Manchester in 1976 to protest against cuts and unemployment. The NSC conference referred to earlier took place in March 1977 and was addressed by academics and national union officials, attended by 200 delegates from 23 different trade unions and focused on the impact of cuts on the social wage.

There were also lobbies of parliament and of trade union and party conferences. The canvassing of parliament on 17 November 1976, for example, was organized by the NSC and repeated as part of a national week of action beginning 21 November 1977. As well as the lobby, this included a rally and the presentation of a 175,000 signature petition to 10 Downing Street.[94] Local and national publicity was again produced for distribution at demonstrations and lobbies and the more regular dissemination of information is evidenced by NUPE's production of internal circulars for local branches and NALGO Publicity Department's bulletins, speakers' notes, leaflets, stickers and posters.

Although opposition to spending cuts did not succeed in preventing or reversing government policy and practice, it did have positive results, including the organization and radicalization of those who were traditional targets for cuts and redundancies. In NALGO, for example, the 1975 conference called for industrial action in branches where jobs and services were at risk. A national campaign committee was also established in December 1975 as a sub-committee of the Executive Council and a campaign launched in early 1976 under the slogan 'Save our Services – Stop the Public Expenditure Cuts'. The following year a Special Conference was convened on 14 January to discuss unemployment and cuts and voted to impose an overtime ban from 1 April and for members to stop covering for vacant posts.[95]

This level of activity contrasts favourably with the Labour Party where the Camden Labour Group provides one of the few examples of opposition when, under the leadership of Frank Dobson, it convened a London-wide meeting to oppose the imposition of housing expenditure controls. From that meeting an organization called Labour Against Housing Cuts was established and although it evolved into Labour Against the Cuts, their operations were limited and practised mainly in London. Trade union delegates also opposed the GLC Labour Group's cuts agenda and secured votes against housing cuts, fare increases and the Labour government's cuts programme at the GLLP's Annual Meeting in 1976.[96]

Opposition was also expressed at the LPAC in motions and debates that were critical of the government's neoliberal agenda. On the whole such resolutions were moved, seconded or received support from CLPs, like composite 25 moved by Richmond and seconded by Bromsgrove and Redditch CLPs in 1976. This particular example called on the government not to implement further cuts in public spending and to prevent further decline in the standards of social, education and community services.

The outlook of party activists is best appreciated by examining the terms of Composite 26 moved by NUPE in the same year. This motion was seconded by Cardiff North West CLP, supported by a range of CLP speakers, and thereby indicates the extent of opposition at this level. Their views were reflected in the wording of the text, with references to the Party's manifesto commitment to improve and expand social services and the rejection of cuts in public spending on houses, schools, hospitals and health centres to provide profits for the private sector.

As part of this proposal, the LPAC was asked to endorse Labour councils that were refusing to implement cuts and to encourage other Labour groups to follow suit. The motion also declared that unity existed in the trade union movement to resist cuts and demanded that the NEC support unions that were taking action. Not surprisingly the NEC asked for the composite to be remitted, but when this was rejected and the motion passed,[97] the national leadership and government ministers simply followed past practice and chose to ignore the decision of the LPAC.

The government's determination to proceed with its plans and its precarious parliamentary majority might help explain the low level of parliamentary dissent over the issue of cuts. In fact, whenever the Labour Party has been in office the PLP has shown a consistently high level of loyalty to its government and, on this occasion, the only revolt of any note saw 37 MPs abstain from a vote on the expenditure white paper in March 1976. Elsewhere, the *Tribune* newspaper provided a vehicle for the expression of parliamentary dissatisfaction and Brian Sedgemore espoused a version of the Alternative Economic Strategy (AES) in April 1977.

Debates also took place in cabinet in July 1975 when Tony Benn, the Secretary of State for Energy, opposed the draft Attack on Inflation White Paper because it 'put forward an economic strategy totally different from that on which the government had been elected.' A year later he also submitted a memorandum to Cabinet proposing a course of action based around the AES, but on both occasions his arguments fell on deaf ears.[98]

With the intervention of the IMF and the proposal to introduce further cuts, Benn was joined in opposing reductions by the Foreign Secretary, Anthony Crosland, and Peter Shore Secretary of State for the Environment. Crosland made his first intervention in the Cabinet Meeting held 23 November 1976 and all three submitted memoranda to a meeting on 1 December. Whereas Crosland argued that further cuts were unnecessary because the government's strategy was working, Benn advocated a programme for economic growth based on an AES formula of planning agreements, expanded industrial investment through the National Enterprise Board, import quotas and exchange controls. Shore also advocated controls on imports, but only temporarily until the balance of trade was in surplus, and all three had different uses for import deposits.[99]

As is now well known, the government's decision to persist with a deflationary approach ultimately paved the way for the return of a Conservative government in 1979. Perhaps it would be too hard an assessment to attribute this outcome to the failure of the campaign of opposition. After all, activity was hampered by the recent introduction and therefore immature nature of rank-and-file structures in both Labour Party and trade unions. On a more positive note, the efforts to build opposition can be seen as important factors that contributed to the development of awareness, activism, shop stewards systems and struggles for democracy. As we shall see, these and other experiences also facilitated a more concerted opposition and resistance on the 1980s.

PART TWO
RETRENCHMENT AND RETREAT, 1979–1984

... the logic of money is asserted without regard for social, political, cultural relations, indeed with a disregard for human dignity itself.
Elmar Altvater, *Financial Crises on the Threshold of the 21st Century*

Chapter Four
THE CONSERVATIVE AGENDA

> See with what heat these dogs of Hell advance
> To waste and havoc yonder world, which I
> So fair and good created; and had still
> Kept in that state, had not the folly of Man
> Let in these wasteful furies
> John Milton, *Paradise Lost*, Book IX

The first Conservative government of the 1980s that ran from 3 May 1979 to 8 June 1983 is generally considered to represent a radical departure from previous governmental practice. In several senses this is true. Certainly the preparedness to allow economic recession to blight the livelihoods and prospects of individuals and families for years to come was something not witnessed since the 1930s. The autocratic predilection of the Prime Minister, Margaret Thatcher, was also somewhat innovative.

When viewed in the context of developments described in the previous two chapters, however, the emphasis on monetary policy and controlling inflation is consistent with the neoliberal agenda that came to the fore in the preceding decade. So too are the reduction of state subsidies, of spending on the NHS and the restriction of state intervention to measures that were intended to establish conditions in which markets could operate without constraint.

Far from being an entirely new phenomenon, therefore, the government's policy and practice can be viewed as building on aspects of its Conservative predecessor and on others honed by the intervening Labour administrations. The similarity also extends to the government abandoning some of its more fundamentalist theories when events seemed to be spiralling out of control; even though some members of its cabinet had lambasted colleagues when they did the same in the early 1970s.

Having been singled out for special attention by previous administrations, local government was once again to bear the brunt of the latest tranche of public spending cuts. The implications of these developments were laid out in a series of legislative interventions that dealt with funding, deregulation, privatization and economic regeneration. Of crucial importance to this study are the ways in which the labour movement attempted to deal with the consequences that these policies had for local government jobs, services and local democracy.

Local Government Funding

From the outset it is fair to say that a chasm existed between the government's stated aims and the practical outcomes of its approach to local funding. This stems in part from an eclectic use of economic devices and is confused further by the categorization of its approach as 'monetarist'. While the use of interest rates to control money supply and therefore inflation can be interpreted in this light, there is no such macro-economic justification for the imposition of spending targets and penalties on individual local authorities.

Similarly, the fact that central government expenditure rose from £73,493 million in 1979-80 to £79,856 million by 1982-83 belies the claim made in a DOE press notice dated 19 June 1980 that public expenditure reductions were central to the government's economic strategy. Closer inspection reveals that this increase was due to spending on defence, payments to the unemployed and the need to pay pensions to people who were now living longer. Reductions in local authority grant provision can therefore be explained in terms of priorities, as the PSBR would have been even higher if the central funding of localities had not been curtailed.[100]

The macro-economic rhetoric also concealed the fact that in the early 1980s Conservative authorities increased spending at a higher rate than their Labour counterparts. In 1982-83, for example, inner London boroughs budgeted for an increase of 4.5 per cent while the mainly Conservative non-metropolitan counties that accounted for nearly 45 per cent of total expenditure, budgeted for an increase of 8.8 per cent. In unusual moments of lucidity, however, Labour local authorities are singled out as 'high spending', 'left-wing', 'lunatic' and 'red'.

In the least hysterical of these examples the term 'high spending' is based on the simplistic calculation of pounds spent per head of population and therefore ignores the different demographic and socio-economic circumstances that require greater local spending.[101] Moreover, the measurement of service provision in terms of price and therefore as a monetary exchange-value is indicative of the Conservative Party's antipathy toward collective consumption and the focus on use-value when services are provided free at the point of contact.

As part of its drive to limit the policy options for Labour authorities, the government introduced abstract formulae and criteria to compute and allocate funding to individual councils. Under the auspices of the Housing Act 1980, for example, central assistance was calculated as the amount a local authority needed to break even on its Housing Revenue Account (HRA), after the deduction of income that was assumed to have been raised through rents, house sales and rates. If by virtue of this calculation an authority's HRA was deemed to be in surplus, general housing subsidy was held back.

These measures were effective in reducing spending on public housing and represent a renewal and extension of a policy that first appeared with the HFA. As with the earlier Act, the new provisions constituted an attack on an area of policy and service provision that was important to Labour controlled authorities like Norwich and Sheffield where new house building was reduced to a virtual standstill. In fact, this strategy was so successful that by 1984-85 only 46 of the 367 local authorities with responsibility for housing received any central funding. What this also meant, however, was that local housing policy moved beyond central control as authorities used rate and rent charges to fund housing provision.[102]

In similar fashion the Local Government, Planning and Land Act 1980 (LGPLA) replaced the old RSG with a block grant that was calculated according to a centrally devised formula known as Grant Related Expenditure Assessment (GREA). As with the HRA calculations, the amount of money allocated depended on the perceived circumstances of each individual authority and corresponded to the balance remaining after a figure for 'locally raised rate fund contribution' or 'grant related poundage' was deducted from the GREA.

The already noted advantage that accrued to rural authorities can now be explained in terms of the attempt to simplify the allocation of funding through an equalization of authorities rateable value per head. In other words, the new GREA employed sterile mathematical models that ignored the effects of population migration and mass unemployment which combined to produce a higher than average proportion of non-working people dependent on council services in urban areas.

Purely by coincidence, of course, rural authorities tended to be Conservative, whereas the impoverished inner cities were represented by Labour councillors who, like their counterparts in the more affluent shires, adopted and applied policies tailored to local needs. The iniquities of this approach became even more apparent when, faced with year on year growth of current expenditure, the government resorted to a system of targets and penalties that singled out labour authorities.[103]

These new devices first appeared with the LGPLA as a grant taper designed to discourage authorities from spending more than 10 per cent over government guidelines and this was followed in January 1981 with individual targets for local authorities in England. The next year, the Local Government Finance Act abolished the right of local authorities to levy a supplementary rate and thereby ensured that authorities could no longer raise extra revenue during the financial year to offset the effect of government formulae, penalties, inflation and interest rates.

The changes in the calculation and imposition of penalties were frequent and complicated and are therefore summarized in the Appendix. Significantly, however, the increasing severity of penalties reflects the extent to which local authority spending continued to exceed government targets. In 1981-82, for example, the level of overspend was 5.3 per cent and by 1983-84 authorities in England were still exceeding government targets by 3.8 per cent. To put this into perspective, it is worth noting that this was at a time when the proportion of local authority current expenditure supported by central government grant fell from 48.5 per cent in 1979-80, to 35.9 per cent in 1982-83.[104]

Local government spending also shrank as a percentage of GDP from 15.9 per cent in 1974-75 to 12.8 per cent in 1983-84, but these figures refer to overall totals.[105] They therefore include capital expenditure over which the government was able to exert more control through the use of cash limits and block allocations introduced under the LGPLA. When combined with the permission to spend only 50 per cent of capital receipts in 1983-84, this had the effect of reducing standards of service by limiting the construction of new buildings and the repair or renovation of existing ones.

Curiously, however, the Conservatives had not learned from the lessons of their Labour predecessors. They therefore allowed limits on capital spending to be compounded by the effects of economic recession and high interest rates that resulted in an underspend of 21 per cent in 1981-82. Faced with a forecast deficit of 33 per cent for 1982-83, the government was forced to urge local authorities to increase capital spending in the October and to raise ceilings on such spending for 1983-84. The relative severity of measures that had the effect of reducing capital spending from £5,952 million in 1979-80 to £2,772 million in 1982-83 is therefore in stark contrast to the rise in current expenditure.[106]

There are two main reasons for this disparity. The first relates to flaws evident in the methods used to control both types of spending and the second is the extent to which the labour movement was able to circumvent targets and penalties. On the one hand, overall current spending was less likely to fall because those rural authorities that benefited from the new formula were encouraged to spend up to their new GREA when it calculated their needs to be in excess of budgeted spending. Furthermore, the fact that targets were based on previous year's budgets also acted as an incentive for authorities to spend more than necessary in order to increase future targets.

Taken together with this last point, the ability and willingness of local authorities to use rates to offset reductions and even create special funds with which to counter the effects of future cuts gives an indication of how Labour groups managed to maintain spending levels. In 1980, for example, Sheffield increased rates by 41 per cent, Liverpool by 50 per cent and Lambeth levied a supplementary rate equivalent to a 70 per cent increase in order to compensate for a £5.6m reduction in grant imposed by the government in July 1980. Sheffield employed the same tactic in 1981 with a 37 per cent increase and in 1982 the GLC approved a 35 per cent rate rise as a one off measure needed to finance future plans.[107]

Perhaps inevitably, however, the tactic proved to be divisive and self-defeating in electoral terms. Labour lost control of both Liverpool and Lambeth in the following year and within the labour movement it was objected that local ratepayers were being used to subsidize central government and that this was proving to be an increasing burden for poorer householders.[108]

As an alternative, a series of financial devices were employed as a way of avoiding penalties, maximizing grant allocation and therefore maintaining spending commitments, jobs and minimizing cuts in service provision. This 'creative accountancy' included: the creation of special funds in one year for revenue purposes in other years; capitalization whereby spending on repairs and maintenance was transferred from the revenue to the capital account; the re-scheduling of debt re-payments to reduce revenue spending on interest payable for capital borrowing; and, deferred purchase schemes to avoid restrictions on a local authority's capital allocation by transferring spending on projects to another year.

Resistance also involved legal challenges mounted by the London boroughs of Brent and Camden, against central government financial orders made under the 1980 Act. Birmingham and Greenwich also undertook separate legal suits which established that the LGPLA had been drafted incorrectly and that all grant paid since 1980 was therefore illegal. This proved to be a hollow victory however, as the government merely introduced retrospective legalization in the form of the Local Government Finance Act 1982.

In the absence of a mobilization or participation of labour movement members, opposition and resistance was focused on councillors and professionals. By depending on increased rates, cuts, financial manoeuvring or legal action, the labour movement also served to obscure the impact that government policy and practice was having on local welfare provision and local democracy. The government was therefore engaged on its own technical ground and this approach resulted in Labour councils making cuts of their own.

Camden, Lewisham and Newcastle, for example combined cuts with rates increases. Similarly, the Labour Group in Birmingham introduced: a moratorium on spending prior to the 1982 local elections; reduced the 1981 education budget by £3 million; privatized Sutton Coalfield Leisure Centre; and introduced both a vacancy freeze and a redundancy programme. In the latter case a broad-based campaign of resistance was attempted under the auspices of a Public Sector Liaison Committee, but this was against a Labour authority rather than the government and not all local unions participated.[109]

The impact of complicated and ever changing targets and penalties was difficult to quantify and explain in terms that were likely to mobilize electors, trade unionists or Labour Party members. This meant that local examples of opposition and resistance also tended to be isolated and focused on more tangible effects. In the early 1980s, however, there was no shortage of government policy and practice that had negative implications for local authority workers and therefore offered the opportunity for a more concerted response.

Deregulation and Privatization

The inability of the government to restrict local spending through its use of formulae, targets and penalties would have been even more apparent if it had not been successful in using deregulation and privatization to drive down wages. In its 1979 General Election Manifesto, for example, the conservatives talked about local direct labour schemes wasting an estimated £400 million a year and of the need to reconcile pay bargaining with cash limits and 'what the taxpayer and ratepayer can afford'.[110]

Several pieces of legislation were used to put this policy into practice. These include the Transport Acts 1980 and 1983, which were aimed at deregulating local bus services. Changes to the operation of DLOs were also introduced by the LGPLA and the Housing Act 1980 promoted the sale of council houses. As the following examples demonstrate, however, each initiative had negative consequences for service standards, job totals and the working conditions of employees.

Ostensibly, the first Transport Act was designed to facilitate the transfer of functions from the public sector by making it easier for private sector operators to obtain licences from the traffic commissioner to run bus services. As a first step, therefore, the Act removed the need for such licences in Devon, Hereford and Norfolk. Lying behind this, of course, was the unspoken neoliberal agenda of restricting state provision to only those services that were incompatible with profit-making and of reducing local spending by cutting operating costs.

In early 1981, this legislation was put to the test when a private company declared an interest in running services on two routes in Cardiff.[111] Not only did the timing of the move display remarkable alacrity, but its preparation and public presentation also showed astute political judgement. To this end, the principle of cross-subsidizing profitable and loss-making routes in the name of public service, which had previously deterred private firms, was used to justify the choice of routes. This also meant that the prospective service provider was able to put their case to the local press as proof that they were not interested in cherry-picking the most profitable routes.

As part of its strategy the local firm also asked the Secretary of State for Transport to exercise powers granted under section 43(2) of the 1980 Act and rescind clause 46 of the Cardiff Corporation Act 1930 on the grounds that it conflicted with the newer act. The Minister duly agreed to this request and thereby set in train a series of events that saw Cardiff City Transport re-organize and re-price its services on the profitable route in order to make it unviable for the private firm to compete.

Of particular significance here is the corollary to this episode that centred on the re-tendering of South Glamorgan County Council's schools transport contract in July 1981. On this occasion Cardiff City Transport won the contract from the same private firm by submitting a lower bid and was able to do so because the TGWU agreed to inferior working conditions and practices in the hope of obviating the threat of broader privatization. This agreement required extra duties to be included in existing shift patterns, together with a reduction in the standard of maintenance checks on vehicles, and therefore provides a perfect example of how the 1980 Act helped reduce costs and standards of provision with the tacit approval of the labour movement.

Local transport policy in London and on Merseyside was also subject to legal challenge by Conservative controlled Bromley Council and Great Universal Stores respectively. In December 1981, for example, the House of Lords upheld lower court decisions that the GLC's 'Fares Fair' policy was ultra vires because it did not comply with the principles of fiduciary duty. Perhaps of more significance for the understanding of how democracy is supposed to work, the judges felt it necessary to declare that representatives should not 'treat themselves as irrevocably bound to carry out pre-announced policies contained in election manifestos'.[112]

Faced with this advice, the Regional Executive of the GLLP and the Labour Group voted to adopt a position of non-compliance, launched a publicity campaign in January 1982 and set up a campaign committee that included London Transport workers. As part of the drive to build support for their position a series of public meetings were held and the Labour Group also met with local trade unions; Labour MPs; community groups; representatives of commuters; and with the Secretary of State for Transport. Local trade unions also mounted their own campaign which began with a one day strike and threatened an indefinite stoppage if the government failed to resolve the situation to their satisfaction.

In the final analysis, however, enough Labour councillors decided to accept the Law Lords advice and voted against Party policy and the wishes of the local electorate. Thus, although the GLLP Regional Executive had voted by 25 to 7 in favour of non-compliance, the Labour Group only voted to continue its resistance by 23 to 22. When the vote was taken in the Council Chamber this meant that enough Labour councillors voted with conservatives and others to overturn the policy.

Emboldened by the GLC case, Great Universal Stores embarked upon similar action in an attempt to overturn Merseyside County Council's policy on local fares. The Council was vindicated in February 1982, however, when Justice Woolf ruled that it had taken into account the impact that the cost of transport would have on those relying on state benefit. This outcome did not prevent threats being made elsewhere, however, and as a consequence West Midlands County Council increased fares when faced with the possibility of legal proceedings.[113]

In South Yorkshire, the concerns were also real enough for the local labour movement to mount a campaign which involved engineering and steel workers in a one day stoppage on 25 January 1982, the distribution of leaflets and a 250,000 signature petition. Buoyed by such support the County Council affirmed its transport and fares policy on 4 March 1982 and waited for the government's next move.

This duly arrived in the form of the Transport Act 1983, which gave the Secretary of State for Transport the power to set annual limits on public transport subsidies; a move that was justified on the grounds that conflicting court rulings needed clarification. In other words, the law was clarified in neoliberal terms and David Howell the Transport Secretary made plain the Conservative's thinking when he stated that:

> The electors are not the same people as the ratepayers. It is the business ratepayers who largely finance these policies. Local democracy is whittled away when many ratepayers do not have a vote in the expenditure of their money.[114]

By way of contrast, however, the votes of those who paid taxes and national insurance were discounted when it came to having a say over the provisions of the LGPLA. In addition to the financial restrictions already discussed, the Act also required DLOs to make at least a 5 per cent return on capital and stipulated that construction and maintenance work had to be offered to the private sector. Up to this point, local authorities had the discretion to invite tenders for work but the new changes were clearly designed to increase the pressure on job numbers, wages and working conditions.

This can be gauged by the reduction in the numbers of DLO employees from 156,606 in 1980 to 121,381 in 1985 and a fall in the value of DLO output from £1.8 to £1.5 million over the same period. Furthermore, of the 90,000 local authority jobs shed in England and Wales between 1979 and 1982, most of the losses involved manual workers and especially those in construction and refuse collection.[115] In other words, jobs were cut in the areas where local authorities were either required or chose to invite tenders from private companies for existing work.

More often than not Conservative councils were more open about their use of privatization to reduce the job security, pay and conditions of the workforce. In Birmingham, for example, 236 refuse collectors jobs were lost in 1982-83 as part of an in-house tender. Other examples include the removal of bonus schemes and the imposition of compulsory overtime at lower rates as part of the Southend refuse collection contract and reduced rates of sick pay and inferior pension provision when Wandsworth's street cleaning was out-sourced. In both cases there was also reduced holiday entitlement, the removal of grievance and disciplinary procedures and, due to the practice of summary dismissal, a loss of redundancy payments.[116]

The different approach adopted by Labour controlled authorities is clearly evident in the statistic that before 1983 no Labour-run council had privatized a contract worth over £50,000. This does not mean that Labour groups refused to co-operate with requirements to submit a percentage of DLO work to private competition. More often than not, private interest was deterred by strict specifications relating to: health and safety; trade union and employment rights; service standards; and penalty clauses.[117] Nevertheless, the cases of Cardiff City Transport and Birmingham among many others show the negative impact that the tendering process had on what are termed 'successful' in-house bids.

Overt opposition to the privatization of council work did occur, but it tended to be localized and reflected the development of the local labour movement, the party controlling the local authority and employer-employee relations. Resistance was attempted in 1982, for example, over plans to privatize refuse collection, school cleaning, school meals and caretaking services in Birmingham. Ultimately, however, its effectiveness was hampered by the fact that full-time officials controlled the joint union committee and were unwilling to put inter-union rivalry and white and blue collar differences to one side.

Perhaps predictably, confrontation was more likely to take place in non-Labour authorities as it did in Wandsworth where there was an alliance of local unions, rate-payers, Labour Party branches and the local Trades Council. The campaign also involved a seven week strike which received support from workers in other authorities who refused to process refuse from Wandsworth. With the Conservative's local election victory in May 1982, however, the action folded.[118]

A similar pattern of events developed in Gloucester the following year when the branches of NALGO, NUPE, TGWU and local MPs helped set up the Gloucester City Public Services Defence Committee to rally local union members, mobilize public opinion and organize a one day strike, demonstration and lobby of the council. Once again resistance collapsed with the Conservative's local election victory, but this was not always the case. In Liverpool, for example, the local labour movement campaigned against privatization of the City's cleansing service in the run up to local elections in 1983 and in this instance a Labour victory spelt the end for Liberal Party plans.

Not content with the deregulation of bus services and privatization of construction, maintenance and other work, the government also identified council housing as an area of collectivized service provision to be targeted by financial restraint and legislative obligations. The first aspect of this approach involved reductions in subsidy and capital expenditure, described above, and the mandatory sale of council houses formed the second. Both were introduced by the Housing Act 1980 but should not be seen as separate aims or processes.

By calculating funding based on a notional income from projected sales, for example, the government either hoped to encourage selling by those authorities that wished to maximize central funding or punish those that did not. Where these incentives proved to be insufficient, Section 23 of the Act gave the secretary of state the power to intervene and ensure that tenants were able to exercise their rights.[119] Analogies have already been drawn between these provisions and those of the HFA, but the similarities do not end there.

From the outset the sale of council housing was opposed in principle by many local Labour parties for whom the service was an important aspect of their electoral base. This stance was consolidated at the 'Local Government in Crisis' Conference in November 1980 which was attended by fifty delegates from Labour groups around the country and agreed that Labour councils should not sell council houses or housing land.[120] The depth of feeling is also indicated by the fact that by May 1981, 39 local authorities had been contacted by the housing minister because they were viewed as not implementing the Act fast enough. As this observation suggests, however, opposition ranged from delaying tactics up to and including outright refusal.

In Norwich, for example, the number of households relying on local authority housing meant that the issue was of central importance in the locality and contributed to the Labour Group's decision not to co-operate. Such was the resolve in Norwich that the government was forced to exercise its powers under Section 23 and, following a House of Lords ruling, the DOE assumed responsibility for sale of council houses in early 1982.

Elsewhere opposition focused on trade union branches and NALGO members in particular as they would be required to process sales applications. With this in mind, the union's 1979 and 1980 conferences both resolved: not to co-operate with new service demands without adequate funding; to oppose council house sales in stress areas; and, to support councils resisting central sales directives. Subsequent action took place in Glasgow, Hackney, Lambeth, Newcastle, Sheffield and Southwark where local branches refused to process applications without extra resources.[121]

Overall, the NALGO action was confined to twelve Labour controlled areas where implicit support was forthcoming from the Labour group, but this should not be misunderstood as representing a uniform approach. On the contrary, different strategies were evident in: Camden where councillors encouraged the slow processing of applications and NALGO refused to process any at all; Lambeth, where councillors agreed to co-operate with the Act, but NALGO took official action over the lack of resources; and in Barking opposition was the initiative of councillors and there was no trade union action at all.

The reliance on localized opposition to financial restraint, privatization and council house sales contributed to the disparity of resistance and a reliance on diversionary tactics. In the absence of a broad-based campaign, opposition became technocratic such as in the use of creative accountancy techniques and strict tender specifications. Similar tactics were used to delay council house sales by: 'counselling' prospective buyers; limiting the number of cases reviewed each month; refusing to use the District Valuer for house valuation; and, requiring council committees to make all decisions. When viewed in the light of these experiences it seems inevitable that disagreements over the best way to stimulate local economic activity would not lead to mass based agitation.

Economic Regeneration

The third and final part of the Conservative government's neoliberal experimentation with the local state involved its application of ideas that it hoped would create the conditions in which economic growth could take root. At the heart of this programme lay the property-led emphasis that had been a feature of the 1970s, but this was now combined with a dogma and rhetoric that, until put to the test, seemed to represent a bold and innovative intervention.

In a refrain that has been repeated by the Conservative led coalition in 2011, the antidote to the combined effects of international economic crisis was promoted as a reduction in public spending and a new relationship between the private sector and the state at national, regional and local levels. For the most part, this centred on the creation of Enterprise Zones (EZ) and Urban Development Corporations (UDC), both of which had been introduced under the sweeping provisions of the LGPLA.[122]

Enterprise Zones, for example, included financial incentives such as exemptions from: development land tax; industrial training levies; and, paying rates on industrial and commercial buildings. There was also a 100 per cent allowance for corporation and incomes taxes for capital expenditure on industrial and commercial building and relaxed planning procedures. Similarly, UDCs were funded by central government, established in designated Urban Development Areas (UDA) and given functions relating to planning, housing, public health and building controls that had previously been the responsibility of elected local authorities.

Underpinning both schemes was the idea that economic growth was inhibited by 'vested interests' and this evidently required certain functions to be moved beyond democratic control. Thus, although EZs had to be requested by local authorities and run locally, central government retained control over their designation and overall operation. The LGPLA also gave the Secretary of State the power to designate UDAs where it was considered to be in the 'national interest' and to provide UDCs with publicly owned land where it was in or adjacent to a designated UDA.

The scope of this form of intervention should not be exaggerated, however, as only 28 EZs were created between 1981 and 1983 and about 20 survived into 1984. Furthermore, although 63,000 jobs were located in EZs during this period, it is estimated that over 50,000 of these had been transferred from other sites.[123]

Similarly, there were only six UDCs in operation by 1987: the docklands on Merseyside and in London that were transferred from local authority control in 1981 and those that followed in Tyne and Wear, Teeside, Manchester and the West Midlands. Significantly, however, all UDCs were designated in Labour-controlled inner-city areas and the fact that 15 EZs were also in Labour-controlled authorities suggests that a degree of targeting had taken place, whether it be political, economic or both.

A number of other initiatives were also tried in an attempt to stimulate local economic activity. These included the Financial Institution Group (FIG) and its offspring Inner City Enterprises, both of which were intended to encourage private and public sector co-operation. Another by-product of FIG, the Urban Development Grant, was used to support private investment in 41 schemes by 1983, while the Business in the Community scheme had created 34 active enterprise agencies by the same year.

Under the latter initiative, regional DOE officers brought together local companies, chambers of commerce, voluntary groups, trade unions and local authorities in schemes designed to assist local communities. The Task Force initiative introduced on Merseyside and in the West Midlands in 1983, on the other hand, involved the Department of Industry, Manpower Services Commission and local firms working together to co-ordinate activity, pilot initiatives and allocate public subsidy.

The removal of economic regeneration from the local electoral sphere is analogous to the transfer of other responsibilities described in chapter one. This later process had been started by the preceding Labour government under the Inner Urban Areas Act 1978, but the direct involvement of ministers and civil servants, the creation of agencies answerable only to the centre and the secondment of private sector personnel was now given a new emphasis.

In a move that paralleled the government's approach to deregulation, privatization and council house sales, the overall reduction of central funding was intended to make it difficult for local authorities to pursue their own regeneration schemes. This is evidenced by the fact that although £361 million was committed to the urban programme in 1985-86, London's local authorities lost the equivalent of £500 million RSG in 1982 alone. Given this kind of institutional and financial shift, any alternative strategy would require an unprecedented level of commitment and ingenuity.[124]

With this in mind, it is perhaps understandable why any Labour movement response might appear to be lacking in co-ordination and ultimately futile. To this can be added an inconsistency of approach that reflected the fact that local initiatives were the responsibility of individual Labour groups and that trade unions were preoccupied with the anti-union nature of the firms that moved between EZs.

Thus, in spite of the Labour Party NEC declaring its opposition to EZs in the Home Policy Statement of August 1980, Bradford Council requested that the whole City be designated as an EZ. Similarly, Salford's ruling Labour Group ignored a campaign by local residents who opposed the designation of an EZ in an area set aside for housing, a school and parkland. Of course, the local response depended on the strength of the local movement, and authorities that had neither the will nor capability of developing their own plans were faced with a dilemma: either apply for EZ status or risk the accusation that they were not tackling unemployment.

Manchester and Sheffield, on the other hand, refused to apply for EZ status and drew up alternative proposals for local regeneration based on the criteria that would have been used as part of the application process. Sheffield also set up an employment committee and department and the GLC and West Midlands County Council established enterprise boards to pursue alternatives to the Conservative government's strategy. In Sheffield, for example, the new department sought to co-ordinate local authority, trade union and community group activity to: prevent further job losses; stimulate new investment; create new kinds of employment; and, diversify job opportunities.[125]

Such initiatives need to be kept in perspective, however, as the differences in scale between the resources available at local and national levels bear comparison to earlier attempts at regeneration. By December 1983, for example, the Greater London Enterprise Board had approved investment worth £18.6m, supported 142 projects and saved or created about 2,000 jobs.[126] The significance of these figures can also be gauged by comparing them to the employment levels of the larger metropolitan authorities and the scope for job creation and protection that these exhibited.

At the end of 1982, for example, full-time employee levels in the largest authorities were as follows: ILEA 40,339; Birmingham 30,508; Manchester

23,360; Liverpool 21,705; GLC 20,666; Sheffield 20,495; and Leeds 20,162. Significant employment levels were also evident among some non-metropolitan county councils and if London Transport is counted in the GLC total it rises to 80,666.[127] These figures are all the more striking because, with the exception of Sheffield, which remained static, they all display a reduction on their 1979 totals.

With the benefit of hindsight, it is fair to say that the Conservative's approach to local government did involve some features that could be interpreted as the centralization of decision-making. These include giving secretaries of state the powers to intervene and take over local authority functions and the removal of responsibilities from the local democratic sphere. What is also clear is that the deliberate contraction of local welfare provision was part of a neoliberal strategy to redirect public funds to the private sector in the form of tax relief and direct payments.

The pursuit of this agenda is the only context in which the full import of financial restraint, deregulation, privatization and regeneration can be appreciated. As has been explained, these policies worked in tandem and were designed to force dissenting Labour councils to comply with the new order. These interrelations were recognized in calls for a comprehensive campaign of opposition to co-ordinate and strengthen localized resistance. Intriguingly, however, the attempt to create the necessary momentum and organization merely served to expose the weaknesses of democratic practice within the labour movement.

Chapter Five
THE DEFENCE OF LOCAL GOVERNMENT

If the government's intentions are to be thwarted, it is essential that a co-ordinated and effective national campaign involving the TUC, Labour Party, and other local government unions is mounted ....
Geoffrey Drain, NALGO General Secretary

The examples of localized opposition and resistance considered thus far serve to epitomize the dilemmas that are inherent in the labour movement's approach to campaigning activity. First and foremost, the stances adopted were by their very nature reactive and defensive, but this was also a consequence of there not being a coherent alternative programme, at least on the part of the TUC and PLP. Their overriding concern with legality and institutional processes also helps to explain why there was an absence of national co-ordination in all but the performance of the usual ritual tasks.

These inclinations are also indicative of tensions within the labour movement over strategy and echo the differing perspectives discussed in earlier chapters. On the one hand, there were repeated calls from activists for national leadership around a set of specific demands. In response, those upon whom such demands were made showed a determined reluctance to have their options for manoeuvre restricted and an equally strong aversion to anything that might give legitimacy to forms of extra-parliamentary activity.

As part of this dynamic both traditions sought to develop structures and alliances through which a broad-based campaign could be conducted in their preferred image. The differences between these approaches are indicated in the motions submitted to the LPAC, the TUC and other conferences. Likewise, the tactics advocated and the likelihood of them being adopted, are also signified by the bodies that were established and used to co-ordinate campaigning activities. The same is also true of the contrasting leadership styles and the alternative interpretations of democratic practice.

Forging a National Campaign

The need for a co-ordinated response to the Conservative government's assault on labour local authorities was widely accepted within labour movement circles and therefore relatively uncontroversial. Indeed, motions submitted to a range of conferences are consistent in their calls for the defence of local government in general. They also agreed that cuts, privatization and deregulation were part of an interconnected strategy and that services had to be defended. Differences arose, however, over how this could and should be achieved.

For the purposes of this account, the divergence can be stylized into prescriptive and non-prescriptive approaches, but the fact that they were often intertwined means that simplistic assumptions of dichotomy should be avoided at all costs. In 1980, for example, emergency motion No. 5 was moved and seconded at the LPAC by Norwood and Sheffield CLPs and instructed the NEC to: co-ordinate a united fight of Labour councils and trade unions on a no cuts position; include industrial action as a tactic; and campaign to unite local communities behind local councils and their unions. A year later, however, emergency resolution No. 3 was also moved by Norwood CLP, but was less specific than its earlier counterpart.[128]

The fact that the 1980 motion was successful contrasts with later years when resolutions making reference to specific tactics were defeated at successive conferences. Thus, although they shared some of the language used in less specific proposals, those that were unsuccessful usually contained one or more of the following demands: that local authorities refuse to implement cuts; that they should not raise rates or rents; and, that trade unions should be prepared take industrial action to defend jobs and services or to support local authorities resisting cuts.

Another feature of these motions was that they were all moved by Liverpool CLPs, but the fact that they were composited and seconded by CLPs from Sunderland (1981), Poole (1982) and Edinburgh (1983) suggests that support extended beyond Liverpool. In approving Composite 30, the 1983 LAPC also signalled a shift toward this approach. Moved by Sheffield and seconded by Glasgow Shettleton CLPs, this motion combined a more combative stance with the less prescriptive approach when calling for the use of 'political and industrial muscle' to 'oppose through all available channels' further legislation against local government.[129]

Calls for a co-ordinated campaign were also echoed in other quarters. In November 1981, for example, proposals for the involvement of council members and local authority trade unions in a campaign against cuts in jobs and services were submitted to a Special General Meeting (SGM) of the Sheffield Branch of NALGO. This resolution was then circulated with a covering letter to all branches considered to be affected by government proposals.[130]

In the same year, the TUC approved a composite motion, moved by the Civil Service Union and seconded by the AUEW, which identified a link between public expenditure cuts, the centralization of RSG decisions, privatization and the use of the voluntary sector and unemployment to depress wages. The motion also called for a campaign involving the Labour Party NEC, trade unions and local authorities to fight cuts and for support to be given to local authorities and local unions working together against cuts.[131]

The origins of the TUC motion provides an opportunity to understand the process by which prescriptive motions reached national forums and therefore the extent to which they were the initiative of grass roots activists. In this case, NALGO's 1981 annual conference had instructed its NEC to: 'call on the TUC General Council to seek joint action with the NEC of the Labour Party in co-ordinating the activities of trade unions and local authority Labour groups in the fight against the cuts'. The NEC then complied with the decision when it submitted a similarly worded motion to that year's TUC.[132]

As part of NALGO's democratic structures, motions that were to be submitted to annual conference were first debated at steward committee and branch level before final submission through District Council.[133] Such bodies were attended by activists, but as is indicated by the annual general meeting (AGM) and SGM decisions of Liverpool NALGO, associated policies were voted on by those who attended general meetings. For motions to arrive at national forums, therefore, some level of local support had to exist; albeit that the attendance of interested members could make such meetings quorate.

In reality and whatever the wording of motions there was enough scope for a variety of tactical approaches to be advocated and practised within a broad-based campaign. Within this range of possibilities, however, a different, more committed and definitive approach became imperative as local Labour parties won overall control of a succession of councils in 1982 and 1983.

This was due in part to the fact that the growing number of Labour councillors elected on a 'no cuts' platform made confrontation more likely, but it was also a product of the government's response. Faced with a serious threat to its plans for local government, it chose to introduce a new range of measures that were designed to reduce the options available to local authorities that wished not only to resist central policy but to pursue their own agenda. Due to the lack of any innovation at the national level, however, attempts to co-ordinate opposition and resistance tended to rely on old methods.

Having been a feature of opposition to the HFA and the policy and practice of public expenditure reductions in the 1970s, this meant that delegate and other sub-national conferences were once again at the forefront of these endeavours. As before, however, the tactics discussed and the decisions taken tended to reflect whether the conference was organized by officials or was primarily a meeting of activists.

One such example is the Local Government in Crisis: National Labour and Trade Union Conference, which was organized by Lambeth local authority trade unions, Lambeth Labour Party and Lambeth Labour Group and took place on 1 November 1980.[134] Although its sponsors included the NEC of NUPE, several NALGO Branches and two NALGO District Councils, the agenda and decisions adopted indicate an attempt to take the initiative by those advocating a prescriptive approach.

To this end, the draft statement submitted to delegates argued that the reliance on rate increases was limited in its effectiveness due to the imposition of government penalties and the tactic's unpopularity. The main aim of the conference was therefore identified as organizing concerted action to secure more central funding for local services and jobs. Whereas the PLP leaders argued that local autonomy and diversity prevented it from offering a lead to those demanding it, the statement acknowledged the importance of differing local circumstances and recognized the need for individual local authorities and trade unions to take their own decisions, but also sought to identify a strategy around which agreement could be found.

In view of the prevailing circumstances, four options for opposition and resistance were presented to the meeting and can be summarized as: rate increases; not increasing rates or making cuts (effectively deficit budgeting); resignation of councillors; and industrial action. These alternatives formed the basis of debate and resulted in the overwhelming agreement that Labour councils should: not cut jobs or services; not raise rents or rates to compensate for government cuts; refuse to sell council houses or housing land; introduce a 35 hour week for all employees; and work with local anti-cuts committees and community groups to build support.

The conference also resolved that trade unionists should: refuse to cover for unfilled vacancies; refuse to deal with increased charges; and consider strike action and occupation to defend threatened facilities. A steering committee of 50 delegates was then elected to oversee the exchange of information relating to action being taken in different labour movement organizations and given the remit to recall the conference in support of councils or councillors penalized by the government.

Although the positions adopted fit with what has been termed the prescriptive approach, there was still a sense of realism. This is indicated by the rejection of a motion submitted by Ted Knight, Labour Leader of Lambeth Council, that called for Labour controlled authorities to refuse to implement cuts provided that trade unions agreed to organize extended industrial action from January 1981. Delegates also defeated an amendment moved on behalf of NUPE by Ron Keating, the union's Assistant General Secretary, which reiterated the national Labour Party's preferred approach and proposed that local authorities should increase rates and blame the government.

Even though the Lambeth conference provides further evidence of the efforts that were being made to galvanize resistance, the outcome was no more concrete than similar meetings convened by officials. These include the December conferences held in Coventry during 1979, and in Leeds a year later, to discuss how Labour groups should respond to cuts in local authority funding. A meeting of controlling Labour groups and their local parties was also convened in July 1981 to 'co-ordinate a sustained campaign against present policies and threatened further legislation'.[135]

In the event, the decisions taken by both kinds of meeting acknowledged the absence of effective structures for the organization of support within the labour movement and among the public. More importantly for the future, the Lambeth conference adds weight to the conclusion that support for the prescriptive and non-prescriptive approaches approximates to a difference between the stances adopted by some local activists and those in positions of leadership.

This inference can be justified on the basis of the background of those attending the conference which included: 450 delegates from local authority unions; 200 from CLPs; 50 from Labour Groups; and 300 observers, and by the nature of Ron Keating's amendment.[136] The number of representatives and the bodies by whom they were sponsored can also be interpreted as indicating that the tactics advocated were designed to form part of a broad-based campaign.

Conversely, however, the fact that Lambeth Labour Group chose to act against the decisions of a conference organized in part by the local labour movement calls into question the authority of the conference. In other words, the evidence of past and future events suggest that people who attended conferences and voted for positions of high principle did so without any mandate for their actions.

In London, for example, Ken Livingstone claimed that the positions adopted by local NALGO BECs were 'out of sympathy with the bulk of its membership' and therefore weak.[137] At this point, it is therefore worth pointing out that while differences existed between leaders and activists, there was an analogous gap between the positions adopted by some labour movement activists and the rank-and-file members they claimed or sought to represent.

Whatever the negative features of the Lambeth conference and other campaign bodies, it should also be remembered that in order to try and win the support of trade unionists, party members and the public there first had to be an agreed position. To this end, such initiatives were also part and parcel of on-going attempts to create effective organizations through which a co-ordinated campaign of opposition and resistance could be conducted.

On the downside, there appears to have been a tendency in some quarters to regard the submission and approval of conference motions as concrete achievements in-themselves. What the contents of such motions indicate, however, is that the importance of co-ordinating activity and developing structures was at least recognized if not always put into practice.

The existence and development of ad hoc committees in the early 1980s are also strikingly similar to those of the anti-cuts campaigns of the previous decade. On Merseyside alone, such groups included: the Merseyside Liaison Committee, which organized public meetings on cuts in 1980; the Merseyside Anti Cuts Committee; a group called Merseyside Education Alliance which, in 1983, included trade unions, community and other groups; and the North West Public Sector Campaign Committee.[138]

At the national level, the TUCLGC encouraged and participated in the creation and development of campaigning bodies. Local government unions, for example, were reminded of the committee's 1976 recommendation that local JTUCs be established to co-ordinate action against cuts. The TUCLGC also encouraged the creation of co-ordination committees at the regional level, to improve TUC-Labour Party liaison and wrote to member unions stressing the importance of liaison with local Labour groups.[139]

A similar, but more tangible development took place in NALGO in July 1981, when the annual National Local Government Group Meeting (NLGGM) was reconvened in line with a decision of that year's annual conference. The NLGGM was attended by delegates from local branches and therefore provided a means by which activists and officers could discuss and agree a response to the government's approach to local government.

This level of participation and interaction is fairly remarkable considering that NALGO had only introduced its shop stewards system in 1976 and, all the more so, because it was instrumental in the call for a '... detailed strategy of national action to defend the jobs and living standards of NALGO members in local government'. As with meetings convened by other organizations during these early stages, the NLGGM was adjourned, so that the National Local Government Committee (NLGC) could draft and circulate proposals on how such a strategy could be formulated and put into practice.[140]

The subsequent report was circulated in September 1981 and outlined a number of options that were expected to maximize unity among NALGO members, while helping to forge solidarity with other local authority unions and with the Labour Party at national and local levels. Perhaps predictably the preferred tactics included the usual focus on institutional processes such as publicity drives, parliamentary intervention and meetings with the local authority associations to encourage opposition to specific measures.

More significant, is the fact that the authors of the report were prepared to acknowledge that a co-ordinated campaign of industrial action might be the only way to change central government policy. Short of this, the type of activity deemed to be feasible was restricted to a repetition of earlier initiatives. Likewise, the options for action that were 'not already being taken as part of the cuts campaign' were therefore considered to be limited.[141]

Once a combination of 'less extreme' measures was discounted as a way of securing concessions, only two alternatives were considered to have a realistic chance of success. The first involved a campaign of 'widespread national strike action by all local government trade unions' and the second foresaw branches encouraging local authorities to resist cuts on the basis that if this resulted in bankruptcy NALGO members would refuse to co-operate with government-appointed commissioners.

In assessing the feasibility of each option, the report concluded that any attempt to stage widespread strike action would be vulnerable to the variable impact of the government's policies and that neither approach could guarantee maximum unity amongst NALGO members. Similarly, it also acknowledged that there were inherent problems in taking action in local authorities considered to be allies in the fight against central government policy. Although not mentioned in the report, to this list of obstacles can be added the implications of withdrawing from users, services that strikers were supposed to be defending.[142]

The report's identification of two distinct approaches: one combative, pro-active and designed to achieve predetermined objectives and the other a more passive resistance based on nuisance value, resembles the choices outlined at the LPAC during the same period. In the case of NALGO, however, the democratic and responsive nature of its decision-making and consultative procedures allowed activists to shape policy and map out a strategy that was designed to be adapted in response to the government's imposition of more punitive measures.

The outcome of this process was evident in the 'National Strategy of Action' that was approved when the NLGGM was re-convened on 5 March 1982. Essentially, this identified eight areas of action, the most prescriptive being: a strict adherence to NALGO policies opposing cuts, including total opposition to privatization and refusing to cover for vacant posts; initiating the creation of JTUCs within each authority to prepare joint action and co-ordinate publicity; and branches taking indefinite strike action in authorities that were severely affected by cuts or where one or more of their members was declared compulsorily redundant.

In addition, the NEC was instructed to: collect a levy from branches to maintain a national Fighting Fund for striking members, once an unspecified level of strike action in defence of jobs and services was taking place; instruct District Councils to co-ordinate support for striking branches; continue parliamentary opposition; and, maintain the provision of publicity material and advice to branches for the mobilization of public and trade union support. Finally, the NLGC was required to seek the support of other local government unions in the implementation of the strategy and to work with the TUC and STUC to co-ordinate support and organize national demonstrations as appropriate.[143]

Like the examples discussed above, the conjectural nature of NALGO's national strategy illustrates the low level of preparedness and co-ordination within the labour movement at the time. Viewed in this light, it seems clear that unless dissatisfaction amongst members could be translated into concrete outcomes, attempts to enact the more assertive types of resistance would have been isolated and disparate. Nevertheless, the fact that such plans were being considered is an indication of how far some people were prepared to go in opposing and resisting central government policy; albeit confined to the aspiration of officers and activists at this point.

When compared to the positions adopted by the national leaders of the Labour Party, the willingness of NALGO officials to consider using industrial action to change government policy is little short of remarkable. The fact that it anticipates the wording of Composite 30 that was approved by the LPAC in 1983 is also important due to the level of activist involvement in the development of NALGO's policy.[144] In other words, the similarity between this policy and the prescriptive demands submitted to consecutive LPACs serves to corroborate the earlier assertion that such tactics were favoured by activists.

While PLP leaders were able to defeat any suggestion of extra-parliamentary action at the LPAC and even dissuade affiliated unions from countenancing such tactics, its influence over NALGO was negligible. Tensions were therefore created by the PLP's refusal to sanction any challenge to the primacy parliament and, although they predated the 1980s, such strains became a constant feature of labour movement attempts to mount a sustained and co-ordinated campaign in defence of local government. What is less clear is the extent to which advocates of the parliamentarist approach actually worked to inhibit the endeavours of others and why they were motivated to do so.

Selective Leadership

Many of the explanations for a lack of leadership in the early 1980s are premised on a myth of betrayal and this is especially true of analyses that emanate from activist quarters. To a degree, this is implicit in the reasoning of the CLPD: that MPs and councillors should be held accountable to the party members and replaced if they refuse. More often than not, however, the parliamentary leadership and MPs were not apostates because they acted according to their core beliefs, even if they were sometimes disingenuous in doing so.

As far as the labour movement campaign against the Conservative agenda for local government goes, the absence of national leadership was manifest in a variety of ways, but most obviously as the lack of a co-ordinated and therefore agreed approach. In part, this reflects the disparate agenda of the government, but the national leadership of the labour movement must bear some responsibility, given its functional roles of decision-making and overseeing the performance of constituent bodies. This is true where their behaviour is analogous to the earlier refusal to offer a lead in the campaign against the HFA but even more so when it involves the deliberate inhibiting of organized opposition.

When there was positive campaigning action it tended to be broad-based and in keeping with the preferred non-prescriptive approach approved by the LPAC and TUC. In one such example, a campaign sub-committee of the Labour Party NEC was established in 1979 and participated in the organization of a series of events to facilitate an expression of dissatisfaction with the Conservative government's approach to local government.

Approved activity included marches, meetings and a demonstration, rally and lobby of parliament in November 1979. The campaign committee also produced a monthly circular entitled 'Cuts Briefing', to provide facts and arguments for spokespeople at the local level and facilitate the sharing of experiences. Similarly, the TUC circulated a 'Cuts Checklist' to local and County Associations of Trades Councils, to provide examples of the kind of cuts taking place.[145]

Each of these examples fit with the institutional approach described earlier and are consistent with the focus on the parliamentary process as the main way of prosecuting campaign aims. This concentration of resources was not so much the inevitable consequence of opposing legislation, however, but an indication of the preferred practice of labour movement leaders.

As far as the Labour Party is concerned its electoral raison d'être and the presence of its leaders in parliament could be taken to imply that this is a natural outcome. Of course, this can be disputed on a number of levels, but that explanation is even less convincing when applied to the upper echelons of the TUC and its almost exclusive concentration on parliament.

Only in specific circumstances, such as opposing the provisions of the Local Government Planning and Land Bill, can the focus on legislative process be understood as reasonable. This assessment also applies to the General Council's approach to the Secretary of State for the Environment before the LGPLA entered the statute books. The same is true of the TUCLGC's liaison with opposition spokespeople and its request that local government unions encourage sponsored MPs to oppose the Bill. Similarly, the fact that, in October 1979, May and December 1980 and November 1981, the TUCLGC held meetings with the Secretary of State for the Environment and other ministers to discuss public expenditure and annual RSG settlements reflects the locus of decision-making.[146]

To a certain extent this was also a reflection of the corporatist practices of the then recent past and the fact that the TUC, if not the Conservative government, was willing to continue such arrangements. No doubt there was also an element of parliamentarism in the TUC's perspective, viewing the House of Commons as the seat of government and therefore offering the best means of amending or influencing government policy and practice. What makes less sense is the fact that in the face of an intransigent government the focus remained almost exclusively on that arena, even when attempts were being made to develop alternative approaches by unions like NALGO.

Equally perplexing is the inconsistent performance of the PLP in opposing particular pieces of legislation. During debates about the Local Government Planning and Land Bill, for example, the PLP leadership failed to offer a distinct line. Indeed, most of the amendments it proposed were provided by the AMA and it was the latter that organized parliamentary lobbying for the local authority associations, not the PLP.

By way of contrast, every clause of the Housing Bill was opposed before its enactment in 1980. This might have been because opposition to the sale of council houses was approved by the 1980 LPAC, but this does not explain why measures introducing central financial control and restraint were opposed in the Housing Bill but not the LGPLA.[147]

This confused approach is symptomatic of a pragmatism that oversaw the introduction of a block grant for Transport funding and the Party leaders' flirtation with and acceptance of neoliberal tenets in the 1970s. In the absence of a clear programme it might seem that the sheer complexity of the Local Government Planning and Land Bill made it difficult to oppose. If this proposition is accepted as true, however, it meant that there was all the more reason why an alternative labour movement campaign of opposition was needed.

In view of the evidence at hand, the most convincing explanation is that the national leaders' room for manoeuvre was restricted by a pre-occupation with the parliamentary process and a preference to merely react to government policy and practice. In their defence the TUC, Labour Party NEC and the PLP could point to the approval of LPAC and Congress motions that called for a campaign without specifying tactics and that the majority of Labour groups were not even considering overt opposition to government policy.

This does not, however, help to explain the leadership's attitude toward those that wanted to take a more combative stance. No doubt it could be argued that the adoption and promotion of a non-prescriptive approach was consistent with the stated preference for a consensual campaign to defend local government services, jobs and local democracy. Even if this was so, it is still something of a contradiction that in order to create such a consensus the demands of a significant number of party and trade union members had to be marginalized and silenced.

The clearest exposition of the Labour leadership's preferred methods is provided by the 1981 and 1983 NEC statements referred to in chapter one. Both offer guidance on how Labour led authorities should deal with cuts in RSG, but by re-affirming the principles outlined in 1981 the latter document demonstrates a lack of development in either the aims or the will of the national party.

Rather than promoting a pro-active approach, the guiding principle of the 1981 statement is clearly ameliorative and non-confrontational. So much so that Labour groups were urged to avoid 'as far as possible' cuts in essential social and public services; compulsory redundancies among the work-force 'in any event'; and, actions that could jeopardize maximum unity. For other service areas, however, the statements warn that: school meal charges should not be increased by more than the rate of inflation; *excessive* rent increases should be avoided, as should measures that might affect a council's responsiveness to tenants' day to day problems.[148]

Put another way, this advice was negative and concerned with what Labour groups should not do, as opposed to what they could do as part of an alternative strategy. Thus, although compulsory redundancies are to be avoided 'in any event', there is no mention of reducing the work-force by means that were less noticeable. Moreover, no account is taken of the impact that job losses would have on the working conditions of those still employed by local authorities.

When challenged about their reluctance to even contemplate the possibility of developing a pro-active campaign, national figures such as Roy Hattersley, Neil Kinnock and Frank Allaun sought to justify the absence of a prescriptive or clear lead on the basis that local authorities had to take decisions according to local circumstances. Hattersley also argued that the PLP could not oppose the LGPLA on the basis that it reduced local government autonomy and then instruct Labour groups how to act.[149]

Similar reasons, including the claim that the Labour Party lacked the machinery to secure concerted action by Labour groups, or hold them accountable to the national party, had been used ten years earlier for not providing a clear lead in the campaign to oppose and resist the HFA. Curiously, however, in both cases the same courtesy or restricted mechanisms of control were not considered to apply to all Labour groups.

In spite of what might have been implied about not being able to hold local parties to account, the national party retained and practised the same powers that had been used to suspend North East Derbyshire CLP in 1974 and hold an enquiry into its affairs. In a similar vein, councillors were suspended from Labour groups in the 1980s and although this happened in Manchester, Bristol and Coventry it only affected those councillors who had voted against cuts.[150]

The manner in which such powers were exercised is therefore conspicuous for the fact that it was used exclusively to penalize those that sought to adopt a more combative response. Likewise, the warning given to the Labour Party's 1982 Local Government Conference that local enterprise Boards should not be allowed to go against national Labour Party economic planning policy was directed at labour groups that were trying to develop alternatives to the neoliberal agenda.

In the final analysis, an explanation for the action taken by Party leaders and the NEC can be found in the fear expressed in the 1970s that if the

Labour controlled local authorities were allowed to disobey legislation Conservative councils might use it as a precedent to defy future Labour governments. This should not be misconstrued as parliamentarism pure and simple, because in the 1980s there was also the added concern that, given the polarization within the party, Labour councils could adopt such a stance when confronted with the policies of a Labour government that they found to be unacceptable; as indeed South Yorkshire had done over transport policy.[151]

On one level, this might help to explain the lack of prescriptive guidance from the national leadership of the Labour Party, but this was not the only reason for the absence of co-ordinated campaigning activity. The fact that insufficient ground-work had been undertaken in many localities can also be seen as a reason for the absence of effective participatory support structures through which a campaign of resistance and opposition could be prosecuted. Furthermore, local campaigns had their own specific and therefore diverse targets that often reflected the importance of particular issues in a given area, as was the case with local authority housing in Norwich.

Even under normal circumstances, action that was primarily focused on local priorities would be difficult to co-ordinate as part of a national campaign concerned with broader issues, but such problems were exacerbated by the overriding concern to accommodate only non-confrontational strategies. In this respect, the generalized non-committal approach adopted by the Labour Party NEC contrasts with the prescriptive tactics advocated by activists and some localities as the only realistic option for preventing cuts and changing government policy.

Stipulations about achieving maximum unity could therefore be interpreted as serving to reduce goals and tactics to the lowest common denominator: that of sympathetic Conservative and Labour councillors who disliked the changes but were not prepared to adopt an overt stance of opposition and resistance. That this left a leadership vacuum for those who favoured a different approach, was not so much a betrayal by those holding national positions, but rather a consequence of the raison d'être of the PLP.

There were attempts to redress this deficit and to develop structures that could be used to prosecute a co-ordinated campaign. Indeed, preparations were stepped up in the face of the government's escalation of the dispute when it introduced the Rates Bill and legislation to abolish the Metropolitan County councils. Then, around the same time, those looking for a workable alternative were bequeathed the exemplar of Liverpool City Council's campaign for more resources in 1983–84.

Chapter Six
LIVERPOOL AS ENIGMA

The mode of production of material life conditions the social, political and intellectual life process in general. It is not the consciousness of men that determines their being, but, on the contrary, their social being that determines their consciousness.
Karl Marx, *A Contribution to the Critique of Political Economy*, Preface

Of all the instances of opposition and resistance to the Conservative government's approach to local government in the early 1980s, one example stands out from the crowd. Whereas attempts at authority wide resistance had failed to materialize in Lambeth and in other areas opposition was mustered over specific issues like privatization, the Liverpool labour movement campaign for more resources between November 1983 and July 1984 managed to attract broad-based support and combine a range of issues under the umbrella of central funding.[152]

For a variety of reasons the significance of the Liverpool experience has been overplayed by some and underestimated by others. In the cold light of day, however, the reasons why and how the campaign happened are firmly rooted in local socio-economic circumstances and developments that do not suit extrapolation to other areas. Nevertheless, the publication of the Rates White Paper in 1983 coincided with events unfolding in Liverpool and the victory claimed in the following year served to galvanize the resolve of others in their preparations for opposition to the latest round of punitive neoliberal measures.

This conjuncture worked to exacerbate those problems that were associated with a lack of national leadership and therefore allowed some of the methods used by Liverpool to be interpreted as a template for action by those seeking a more combative response. Viewed in a sympathetic manner the conflation of the two approaches could be understood as a consequence of the circumstances at hand, but this would be to miss the point.

The full implications of this development can only be appreciated if the socio-economic context within which the Liverpool labour movement evolved is compared to that of others involved in campaigning activity. These similarities and differences not only provide an insight into those elements that can be identified as prerequisites for concerted action. They also help to identify the connections between historical developments and the organization, practice and tactics that were employed as part of an apparently successful campaign.

Liverpool Labour Movement

Observed from a distance, developments can appear to be very similar. As a consequence of the Trade Disputes and Trade Unions Act 1927 and its distinction between industrial and political action, for example, there was an almost universal separation of trade union and Labour Party roles at the local level. While this might appear to be a uniform process, it nevertheless conceals a multiplicity of variations and complexities that included the experiences of Liverpool and Sheffield where joint organizations were maintained until the 1970s.[153]

In the case of Sheffield, the domination of the engineering and steel unions reflected the industrial landscape and provided the basis for a strong and determined local labour movement which maintained a consistent level of membership and support through its representative structures. By way of contrast, however, the Trades Council and Labour Party in Liverpool was little more than an alliance of trade union and party officials, premised on moribund party organizations, such as the Liverpool Exchange Constituency, which had no members.

Whereas the circumstances in Sheffield contributed to the relatively peaceful development of a coherent and consistent party programme, the weakness of the position in Liverpool made for vulnerability and volatility in the face of local social and economic change. In one respect, this becomes apparent from the 1960s when the TGWU allowed local branches to send rank and file delegates from the docks and car plants to the Trades Council and Labour Party, and this at a time when white collar affiliates were growing.

Underpinning these developments were the historical reliance on the seaport as a source of unskilled, casualized employment and the post-war introduction of manufacturing industry to the city. The latter initiative was part of a regional economic policy designed to offset the loss of port related industries and jobs, but had the unintended consequences of serving to radicalize those affected.

This was due in part to a clash of cultures based on the social relations of production. There was, for example, a world of difference between the nature of dock work and the discipline of the production line. Perhaps less expected was the resistance to factory closures and job losses that resulted from public expenditure cuts and the consequent withdrawal of public subsidy in the form of regional aid in the late 1970s and early 1980s.

Although Liverpool was not alone in experiencing economic decline the contraction there was particularly severe. While the whole of Merseyside witnessed a decline in its manufacturing, construction and service sectors of 42 per cent, 17 per cent and 5 per cent respectively between 1971 and 1984, Liverpool lost 57 per cent, 47 per cent and 33 per cent of the same categories. As might be expected, this collapse had an equally drastic effect on employment in the city, which fell by 33 per cent between 1971 and 1985, as opposed to a national decline of just 3 per cent.[154]

The process in Liverpool was also exacerbated by the relocation of large scale enterprises as part of past regional economic policy. So much so, that by 1979 around 40 per cent of employees were working for less than 1 per cent of the City's employers and as these firms either failed or shrank in size, Liverpool City Council was left as the largest single source of jobs on Merseyside. This then is one reason why the local authority became the focus of attempts to create or preserve jobs.[155]

Faced with the local consequences of economic crisis, sections of the Liverpool labour movement engaged in campaigns to prevent factory closures or redundancies at British Leyland, CAV Lucas, Fisher Bendix, GEC, Plessey, Rank-Hovis, Tate and Lyle and Western Ship Repairers. Although these rearguard actions failed to achieve their immediate aims they had a broader impact of radicalizing trade union activists who, in parallel to similar developments in other areas, subsequently joined the Labour Party in search of a broader political strategy and moved into local government as the main chance of employment.[156]

The influx of new members helped those wishing to challenge the established arrangements within the Liverpool labour movement and contributed to the separation of Trades Council and Labour Party in 1970. This process was also assisted when the Labour Group split over its response to the HFA in 1972, when only 21 out of 49 councillors voted in line with Party policy and opposed the proposal to increase rents. That minority was then supported by the DLP and the episode used to provide added impetus to the campaign to make the Labour Group accountable to the wider party.[157]

An essential feature of the ensuing struggles and a deciding factor in the transfer of power from Labour Group to DLP was the move to give the latter control over the selection of prospective councillors. Under the new arrangement, candidates were only accepted if they agreed to vote in line with DLP policy and in the early 1980s some of the activists who joined from struggles against factory closure were selected as councillors. The resultant control exercised over the Labour Group in Liverpool, with the consent of prospective councillors, resembles practice in Clay Cross, London, Manchester and Sheffield. Finally, the ascendancy of the DLP also saw the creation of policy sub-committees which mirrored the departmental structure of the local authority.[158]

Like Liverpool other areas also experienced changes in membership totals and composition. Sheffield and Southwark Labour parties, for example, witnessed an influx of new members that included manual workers and public sector professionals. In Sheffield, job losses in the steel and engineering industries affected the composition of the Trades Council as NALGO became the largest member and other public sector unions increased their affiliations. In London too, the two largest block votes at the GLLP conference were held by the TGWU and NUPE; amounting to around 25 per cent of the total.[159]

One other factor that should not be overlooked in any discussion about the development of the Liverpool Labour Party is the impact and role of Militant Tendency. Although moribund parties, of which there were many in Liverpool, were considered to be easy targets for entryism it is too simplistic to assume a causal connection between the two. As has already been noted, the main policy and organizational influences came from the input of activists radicalized through industrial struggles and Militant's influence was that of a minority that depended on the support of a broader spectrum.[160]

Caution should therefore be exercised where Militant's role is concerned. The pretence of control not only served the interests of the Tendency itself but also those of the Conservative and Labour Party leaderships who sought to discredit the Liverpool campaign. This kind of misrepresentation is also evident in journalistic and non-critical academic accounts and takes no account of the disproportionate role played by other groups like the Communist Party, whose members held influential positions in several unions.[161]

Of much more significance are those developments and experiences that resulted in a strong working relationship between the Labour Party and local authority trade unions. Instead of being merely an alliance of officials, as had been the case on the Trades Council and Labour Party in the past, the new understanding was based on the involvement of activists, some of whom were members of both. More than any other factor, it was this bond between the Labour Group and the representatives of the local authority workforce that underpinned Liverpool's ability to mount a concerted campaign between November 1983 and July 1984.[162]

While it is true that the Labour administration agreed to improvements in employee conditions of service and enhanced the role of union representatives, it would be wrong to suppose that this is the only or even the main reason why trade unions supported the campaign for more resources. In reality, the developing relationship between the Labour Party, Labour Group and local authority trade unions was much more complex than this, being influenced by the decline of the private sector and by disputes with the Liberal administration 1981-83.

As part of the overall socio-economic impact, the effective disappearance of large size firms meant that the bulk of the trade union movement in Liverpool was now based in the local authority. This was also reflected in affiliations to the Labour Party where GMBATU and the TGWU had 85 delegates between them, more than the others put together.[163] Of the two unions, however, GMBATU had most delegates, because representation was based on the number of members and on how many branches the union had.

Nevertheless, it should not be assumed that GMBATU's influence stemmed from its status as the biggest union in terms of total membership and the fact that it was organized into several branches. Stated simply, the more branches there were, the more room there was for the adoption of different policy positions, and it was therefore the political composition of certain branches that afforded it a pivotal position in policy making. Suggestions that there was a 'sweetheart relationship' are therefore superficial, misleading and ignore the fact that GMBATU was forced into disputes with the authority to ensure that promises of improved conditions, such as a 35 hour week, were honoured.[164]

Such assertions also fail to explain NALGO's relations with the Labour Party. The Chairperson and Secretary of the Liverpool branch, from the late 1970s and throughout the 1980s, for example, both refute the idea that service conditions improvements played a part in securing NALGO's support for the campaign for more resources. On the contrary, they contend that improvements were easier to negotiate with the Liberal administrations, but agree that Labour afforded more job security.[165]

In the context of the campaign, the most important arrangements introduced by the Labour administration are identified as those that were advantageous, not to the conditions of service of any particular trade union members, but to trade union activism in general. These included: paid time off for trade union duties; Joint Shop Steward Committee (JSSC) observers on the Council's Personnel Committee; trade union nomination rights in the filling of vacancies; non-voting trade union observers at recruitment interviews; and departmental stewards committee representation at Personnel and Performance Review Committees considering the filling of vacancies. Most crucial of all, however, was the provision of paid time off for people who attended and organized workplace meetings and courses promoting the campaign.[166]

Even so, it would be sheer folly to imply that NALGO's policy development was dictated by such arrangements, especially as it was not affiliated to the Labour Party. That said, NALGO did on occasion respond to party policy, such as in February 1980 when a SGM was called to discuss opposition to 'huge rent and rate increases' that were designed to compensate for cuts in RSG. This meeting received a report entitled 'The Rate, the Cuts and the Government', which discussed the Party's policy in the context of developments in local government funding since 1975 and outlined the case for and against cuts.[167] The approval of branch policy through meetings open to all members is evidence of the democratic practice of Liverpool NALGO, but as no attendance figures are available it is impossible to gauge the level of support.

In November 1983 NALGO departmental delegates also took part in a special Service Conditions Committee that was convened to consider a Labour Party document entitled 'Jobs, Services and Rates'. The meeting agreed to circulate the document to all NALGO stewards and to submit motions to NALGO's North West and North Wales District Council and to the North West District Local Government Committee calling for national support for the campaign in Liverpool.[168]

Neither the records of the SGM nor the Service Conditions Committee give any indication of a predetermined consensus between NALGO and the Liverpool Labour Party. What they do show is a level of support among union activists for similar policies. For the purposes at hand, however, there is little to be gained from speculating about the reasons for this. Except, that is, to say that NALGO's support cannot be explained in reference to affiliation to the Labour Party or to nomination rights, which it rejected. On the other hand, it should also be acknowledged that a number of activists who were Labour Party members also played a leading role in the campaign.

In general terms, the main factor that helped draw together the Labour Group, DLP and local authority trade unions was the latter's dealings with the Liberal and Conservative administrations between 1980 and 1983. An early example of this development involved the re-negotiation of the local authority's 'no redundancy agreement' when, although involved in a council-wide dispute over the issue, NALGO reached their own favourable settlement with the City Council in August 1980.

As part of this process, NALGO agreed that they would not undermine action that was taken by other unions in furtherance of this dispute, but the Labour Group voted against the NALGO deal because vacancies were not being filled and because it had not been consulted as part of the negotiating process. These events, it is worth noting, took place at a time when the Labour Group was at odds with the DLP, but its actions on this occasion were deemed to have stemmed from a misunderstanding. As a result it was acknowledged that there had been a lack of co-ordination between NALGO and the Labour Party and John Hamilton, the leader of the latter, agreed that there was a need for better liaison in the future.[169]

The next event that served to cement the co-operation and understanding between the party and the unions was the successful campaign mounted against Liberal Party plans to privatize the housing management and cleansing services. This drive against privatization is also credited with contributing to Labour's local election victory of 1983[170] and, like other areas, involved joint trade union action and committees. First and foremost, however, this campaign is credited with raising the consciousness of union members through the successful prosecution of joint initiatives, such as delivering leaflets and boycotting work associated with privatization.[171]

The developing relationship between the Labour Party and NALGO is also indicated by the invitation of speakers to address meetings. As part of this arrangement Derek Hatton, the then Labour Party Personnel spokesperson, was allowed to speak about budget issues at the Branch Executive Council (BEC) in February 1981 and John Hamilton also spoke in July 1982. This trend was continued when Hatton, as Deputy Leader of the Liverpool Labour Group, and Tony Byrne, the Chair of Finance, were allowed to address BEC meetings about the campaign for more resources. The later meetings in particular can be seen as part of a gathering of momentum that followed the local election victory in 1983 and of a process that was pivotal in shaping the way that support for the campaign was built.

Campaigning Activity

Although the names and titles might sound familiar, the actual conduct and composition of campaign bodies in Liverpool bear an indelible local stamp. In particular, the roles played by activists, the tactics employed, the way in which decisions were taken and the constituents that such committees represented were all indicative of the City's recent socio-economic history.

That said, the importance of these factors extends beyond establishing a simple differentiation between geographical areas or identifying successful mechanisms for the resistance of central government policy and practice. The Liverpool experience actually provides further evidence of the inconsistent approach of national Labour Party figures and therefore demonstrates the importance of local determination, commitment and support in overcoming attempts at manipulation.

As has been noted, broad-based committees formed to organize, promote and carry out opposition and resistance to central government were common features of campaigning activity in the 1970s and early 1980s. In general terms, therefore, Liverpool was no different in so far as these roles were performed by Liverpool City Council JSSC; the Merseyside Trade Union and Labour Movement Campaign Committee (MTULMCC); meetings between councillors, full-time and lay trade union representatives; and the Campaign Working Party established by the local authority.

The JSSC, for example, was formed and developed in the late 1970s as a response to attacks on jobs and working conditions by an earlier, local form of Liberal and Conservative coalition. Strictly activist led, it eschewed full-time officer participation, included both manual and non-manual trade unions and organized joint union campaigns against redundancies, cuts and privatization.[172]

Elsewhere, JTUCs that had been set up in response to the effects of public expenditure cuts were few and far between and rarely involved both employment categories. In Sheffield, for example, the JTUC representing local authority workers involved only blue collar unions and a joint union campaign committee formed in January 1985 involved full-time officers. Bizarrely, Birmingham even had two committees: the Public Sector Liaison Committee founded by lay members, and a committee dominated by full-time officials.

Local campaigns and protests against public expenditure had also been organized through Trades Councils in the 1970s. Such activity extended into the 1980s in Croydon and in opposition to privatization in Basingstoke and Wandsworth. Similarly, the Liverpool Trades Council established a Co-ordinating Committee Against Cuts in September 1979; supported a one day strike called by South Yorkshire Trades Council to oppose cuts on 18 February 1980 and helped found the MTULMCC in 1983.[173]

As the minutes of Liverpool NALGO meetings testify, however, the JSSC replaced the Trades Council as the main co-ordinating body for local unions.

This is evidenced by the fact that mention of the latter tails off from April 1981, while references to the former increase. With the demise of the private sector, the shift of attention to the local authority arena and a preoccupation with sectional in-fighting, it therefore seems almost inevitable that the Trades Council would be eclipsed by the JSSC.[174] In practice, though, the Trades Council co-existed with the JSSC, albeit as a junior partner, and was used to obtain support from the wider labour movement.

One of the main functions of the JSSC was the role it played in co-ordinating activities and policies among member unions, as evidenced by NALGO's fight to stop cuts and redundancies in 1980. In specific terms, this meant ceasing to serve Council committees and sub-committees after 4.45 pm and not co-operating with: councillors who voted for cuts; working parties on cuts; work on the transfer of housing repairs to private contractors; and the processing of redundancies. More generally, a programme of action undertaken with other unions included one-day strikes, demonstrations, lobbies of council meetings, and mass meetings.

Such polices were developed at meetings attended by stewards representing affiliated trade unions and then presented to union members for approval. The activities described above were agreed in this manner, when NALGO held meetings on 4 June and 25 June 1980, to vote on a JSSC call for industrial action in response to 600 threatened redundancies in the Minor Works Department.

The JSSC itself organized a conference of all shop stewards on 28 June and a meeting of all local authority trade union members on 10 July 1980. Similar consultative processes were also used in 1984 when a NALGO SGM held on 6 March supported the Labour Group's case for more resources and approved strike action for 29 March. This day had also been designated as national 'Democracy Day' by the TUC and was the date that the council was due to meet and decide its budget options for the forthcoming financial year.[175]

The JSSC also helped establish the MTULMCC and was joined in this endeavour by the Labour groups of Liverpool City and Merseyside County councils, the Trades Council, Liverpool's DLP, the City's MPs and by the Merseyside Trade Union and Unemployed Resources Centre (MTUURC).[176] Originally formed to oppose public expenditure cuts and anti-trade union legislation, the MTULMCC was the broadest based group involved in Liverpool's campaign for more resources and undertook a role that is comparable to that played by the NSC in the 1970s.

Whereas the primary role of the JSSC centred on the co-ordination of activities and policies at local authority level, the MTULMCC had a wider reach. As well as producing and distributing publicity, it also helped arrange meetings at which representatives from stewards committees, union branches, district committees, community groups, tenants associations and unemployed centres could discuss issues and exchange views.

On many occasions the JSSC and MTULMCC can also be seen to complement each other's activities, such as when they helped organize: a rally and demonstration in Liverpool on 19 November 1983; the 'Liverpool in Crisis' delegate conference held 27 February 1984; a meeting of activists on 9 February 1984; various lobbies of City Council budget meetings; public and factory gate meetings; and a lobby of parliament on 22 March 1984.[177]

Regular meetings between councillors, full-time union officials and activists also took place outside the above structures and were used to discuss the tactics, direction and progress of the campaign for more resources. The fact that they involved full-time officers and shop stewards helps to show how the perspective of rank and file union delegates differed to those of officials.

At a meeting held between councillors and full-time officers in February 1984, for example, the full-time GMBATU representative announced that the policies presented to councillors were not necessarily official union policy, because full-timers had not been involved in the decision-making process. The same meeting also provides evidence of tensions within NUPE, with the full-time representative expressing concern over the lack of involvement in the JSSC and indicating that there was national pressure for local policy to be reversed.[178]

Established under the auspices of the local authority to assist with co-ordinating activity and disseminating information, the Campaign Working Party is the other broad-based committee that played a leading role in Liverpool during the period. As indicated by its terms of reference, one of its main functions was helping the council's communication sub-committee to create and develop links with local authorities and other bodies that shared the aims of maintaining and expanding jobs and services. Because it was an official organ of the Council, however, the Working Party was tasked with promoting and securing support for its policies, as well as helping to develop an effective campaign.[179]

Like the MTULMCC, the Working Party was designed to be inclusive and was therefore open to councillors from Knowsley, Liverpool, Merseyside and Saint Helens councils. Members of the executive of the JSSC and representatives of the trade union movement outside the city council were also eligible to attend. So too, delegates from local community based organizations such as Merseyside Community Relations Council, the

Liverpool Council of Voluntary Services and Merseyside pensioners groups. The council's Central Support Unit (CCSU) also played a similar role developing links with service users via the council's departments, liaising with voluntary organizations, community groups, the MTUURC and by providing speakers for meetings on the campaign.[180]

Of course, similar committees were also used in the organization of campaigning activities undertaken elsewhere. A particular feature of the Liverpool experience, however, was the extent to which activists drove the conduct of the campaign and therefore influenced the kind of tactics employed. As has already been noted, this was a reflection of the way the local labour movement developed and how this influenced the struggles for rank and file control of unions and party.

Another similarity was the fact that the Liverpool campaign replicated earlier labour movement activity in so far as it staged a number of delegate conferences. Given the labour movement's predilection for such events, this comes as no surprise, but again there were differences. The 'Liverpool in Crisis' conference that took place on 27 February 1984, for example, was aimed at local authority workers from other areas and open to delegates from interested stewards committees.[181] This focus on shop stewards and lay members is symptomatic of an overriding concern with the mobilization of activists to develop the situation in Liverpool and build support for the campaign in general.

In similar fashion, the National Fight Back Conference was held on 23 June 1984 and open to activists from: trade union branches; stewards committees; Trades councils; Branch, Constituency and District Labour parties; Labour groups; Labour Party Young Socialists; trade union youth sections; community groups; tenants associations; and unemployed centres. Organized by the Liverpool CCSU, the event was supposed to consist of opening speeches, followed by four group discussions focusing on: defending local authorities; protecting public services; campaign building; and fighting factory closures and redundancies. On the day, however, the workshops were cancelled and the event took the form of a rally which left little room for meaningful discussion of tactics or issues.[182]

Much of the publicity and education practices employed as part of the Liverpool campaign are also reflective of activity undertaken elsewhere. On a general level this involved the production and distribution of leaflets, stickers, posters and badges and the compilation of a petition containing 20,000 signatures.[183] Once again, however, the involvement of activists meant that the campaign message was able to reach out to a wider audience.

In Liverpool NALGO, for example, a Branch Campaign Committee was set up in December 1983 and attended by delegates from departmental stewards committees who helped to produce ad hoc circulars as well as the regular bulletin, 'Our City Our Fight' (OCOF). Distributed to local branch members, OCOF explained issues, provided a running commentary on developments and catalogued support from elsewhere. The committee was also instrumental in publicizing the campaign outside the local authority.

As part of its latter role, the committee arranged for activists to visit the Norfolk Branch of NALGO and to address meetings of the union's North East District and South West District councils. This initiative also formed part of a reciprocal process, with Liverpool receiving speakers from Merseyside County Council and Hackney branches. Similarly, Glasgow District Branch requested speakers from Liverpool, Lothian and Sheffield.[184]

In Liverpool itself, the run up to the local elections in 1984 represented a period of peak activity as all efforts were geared toward maximizing support for the campaign and therefore Labour candidates. NALGO activists were again involved in organizing and addressing workplace meetings that were attended by an estimated 4,000 members and running campaign courses for 180 shop stewards. An all steward meeting was also convened on 12 April 1984 to discuss the situation after the council agreed not to set a rate.[185]

Perhaps the most innovative role was played by those activists that took part in the NALGO Jobs, Services and Rates Road Show, which leafleted various parts of the city in the week prior to the local elections in 1984. Advertisements were also placed in the local media asking people to vote for Jobs and Services and a circular issued to NALGO members stressed that NALGO was independent from the Labour Party, but that both supported the same issues in the May elections. Finally, Liverpool NALGO also wrote to dissenting Labour councillors enquiring after their positions on cuts and redundancies.[186]

The positive effects of all this activity effort can be seen to have borne fruit on a number of fronts. First and foremost the Labour Party increased its majority by seven and secured 46 per cent of the vote in a higher than normal turn-out of 51 per cent in the 1984 local election.[187] This was an important boost for the campaign and especially those Labour councillors who were asked to risk illegality and surcharge. Likewise, the numbers of people attending demonstrations and lobbies of council meetings on 29 March, 25 April and 11 July 1984 served to strengthen resolve and can be taken as an indication of how effective campaigners were in publicizing events.

Activists were a central part of this process and therefore contributed to the mobilization, not only of trade union and party members, but of sections of the broader public as well. Their success in achieving such levels of support was no doubt due in part to the fact that the campaign played on the unfair treatment of Liverpool. Whatever those reasons were, however, the involvement of rank and file members proved to be a crucial factor in determining the outcome of dealings with the national leadership of the Labour Party.

National Interference

In keeping with the established practice of their forebears in the 1970s and 80s, national figures began by refusing to support the Liverpool campaign. This should not be understood as a failure to provide leadership, because clear guidance was on offer. Indeed the stance taken was consistent with the examples cited in previous chapters and was clearly more to do with avoiding confrontation than securing a just outcome or protecting people who faced losing the jobs or services upon which they relied.

The attempt to undermine the Liverpool DLP and Labour Group began in March 1984 when the General Secretaries of five unions with members in Liverpool City Council were contacted by the office of Neil Kinnock, the Party leader. A meeting was then arranged between Jack Straw and John Cunningham for the PLP and the Assistant General Secretaries and National officers from GMBATU, NALGO, NUPE, the NUT and the TGWU. At the meeting, Cunningham and Straw made a mockery of the previous argument that respect for autonomy prevented the national party from interfering in local affairs and sought trade union support for an attempt to restrain the leadership of Liverpool Labour Group.

Although a minority in terms of union membership in the city council, and probably because the first two unions were not part of the campaign, the:

> representatives of the NUT, NUPE, and TGWU agreed with John Cunningham that they should seek a meeting with leading members of the Labour Group ... to indicate that the Labour Movement would not support illegality nor would it be willing to bail anybody out if things went wrong.[188]

In contrast, Dave Prentis for NALGO and John Edmonds for GMBATU refused to support the proposal on the grounds that their members were in favour of the policies adopted by the council. They also argued that neither Cunningham nor Straw appreciated the issues involved or strength of feeling aroused by the problems in Liverpool.

As a consequence of these representations, it was agreed that a fact finding meeting should be held with leaders of the Labour Group to explore the choices available for the impending budget. Prentis and Alan Jinkinson, NALGO Assistant General Secretary, attended the subsequent meeting with councillors and the latter described the trade union presence as 'conciliatory'. The NALGO representatives also stressed that the Liverpool Branch was strongly in support of the council's policy not to cut either jobs or services.

Far from promoting the rights of local parties to vary policy based on local circumstances and democratic mandates, the PLP representatives proposed compliance with national Labour Party policy. Despite the evidence from other areas where voters punished local councillors in the polls, this advice consisted of an unchanged and implausible formula of a 60 per cent rates increase and reductions in service provision to minimize the impact of central government measures.[189]

Following the Liverpool Labour Party's electoral success in May 1984, however, the PLP approach underwent a noticeable change from dissuader to that of facilitator and intermediary. Cunningham, for example, liaised between the Liverpool Labour Group, PLP, GMBATU, NALGO, NUPE, NUT and Patrick Jenkin, Secretary of State for the Environment. As a result of this initiative Cunningham was able to establish room for manoeuvre after holding informal talks prior to a meeting of all parties on 17 May 1984.

Although it has been argued that, following the general Election defeat in 1983, the leadership of the PLP had exhibited a wariness of 'anything that smacked of radical or revolutionary politics', the attitude toward Liverpool's chosen tactic of refusing to set a rate is also consistent with a visceral dread of even the perception of illegality.[190] Indeed, this position had been restated by Cunningham at the Party's Local Government Conference held in Nottingham in February 1984.

Paradoxically and somewhat speciously the overlap between Liverpool's campaign and preparations for the resistance of rate-capping was also used as an argument to defer Liverpool's resistance. There is therefore a certain irony in the fact that the PLP worked to facilitate a legal settlement that was heralded as a victory for the Liverpool campaign. In other words, having failed to deter the Liverpool Labour Group, the outcome of the PLP's intervention inadvertently served to galvanize the resolve of others who were contemplating non-compliance in 1985 and proved to be instrumental in their choice of the no rate tactic.[191]

Above all else the Liverpool campaign showed that it was possible, at least in the short term, to combine activity in and through official channels with a level of mass agitation and support. That the local Labour Party, GMBATU and NALGO were able to achieve this synchrony was due to the fact that neither group focused exclusively on the political process at the expense of popular participation. In the final analysis, it was this that distinguished the Liverpool experience from previous campaigns and proved to be a major disappointment to national political figures.

If the implications of economic decline and changes in the membership, organization and accountability of labour movement bodies are viewed on a general level, it is hard to see any differences between regions, cities and localities. The Liverpool experience, however, was marked out by the growth of shop stewards systems and broader forms of activism that were, in part, a response to the socio-economic consequences of national and regional government policy.

In other words, the local authority trade unions and the Liverpool Labour Party were embroiled in the broader clash of collectivist and individualist cultures. People radicalized through local struggles joined the Party and, having found that the local authority represented the main opportunity for work, became active in the unions too. This is nowhere more apparent than in the different approaches adopted by NUPE and the NUT on one hand and GMBATU and NALGO on the other. In the latter two unions, the development of activist structures and the support they were able to muster was impossible for national figures to ignore.

These and other factors were therefore instrumental in shaping opposition to government policy and practice in Liverpool. In much the same way, the interaction of local and national socio-economic struggles were reflected in the stances adopted by other localities like Clay Cross in the 1970s and the GLC and Sheffield in the 1980s. More importantly, the differences that each area exhibited were significant enough to mean that there was no single model that could be applied universally in an attempt to guarantee campaign success.

PART THREE
THE PRIMACY PARLIAMENT 1983-1987

Of political parties claiming socialism to be their aim, the Labour Party has always been one of the most dogmatic – not about socialism, but about the parliamentary system.
Ralph Miliband, *Parliamentary Socialism*, Introduction

Chapter Seven
THE VAGARIES OF RATE-CAPPING

It is ... essential for those whom, for want of a more accurate term, we call the ruling class to transform all serious conflicts from struggles over concrete issues into challenges to the rule of law.
Leslie Sklair, *The Struggle Against the Housing Finance Act*

The theory and practice of rate-capping epitomizes the Conservatives' confused approach to local government in the first half of the 1980s and should be understood in that context. In spite of all the evidence to the contrary, the government still maintained that local spending and taxation was inimical to economic recovery. Moreover, the answer now appeared to lie in the limitation of domestic and non-domestic rates raised by Labour-led local authorities and in condensing the issue of local government funding into one piece of legislation.

These restrictions had been threatened as part of earlier attempts to control spending and in keeping with past and future practice Scotland was used as a testing ground when the provision was included in the Local Government and Planning (Scotland) Act 1982. Taken together, the combination of rate limitation with a harsher system of targets and penalties represented a serious challenge to established notions of local autonomy and democracy. When considered in conjunction with the other legislative measures that were at that time unprecedented in their severity, the outcome was effectively one of emasculation.[192]

In England and Wales, the Rates Act 1984 provided the opportunity for a level of focus that was absent from the hitherto fragmented resistance and necessary if it was to be transformed into a co-ordinated response. Curiously enough, however, the fact that the government had apparently exhausted all other options meant that the earlier struggles had achieved a modicum of success. Understood in this way, the issue of rate-capping constitutes the decisive stage in the struggle between the social democratic and collectivist inclinations of Labour led local authorities and the individualistic neoliberal agenda of central government.

This can be illustrated by comparing the motivations that informed the Conservatives' justification of the Rates Bill with those that underpinned the positions taken by sections of the labour movement. The stances adopted by both sides were inevitably influenced by the experiences gained as part of earlier struggles, including events in and around Liverpool. These lessons can be seen clearly in the tactics debated and employed as part of the labour movement's strategy of opposing the Rates Bill and Act prior to implementation and, if necessary, resisting its operation.

Pros and Cons

The Conservatives' reasons for imposing rates limitation is to be found in a variety of sources, but the arguments and their inconsistencies make familiar reading. At the macro-economic level, for example, limitation was advocated as a means of bringing the overall level of spending into line with public expenditure plans. Considering the fact that local rates were not part of the PSBR calculation and that selective rate-capping was estimated to reduce taxation by only 0.5 per cent, it is difficult to substantiate this claim.[193]

In an argument that is similar to the one laid against the 50p tax rate in 2011, the British Chamber of Commerce was also cited as supporting rate-capping on the basis that rates stifled growth, cost jobs and damaged industry. Another justification resembles the public choice view of so-called vested interests and laments the apparent injustice that those who pay non-domestic rates 'have no direct influence on councils'.[194] Further insight into Conservative thinking on the operation of democracy is also available from Kenneth Baker who as Minister for Local Government argued that local mandates were illegitimate because some rate-payers received rebates.[195]

Such reasoning appears to be a contrived version of the no taxation without representation tenet and although it shows a dislike of the principle of one person one vote, the government was not willing to reveal the Party's true colours by re-introducing the 'business vote'. Perhaps as the next best thing, it did propose to limit the level of non-domestic rates levied by individual local authorities and require representatives of industrial and commercial rate-payers to be consulted over expenditure and finance plans.

While it was argued above that earlier attempts to control the spending and activity of local authorities had been misinterpreted as centralization, it would require an act of faith to deny that the imposition of rate limits represents an unambiguous transfer of power and control to the centre. To this end, the Rates Bill was specifically designed to prevent certain communities from supporting their own levels of service provision through local taxation and therefore represents a new approach that was specifically designed to reduce local autonomy.

The proposals were so stringent that even if authorities decided to use the right of appeal, they would have to agree to a central inspection of local finances and thereby run the risk of having their spending curbed even further. This was no doubt intended to work as a disincentive to the 13 authorities whose rate-cap was lower than the amount they had levied in 1984-85. All in all, the combined effects were also similar to those of cash limits, described earlier, because they were exacerbated by the fact that they took no account of inflation or increased labour costs.[196]

As if that wasn't enough, there was also a tougher system of targets and penalties for local authorities and other pieces of legislation that were perceived as threatening local democracy, jobs and services. The full implications for local authority spending are outlined in the Appendix, but can be illustrated in reference to Merseyside County Council where the maximum capped precept increase of 18p would incur 16p in penalties.[197]

Once again, however, there were irregularities and inconsistencies that meant that in some circumstances the measures contained in the Rates Bill could appear to be counter-productive. This was so for the capped authorities that had their targets frozen at 1984-85 levels which, in spite of rhetoric to the contrary, meant that if they complied with the restrictions they could receive more grant. In other words, by preventing them from increasing rates to fund spending and freezing their targets, they would no longer be subject to penalty reductions. This might be interpreted as an incentive to comply, but in reality it was not likely to happen because it did not allow for the amounts hidden by creative accountancy and other techniques.[198]

The new drive toward central control was also reinforced by the London Regional Transport Bill, which was designed to give the government overall responsibility for the capital and had been described as removing local control over service provision under the guise of creating a regional transport system. Likewise, the Education (Grants and Awards) Bill implied an increase in central influence and therefore control of local education policy, by withholding 0.5 per cent of the annual RSG education settlement and requiring local authorities to compete for allocation according to central priorities.

Ultimately, however, abolition of the Metropolitan County councils constituted the most overt attack on local democracy, accountability and representation. As part of this proposal 21 boards, three new quangos and up to 100 joint local authority bodies were to be formed to run local services in place of directly elected authorities.[199] This aspect of Conservative policy is therefore consistent with the neoliberal agenda of limiting the overt role of government, but it also reflects the expressions of antipathy towards local mandates.

The approach should also be seen as part of the attempt to limit the opportunity for collectivist provision and as a continuation of the removal of supposedly contentious state functions from the local electoral sphere.[200] In this instance, strategic services – such as fire, police and public transport – were taken out of democratic control, and the appointment of people to joint boards and quangos meant that central government had the power to choose those who were sympathetic to their objectives.

Nevertheless, it is only fair that credit is given where it is due and, with this in mind, it should be recognized that not all Conservatives supported rate-capping and its associated measures. Although the Party dominated the Association of County Councils and the Association of District Councils, for example, both expressed opposition and some back-bench Conservative MPs also raised doubts about the proposed legislation.[201]

Significantly, however, the concerns that were expressed reflect the differences between the 'one nation' and neoliberal tendencies within the party. Conservative opponents were therefore more worried about the constitutional implications of the legislation than its potential effects on local communities in general and vulnerable people in particular. This unease is also reflected in the anxieties expressed by sections of the labour movement about constitutional equilibrium. NALGO, for example, portrayed the constitutional position of local government as an integral part of the balance between centre and locality and as playing a counteracting role equivalent to that of judicial, legislative and executive functions within the state apparatus.

In other words, removing the right of authorities to set their own levels of tax and standards of service provision in accordance with local electoral mandates was seen as a threat to this arrangement. Similarly, the requirement for local authorities to consult with representatives of local business was considered to: be tantamount to a business veto; threaten the principle of one person one vote; and signal the re-introduction of property qualifications.[202]

Of course, Labour movement opposition was part of a broader perspective and the limited common ground with Conservative sceptics therefore raises questions about the thinking behind John Cunningham's statement to the TUCLGC that it was 'vital to maintain the all-party support which had been developed for the campaign against the government's rate-capping and abolition proposals'.[203] While this was conditioned by the focus on parliament as a means of defeating the bill, it is also worth noting that this approach ran the risk of reducing campaign aims to the lowest common denominator. In courting Conservative MPs, the PLP also exposed itself to their differing interpretations of the role and functions of the local state.

Of particular significance here is the neoliberal view that the state should only intervene where it is impossible for the private sector to profit from the provision of local services. Indeed, some Liberal Party MPs supported rate-capping on this basis, arguing that:

> on the evidence so far available it is possible for authorities to budget for the preservation of all statutory and essential services and jobs in the forthcoming financial year while complying with the rate-capped limit.

In other words, they were happy to reduce welfare provision to the bare minimum.[204]

Also worthy of note is the extent to which this represents a transformation of the process outlined in Chapter One whereby infrastructural provision and the social wage constituted an indirect subsidy to businesses. Under the neoliberal schema, for example, the emphasis on reducing costs translated into inferior standards of provision and, in the case of privatization, assistance to private firms now took the form of direct payments for the running of services. What this also meant was that health, social care and welfare provision was no longer valued for its redistributive effects, but was viewed purely as an infrastructural function.

All this put the PLP in an invidious position as it tried to reconcile its increasing acceptance of neoliberalism with the demands of Labour-controlled authorities, trade unions and others who sought its support for their campaign to protect redistributive policies. This is epitomized by the advice to Liverpool in 1984 that it should increase rates, even though the tactic had been discredited in social-democratic terms and had led to the loss of council seats in the past. In view of its record of suppressing advocates of resistance, it seems somewhat suspicious that the PLP should advise similarly minded Labour groups to adopt a tactic that could cost them votes and therefore control of the council chamber.

The position adopted by party leaders came under further scrutiny when it became apparent that the selective limitation of local authority rate levels was designed to restrict the options of those Labour authorities that had consistently defied the government. Any semblance of remaining credibility was then stretched to breaking point by the impact that the new round of measure was expected to have.

A joint statement issued by NALGO, NUPE, TGWU, GMBATU, FBU, NUT and NATFHE, for example, predicted that 75,000 jobs would be lost and that services for the old, young, sick and disabled would be cut. Similarly, the TUC identified roads, fire brigades, schools and social services in its list of areas threatened by the provisions of the Rates Act. More specifically, Merseyside County Council's cap was estimated to require £23m worth of cuts, an increase in public transport fares, a redundancy programme, and an overall reduction in services of 10 per cent.[205]

Taking into account the scale of the problems faced and the concerted nature of the attack, if any opposition was to have a realistic chance of success it would require a degree of focus and co-ordination not seen in recent labour movement history. This also meant that new levels of organization, participation and mobilization became imperative as they constituted the foundation upon which the success or failure of any campaign would depend. Once again, however, the desire for maximum levels of unity within a broad-based campaign made these tasks more difficult to achieve.

This problem was compounded by the fact that many participants had conflicting agendas, but in spite of this it is possible to identify a set of consistent aims that were elaborated at various meetings and conferences. These examples are too numerous to survey in any detail here, but they are clearly summarized in a document that was prepared by representatives of local authorities and trade unions and presented to Patrick Jenkin, the Secretary of State for the Environment, on 4 February 1985.

In total, the paper listed seven demands: abandonment of targets and penalties for 1985-86; publication of financial assumptions upon which maximum rate level calculations were based; disclosure of the anticipated impact of financial limits on services, clients and jobs; abandonment of the Rates Act; restoration of grant levels to those inherited by the Conservative Government in 1979; that a commission of enquiry be established to resolve the financing of local government; and abandonment of the timetable for implementing the Rates Act.[206]

If achieved in their entirety, this broad range of objectives would have neutralized not only the Rates Act, but also the government's whole prospectus for local government since 1979. Although intended to facilitate maximum unity, such an approach also had implicit weaknesses. On the one hand, the fact that the demands boiled down to a reversal of the government's entire policy made it less likely that it would listen. On the other, their all encompassing nature meant that there had to be differences between campaign participants over the desirability of certain aims, the commitment to campaigning and the minimum level of concessions expected.

Despite this confusion, there was a growing resolve among the Labour authorities selected for capping and, in so far as their aims sought to reverse the Conservative's programme of financial restraint, deregulation and privatization, it meant that aspects of the earlier campaigning activity could be developed. In the meantime, however, the successful mobilization, participation and support of trade union and Labour Party members, activists, service users and members of the general public remained the task upon which the prospects of any opposition would rest.

For this to happen, it also required the agreement and involvement of full-time officials and councillors, but once more the effect was to highlight divisions as the goals of the former tended to differ from those of rank and file activists. What all this meant in practice was that opposition to the Rates Bill and subsequent Act became focused on a minority of determined campaigners, all of whom were involved in the labour movement.

Opposing the Bill

The Rates Bill was published in 1983, enacted in 1984 but not actually enforced until the financial year 1985-86. As a result, the activities that formed part of the campaign of opposition were largely concerned with defeating or amending the Bill, but they can also be understood as the precursor of a campaign of non-compliance. In either case, the selection and utilization of tactics was informed by the need to create a level of support that could be used to exert pressure on the government.

Although this was a multi-dimensional process that operated on a number of different levels, it can be summarized as involving the pursuit of objectives through official channels and the mobilization of popular participation and support. Curiously enough, these two options tended to reflect the preferences of full-time officers, MPs and councillors on the one hand and activists and rank and file participants on the other. In reality, however, neither strategy was ever premised on the exclusion of the other, so the crucial question was how the two strands could be joined together in a way that maximized the overall potential for success.

As had been the case in the late 1970s, trade unions were once again at the forefront of this activity. On that occasion the Labour Party had been in government, but there was no such excuse for the quiescence of its national leaders in the 1980s. Into this void stepped the TUC and NALGO as the most prominent proponents of and participants in oppositional activities.

The development of the TUC's response to rate-capping can be traced through its Annual Reports which record how decisions taken at annual congress were put into practice by the General Council and other committees. As part of this process, the interests of trade unions organizing and recruiting in local government were brought together under the auspices of the Local Government Committee. This body was responsible for overseeing campaigning activity on related issues and was attended by full-time officers of the TUC and those of member unions.

In keeping with a 1983 Congress decision to oppose the Rates Bill and abolition of the Metropolitan County councils, the TUCLGC also created a Local Government Campaign Co-ordinating Committee (LGCCC) that consisted of one national representative from each local government trade union and the secretaries of the TUC's regional councils. The main purpose of the LGCCC was to assist liaison between individual trade unions, co-ordination and development of national initiatives, and the promotion of a unified trade union response. This function also stretched to maintaining contacts with the PLP, the Local Government Campaign Unit (LGCU),[207] rate-capped Labour authorities, and the local authority associations. Further down the line, TUC initiatives were also developed and co-ordinated through its regional councils.

Within NALGO the campaign was directed at the national level by the NLGC and the union's economic, education, publicity and law and parliamentary committees. As has already been discussed, special NLGGMs were also called and recalled for activists to participate in the decision-making process. Campaigning strategy and activity was also progressed at the regional level through district councils, district campaign co-ordinating committees and, in the case of abolition, by district delegate meetings attended by Metropolitan county, district and London borough branches.[208]

The NLGC also called a series of National Delegate Advisory Meetings (NDAM) that started 30 November 1983 and were dedicated to the issue of rate-capping. These meetings provided a forum for national officials and representatives from local authority branches to exchange views, consider progress and make recommendations for consideration by the NLGC. Leaders and representatives of councils on the rate-cap hit-list were also allowed to attend and speak, but were not able to cast a vote.

Another significant innovation involved the convening of monthly Rate-Capping Liaison Group Meetings (RCLGM) as a body that was independent of the normal national committee structure. Attendance at RCLGMs was based on two delegates from branches identified for rate-capping and one from those severely affected by targets and penalties. The RCLGM was also allowed to send two observers to the NLGC if the latter was discussing rate-capping or the campaign for the defence of local government.[209]

In spite of these and other positive attempts made by national leaders to encourage and support local initiatives, NALGO was not exempt from the unevenness of activity and organization that was prevalent elsewhere. This is evident in the expressions of concern that in non-metropolitan branches and those not affected by rate-capping there was 'little or no action' and, perhaps more significantly, that the 'activity of other unions at national level is similarly lacking'.[210]

Similar reservations are also apparent in calls for local joint union campaign co-ordinating committees to be established 'as a matter of the utmost urgency'. That this exhortation was necessary in March 1984 is a reflection of the general state of preparedness and the ineffectiveness of the TUCLGC's letter to public sector unions on the matter in late 1983.[211] Although not necessarily a definitive guide, the records of the inaugural conference of the National Local Authority Co-ordinating Committee (NLACC), held a year later in Liverpool, implies that matters had not improved much by then. The meeting on 30 March 1985 was attended by representatives from 40 local authorities and only 19 JTUCs had affiliated by the time the first meeting was held in Sheffield 13 April 1985.[212]

Public sector trade unions were instrumental in setting up the LGCU in November 1983, however, and a year later COHSE, CPSA, FBU, GMBATU, NALGO, NATFHE, NUPE, NUT and the TGWU had all affiliated, along with 70 local authorities. The move to set up a national campaign unit followed the Labour Party's 1983 general election defeat and reflected the urgent need to establish some means through which a national lead could be developed. In purely functional terms, this involved co-ordinating the activities of local authorities, professional associations, the voluntary sector, trade unions and the TUC to avoid organizational conflicts and unify separate initiatives to common time-scales.[213]

Analogies can therefore be drawn between the roles played by the LGCU, the NSC in the 1970s and the MTULMCC in Liverpool, but in this instance there was a degree of national co-ordination and co-operation hitherto unseen in local government campaigns. At a general level, for example, the LGCU Management Committee was attended by leading councillors, full-time trade union officers, officers from the AMA and ALA and employees of the Unit. This committee oversaw the conduct of campaigning activity, but a strategy sub-group was also established for those with a direct involvement in the campaign and to deal with specific issues. Both forums provided an opportunity for the leaders of the Labour groups to share their views and experiences and this was complemented by a joint union campaign officers group that helped co-ordinate national activities against rate-capping and abolition.[214]

All of the bodies discussed so far operated at the national level, while localized struggles continued to focus on specific issues related to services, jobs and local democracy. For the purposes of defeating or amending the Rates Bill, however, the chances of success depended on the ability to put the government under pressure and on its willingness to make concessions. In the final analysis, this boiled down to two interlinked tactics: using education and publicity to engage and mobilize mass support, and pro-active interventions such as lobbying, litigation and industrial action.

On a day-to-day basis, attempts to engage and mobilize support faced two central problems. The first of these involved the challenge of raising the profile and value of local government services to those who benefited from them but did so only indirectly. Perhaps more difficult was the mobilization not only of people who, due to infirmity or vulnerability, used and relied on services as part of their daily lives, but also of the people who cared for them as local government employees.

Rather than a mass campaign that began as the expression of popular grievance, therefore, opposition to rate-capping was essentially a top down affair, but this also reflected the labour movement's preference for process over participatory decision-making. This is apparent in the cascade approach whereby much of the information used in local education and publicity initiatives originated with full-time officers and was passed on to activists and then to union members and the general public.

Joint TUC and LGCU workshops held in London, Southampton, Cambridge, Sheffield, Liverpool and Preston during 1985 on the subject of local government finance fall into this category. So too, do the circulars, bulletins, pamphlets, information and briefing packs produced and distributed by the LGCU, ALA and AMA.

In addition to more than 40 issues of 'Fight to Defend Local Democracy' distributed between September 1983 and March 1985, NALGO full-time officers produced and circulated briefing packs and fact sheets on: rate-capping and the Rates Bill; abolition of the Metropolitan County councils; the Education (Grants and Awards) Bill; and RSG settlements.[215] As well as the ubiquitous posters, leaflets, badges and stickers, this literature provided updates on local developments, publicized the availability of campaign materials and advised local groups and organizations how to campaign. Much of the information provided by NALGO's national officers was evident in Liverpool NALGO's Campaign News '85, for example, and in other active branches like Islington it formed the bedrock of education and information programmes run by activists for the broader membership.

Efforts were also made to reach beyond local authority workers through civic newspapers, briefing and information packs, booklets, pamphlets and adverts in local media. Petitions formed part of this approach in Haringey and Islington where service-user signatures were collected at the point of contact. Other compilers included Manchester, Leeds and Greenwich which recorded 300,000 signatures. Such initiatives were dependent on activist involvement and NALGO encouraged local branches to include petitions along with leafleting, public meetings and rallies as part of their promotional activities.

The need to build sustained involvement outside the labour movement informed attempts by a number of authorities to develop new ways of engaging the public. Lambeth, for example, produced a public consultation document entitled 'Rate-Capping and Lambeth', and Sheffield's community inquiry took evidence from three hundred local groups via an open ended questionnaire and two day conference. Greenwich, Lambeth, Lewisham and Southwark also conducted local opinion polls on the issues of local finances and service provision and held a joint press conference to compare new RSG levels with local opinion.[216]

Such innovations resemble the Open Forum and Communiplan initiatives practised by Clay Cross in the 1970s. In that case, however, the structures were well established and therefore better placed to facilitate inclusion and participatory decision-making. The very fact that such ventures in the 1980s tended to be new and transitory meant that they were not embedded in the locality. This observation is equally true of the community and other conferences that offered little scope for on-going mobilization and participation.

Examples of this latter approach include the London Voluntary Sector Conference which was organized jointly by the LGCU and London Community Work Service and held on 13 February 1984. There was also Lambeth's 'Fighting for the Future' community campaign conference which attracted over 100 local groups on 11 December 1984. Likewise, Camden, Fulham, Hammersmith and Lambeth established umbrella assemblies of delegates and representatives from the local community, trade unions, unemployed groups and others.[217]

In addition to the aforementioned activities, labour movement delegate conferences were again used to develop strategy and organization, but they displayed little consistency. The supposedly London-wide conference called by Southwark in 1983, for example, was attended by only six Labour groups and all local government unions except NALGO. Those who did attend voted to oppose cuts, redundancies, increases in rent or rates over the rate of inflation and agreed to establish a steering committee. This stance contrasts with a conference of hit list authorities on 23 May 1984 that failed to adopt a clear strategy and an LGCU strategy conference held 13 November 1984 which called for the withdrawal of powers granted under the Rates Act, abolition of targets and penalties and the restoration of RSG to 1979 levels.[218]

Despite this variation, or more probably because of it, there are two events that stand out from the rest. The first of these is the 'Forging the Links' conference that was organized by Sheffield and the LGCU and attended by delegates from 40 Labour authorities.[219] This meeting was important because it signalled a willingness to defy parliament when it agreed that Labour groups should not comply with rate-capping, penalties or targets.

Interestingly, Sheffield had also played host to a similar conference to coordinate opposition to the HFA in 1972 and, although NALGO had adopted a position of non-compliance, the decision of the latest Sheffield conference points to a growing resolve and a disillusionment within the Labour Party over the approach of the PLP. To a certain extent, the move represents an attempt to fill the leadership vacuum, but campaigning activity was not dependent on the national organs of the Labour Party alone. To suggest otherwise is to subscribe to, or foster, the myth that political actions take place only through political parties and their parliamentary or national bodies.

The National Consultative Conference on the Rates Act and the Defence of Local Government is the second important conference referred to. This took place on 4 December 1984, was organized by the TUC and attended by 200 delegates from local authorities and local government trade unions.[220] Representatives also supported a strategy of non-compliance for rate-capped councils, but in common with others who adopted this position, a question mark hangs over the mandate they had from those they claimed to represent.

Before non-compliance was put to the test, however, a series of legal challenges to rate-capping and its associated measures were mounted as part of the strategy of building pressure on the government. These included the GLC's contention that the deadline for appeals against specific rate-caps was arbitrary, unjust and unreasonable. Sheffield also argued that GREA calculations were inconsistent and in Sheffield's case did not take all the factors into account. Leicester and Greenwich also considered challenging the assumptions made by the Secretary of State about authorities' balances and reserves when selecting authorities to be capped.[221]

Like creative accountancy before it, however, such moves served to emphasize the divide between arguments over technical issues and the broader perspective needed to engage activists and the public. A similar dilemma was also evident in those instances where campaigning activity amounted to little more than writing to, lobbying and meeting MPs and peers. In this case the focus on the parliamentary process exhibited a detachment from the real social world that extended to a distribution of information packs in the forlorn hope that this might disrupt the passage of the Rates Bill.

Starting in February 1984, for example, the LGCCC and LGCU arranged for delegations of activists and councillors to visit parliament each Wednesday that relevant legislation was scheduled to be discussed. These interventions were supported by local JTUC and district campaign co-ordinating committees and, by and large, were the responsibility of full-time officers. The same is also true of the adverts placed in the Houses of Parliament Journal and, more obviously, when general secretaries wrote to members of standing committees.[222]

With an overall parliamentary majority of 144 and of 188 over the Labour Party there was never any realistic prospect of using parliamentary intervention to defeat or even secure significant amendments to the Conservative government's legislative programme. This is borne out by the fact that debate was curtailed when the Rates Bill was guillotined in March 1984 and justifies NALGO's observation in October 1983, that political and parliamentary resistance of the government would need to be backed by a strategy of non-compliance.[223]

To a certain extent, this view was implicit in the fact that parliamentary intervention was combined with legal action, public protest and industrial action as part of the attempt to put pressure on the government. Examples of the latter strategy include the focusing of events during the TUC's Democracy Week in March 1984. This culminated in 60,000 people marching through London on 29 March, which was the day that the House of Commons was scheduled to approve the Rates Bill and the date the abolition paving bill was due to be published.

In this and other instances, protests were called in conjunction with one day strikes, like the action organized by Metropolitan County branches on 24 January 1984 to express opposition to abolition. In July 1984, the TUCLGC, NALGO and NUPE also called a one day strike to protest at the crisis in local government and NALGO members employed by Merseyside

County Council took strike action on 7 August 1984 to protest against the imposition of a rate-cap on the authority.[224]

At the local level, such action was often co-ordinated with important council meetings, and public rallies were called to show support for councillors and to help strengthen their resolve. In terms of alerting and mobilizing trade unionists on a temporary basis one-off isolated days of action might have been effective, but they did little to pressurize the government into changing tack. This reality was neatly summarized in NALGO's assertion that: 'a coherent programme of militant industrial action against the government's attack on local democracy, services and jobs is imperative.'[225]

On a more positive note, it is fair to say that although it could not prevent the Rates Bill becoming law, the campaign did achieve unprecedented levels of interaction and co-operation between activists and full-time officers. In the case of NALGO, this also included the agreement of a strategy that countenanced extra-parliamentary resistance and the development of structures through which it could be organized.

Viewed in this light, the range of activities undertaken in opposing the Rates Bill can also be understood as preparations for the attempt to resist the implementation of rate-capping. At the national level, for example, this included the evolution of existing mechanisms and the creation of ad-hoc committees by NALGO, the TUC and LGCU. Within NALGO these processes even contributed to a situation whereby full-time national officers responded to and agreed with the demands of activists in branches where campaigning activity was underway.

Less encouraging was the assumption, made by the NLGC, that where formal arrangements existed they were sound and effective. As will become clear, this would turn out to be a crucial mistake if delegates attending NALGO's NDAMs and RCLGMs voted for policies that did not represent the views of their members and for which they could not mobilize them in support.[226]

At this juncture, therefore, it is worth drawing an analogy between the labour movement's reliance on abstracted decision-making processes and the practice of constitutional democracy whereby parliamentary and local authority structures are removed and insulated from the forces at play in society as a whole. Whereas representatives in parliament or the council chamber are supposed to take decisions according to their interpretation of the will of the people or the national interest, it seems that some activists, councillors and full-time officers preferred to act according to their view of how things should be.

This conclusion does not mean that campaigns should be undertaken only when there is pre-existing support, but it recognizes the extent to which tensions between the aims and aspirations of full-time officers, activists and their members became all the more acute when the Rates Act was due to be implemented. At that point, the focus of the campaign shifted from the direct involvement of activists in deciding policy, to a reliance on the resolve of councillors and Labour groups for non-compliance.

Chapter Eight
THE CAMPAIGN OF NON-COMPLIANCE

> Without the prospect of an alternative government with realistic policies, offending neither against common sense nor against the instincts of the majority, the very survival of parliamentary democracy could be threatened – by the increasing alienation of the electors, if not in the end by direct action from exasperated pressure groups.
> Conservative Party, 'The Right Approach'.

The emphasis and practice of the campaign of non-compliance represents a move from generalized opposition to a real challenge to central government authority.Whereas sections of the labour movement had sought to encourage mobilization and participation as a way of preventing the Rates Bill becoming statute, the next stage of the campaign required Labour councillors to resist the Act's implementation.

As part of this approach, a fallback position of sustained industrial action was requested and promised should concessions not be won, councillors surcharged or commissioners introduced.[227] The immediate prospects of the campaign therefore rested on the commitment of elected representatives, but in the long term it presaged an unprecedented level of mobilization and participation, not just of activists, but of the membership of local government trade unions involved in the campaign.

This newfound preparedness to use extra-parliamentary tactics represents an important shift within the labour movement. Of particular significance is the intention to use industrial action to secure concessions from government, not only because it harked back to the General Strike, but because it also threatened the constitutional and ideological primacy of parliament. That this was a drastic step to take merely confirms the fact that the struggle to prevent neoliberal domination was entering its final and decisive stage.

Whether all those involved realized this or intended to challenge the legitimacy of constitutional democracy based on a universal suffrage exercised at least once every five years is irrelevant in practical terms. A victory for non-compliance would have offered a serious choice for the future direction of social and economic policy, both within the labour movement and the country as a whole.

In theory then, non-compliance was conceived as a two stage process. As part of the first phase, Labour local authorities planned to employ a range of blocking tactics within existing constitutional arrangements. While this was taking place, the threat of industrial action was intended to help elicit a negotiated settlement, but for it to have the desired effect it was necessary to make detailed preparations for the instigation and co-ordination of the ultimate weapon.

Constitutional Confrontation

While it was not inevitable that Labour local authorities would be left in a weak position if they failed to prevent the enactment of rate-capping, it certainly limited their room for manoeuvre. This, as we shall see, is apparent in the tactics considered and was a consequence of the subordinate constitutional status of local government within the British state system. To some extent, these limitations might help explain the preference for a negotiated settlement that would have averted direct confrontation, but it is not the whole story.[228]

A number of other factors can be identified as contributing to the eventual breakdown of negotiations, not the least of which was the practical prospects for non-compliance given the local circumstances of authorities and Labour groups contemplating resistance. In particular, the choice of the 'no rate tactic' brought to the fore the importance of local decision-making, levels of activity and commitment and, most significantly, the internal divisions that affected the campaign.

From the outset non-compliance had been endorsed in principle by the Labour Party NEC and the party's local government conferences in 1984, but in keeping with past practice the national leadership failed to offer guidance as to what form it should take. The fact that the options were limited meant that this was less of a problem than it might have been, albeit that it placed the onus fairly and squarely on councillors and officers. After the wholesale resignation of councillors had been ruled out at an early stage, Labour groups faced a choice between withholding information, not honouring financial obligations, not setting a rate, and deficit budgeting.

The pros and cons of not providing information to central government departments and not honouring financial contributions or obligations received extensive consideration at the LGCU. In particular, the question of withholding financial contributions was debated at several meetings and these covered the possibility of not paying precepts to police authorities; not honouring interest payments to financial institutions; or not paying income tax and National Insurance contributions.Ultimately, however, and despite the fact that the tactic was countenanced and support sought from the TUC, this line of action was not actually attempted.[229]

Also discussed was the possibility of refusing to return routine information to central authorities, especially if it was expected to assist abolition of the Metropolitan County councils and implementation of the Rates Act. There were serious doubts about how effective this would be, however, as much of the information relevant to abolition was already in the public domain and made non co-operation virtually irrelevant. Similarly, although NALGO had a policy of not co-operating with information requests relating to abolition and rate-capping, it was recognized that individual legal culpability meant that the officers affected could be prepared to defy union and councillor instructions.[230]

The tactic was also considered to be impractical because the amount of information provided to central agencies made it difficult to identify crucial data. There were other complications as well, such as the fact that: certain local authority funding was dependent on returns; some returns could benefit one authority, but be detrimental to another; and non-receipt of information could be used by employer bodies to stall negotiations with trade unions. Even so, efforts were made by LGCU, AMA and ALA officers to identify information that could be withheld and a questionnaire was distributed to local authorities.[231]

Where it was adopted, the practice varied between individual authorities with routine forms scrutinized by councillors and officers in some and, despite pressure from District Audit, forms delayed or withheld in others. The one area where action was considered to be feasible across the board, involved delaying submission of the Capital Estimates and Commitments Return. This was intended to hamper government plans to restrict capital spending, but as the information had been delayed on a regular basis since 1983 it added nothing new.

What all this meant in effect was that non-compliance boiled down to a choice between authorities refusing to set a rate, or adopting a deficit budget. This was reflected in the observation made in the Labour Party NEC statement that 'Non-compliance could lead to some Councils being unable to fix a rate. For others, it could mean running out of money for essential services.'[232] While this and other accounts imply that the tactics were mutually exclusive, in the long term not setting a rate could also mean running out of money.

Either way, the perceived advantages and disadvantages of both strategies were debated at length and focused on their expected compatibility with achieving maximum unity among authorities. To that end, the no rate tactic was favoured by the South London boroughs, appeared to have worked for Liverpool during 1984 and was expected to allow authorities to work to a common timetable and maximize public pressure for a negotiated settlement.[233]

By way of contrast, deficit budgeting was considered to be a recipe for suspicion, based on past experiences when some local authorities had claimed to be maintaining services while implementing surreptitious cuts. For the tactic to be successful, therefore, authorities would have to stick rigidly to their budget strategies, fulfil promises on maintaining services and establish joint monitoring arrangements between Labour groups and trade unions. More difficult to overcome was the fact that each authority would run out of money at different times and had a legal requirement to demonstrate steps taken to match expenditure and income.

Other arguments for and against a deficit budget were ambiguous. As there was no time-scale before authorities ran out of money, for example, it might mean that any local crises could be deferred and, although this increased the pressure on councillors, it would also test the will of the government throughout the financial year. It was also expected that at some point drastic cuts would be required to deal with the deficit and comply with government targets and penalties. If this was at the behest of Commissioners, however, it could place the government in an invidious position 18 months before a general election. Finally, if deficit budgeting was likely to cause confusion at the local level, it would also mean that the government would not be able to judge the financial position and viability of local authorities.

As a result of this debate the no rate tactic was considered to be the best option, but when it was put to the test it proved to be less than straightforward. At the root of the problem lay the focus of risk on councillors and officers, as opposed to the broader movement and the desire to maximize the number of Labour groups willing to adopt the same stance. The effect of both these factors was evidenced in the decision, taken by council leaders meeting at the LGCU on 19 February 1985, to change their stance from refusal to deferral.

Selection of the deferral tactic was also premised on the assumption that the government would negotiate and that it would continue to pay grant instalments as it had with Liverpool in 1984. Based on the only available evidence, it was assumed that: 'negotiations would commence at an early date and that the pressure of council action would ensure a favourable settlement'. To enhance the chances of this happening, attempts were made to give the impression of a united front, by synchronizing council meetings called to discuss non-compliance and adopting a collective approach to negotiations.[234]

Within the confines of the LGCU, however, it was admitted that non-compliance was merely intended to be a process of 'bluff and counter bluff' designed to achieve concessions. If there had been any chance of the government being fooled by this approach, such illusions were shattered when the precepting authorities of the GLC, ILEA, Merseyside and South Yorkshire all complied with their statutory obligation to set a rate by 10 March 1985. Furthermore, the government had also learned from its dealings with Liverpool, as the charade that passed for negotiations make clear.

To begin with, the uncertain position of participants was indicated on 23 January 1985, when the LGCU exhibited undue haste in asking Patrick Jenkin, Secretary of State for the Environment, to open negotiations. At the subsequent meeting on 4 February, representatives presented their case for the: abandonment of targets and penalties for 1985-86; disclosure of assumptions; abandonment of the Rates Act; a commission of inquiry into local government funding; and, the restoration of grant to 1979 levels.[235]

Jenkin, however, refused to enter into negotiations on any of the matters raised and simply dismissed the proposals out of hand. In response, the LGCU resorted to a predetermined plan for media activities and issued a press release which attempted to portray the minister as precipitating confrontation. As if to emphasize the weakness of their own bargaining position, the LGCU then wrote to Jenkin the very next day and asked for the local authorities' case to be reconsidered and for an independent commission of inquiry to be set up as a means of avoiding confrontation.[236]

The subsequent exchange of letters between the LGCU and Jenkin is instructive in so far as it suggests a degree of desperation on the part of the former, both in the rapidity of its responses and in the repeated offers of further meetings. In contrast, the Secretary of State exhibited an air of self-assurance when, on 21 February 1985, he wrote that he would agree to further meetings, but only on the basis that there would be no changes to the Rates Act or RSG settlement and local authorities were not proposing or threatening illegal action. Then, after parliamentary approval of rate limitations on 25 February, he suggested that consultation should be undertaken by individual authorities or through the local authority associations and CCLGF.²³⁷

Further evidence of this power relation is provided by the treatment of other labour movement representatives, such as when Norman Willis, General Secretary of the TUC, wrote to Jenkin and requested a meeting to discuss ways of overcoming the impasse. In his answer, Jenkin stated that he was unwilling to meet the TUCLGC because this could be misrepresented as negotiations and provide local authorities with a reason to delay making a rate.²³⁸

As it had done with Liverpool the previous year, the PLP engaged in a number of initiatives aimed at precipitating a negotiated settlement. John Cunningham, Labour's Shadow Secretary of State for the Environment, was again involved, tabling a series of parliamentary questions between December 1984 and February 1985. In January, for example, he asked for the publication of assumptions made in relation to the calculation of individual authority grant allocations and rate limits. This was followed up in correspondence with Patrick Jenkin, but the Minister's response was that such information would only be disclosed to authorities that sought derogation.²³⁹

Following a complaint by Jack Layden and Margaret Hodge on behalf of the AMA and ALA that Jenkin refused to meet outside the regular CCLGF cycle, Cunningham wrote and asked Jenkin to meet with them to discuss the financial problems members of the two bodies were experiencing. By way of a reply, however, Jenkin simply reiterated earlier points about meetings being misrepresented as negotiation or used to justify delays in setting a rate and on that basis refused the request. The same stance was also adopted at the CCLGF on 17 April 1985 when government representatives refused to discuss the operation of the Rates Act or the RSG settlement for 1985-86.²⁴⁰

In conjunction with its strategy of not negotiating, the government sought to exploit the fragile unity amongst campaigning authorities by trying to encourage splits. This involved approaches to Thamesdown by the minister for local government's parliamentary private secretary and to Lewisham through the Chartered Institute of Public Finance and Accountancy, to encourage applications for derogation. The resolve of selected councillors was also tested in February 1985, when the rate limits of ILEA, Hackney, Haringey, Islington, Leicester and Lewisham were raised.²⁴¹

Such carrots were also accompanied by the stick when, on 1 March 1985, the district auditor wrote to warn local authorities threatening non-compliance that failure to set a rate could be construed as wilful misconduct. This threat was reiterated to those authorities that were still resisting in May and served to increase the pressure exerted by the fact that block grant and housing subsidy instalments had been withheld since April.[242]

Each of the measures described above were clearly designed to exploit any weaknesses that existed in the resolve of councillors, officers and the commitment of local labour movements. In effect, however, the decision to concentrate on official channels played into the government's hands by allowing it to take the initiative in refusing to talk and using existing powers to exacerbate the predicament faced by each authority. At this point, therefore, the focus shifted to the means by which councillors and Labour groups were to be supported or encouraged in their non-compliance.

Rather than take the campaign to another level, as might have been expected, what this revealed was a lack of preparedness amongst high profile authorities and a less than constructive dialogue with their trade unions. Taking the GLC as an example, Labour Party activists were described as a driving force and their involvement in community based struggles as the bedrock of the Labour Party's support in London.[243]

Although the more tangible threat of abolition is given as a reason for the failure to develop internal support for the campaign against rate-capping, there was also an evident distrust between the Labour Group and the authority's trade unions, especially the Staff Association. This might explain why little attempt was made to develop relations with lower paid staff and why efforts to build a trade union campaign against abolition bypassed committees dominated by the Staff Association. Less clear are the reasons why more use was not made of the London Bridge JSSC or events like the assembly of London trade unions and voluntary groups that was convened on 23 February 1985.

All in all, this meant that the fate of non-compliance rested with the Labour Group, but to say that its commitment was uncertain is something of an understatement. The situation was so perilous that budget discussions had to be suppressed prior to the March deadline and when the matter eventually came to a head after the GLLP Conference held in March 1985, 24 councillors, including some that had defied the Law Lords over the Fares Fair policy, voted to set a rate.

The analogy between the 'Fares Fair' and rate-capping campaigns is worth developing further, because in the former case councillors were exposed to the views of trade union activists in London Transport and the GLC in attempt to stiffen their resolve following the Law Lords' decision. Even then it had not been enough to persuade all councillors to vote in line with Party policy, but for the campaign of non-compliance the tactic was not even considered worth trying.

Despite their differing circumstances, there are interesting similarities in the way the GLC and Sheffield approached the campaign of non-compliance. In both authorities, additional factors were cited as reasons for inhibiting campaign preparations and for Sheffield this was attributed, in part, to an on-going focus on the miners' strike. Like the GLC, there was also a lack of constructive dialogue between the Labour Group and local authority unions.

Manual and white collar representatives in Sheffield, for example, complained that they were not mobilized in the development of council policy and that decisions taken by councillors were presented as complete. This fact is reflected in the belated attempt by councillors to develop links with the local authority workforce by holding meetings before and after the council budget meeting scheduled for 7 March 1985.[244]

Such factors were also instrumental in delaying the formation of a joint trade union campaign committee until January 1985 and, once again, this meant that councillors were at the forefront of non-compliance. In another similarity, the make-up of the Sheffield council chamber resembled that of the GLC in so far as it only required a minority of Labour councillors to vote with opposition parties and the no rate strategy would fail.

This happened following the DLP's rejection of the Labour Group and local party leadership's deficit budget proposal on 30 April 1985 and its decision that a rate not be set: 'until the government provided sufficient resources for the fulfilment of the capital and revenues programmes for 1985/6 and subsequent financial years'.[245] At this point the continuation of the campaign appears to have been rejected in favour of a position of principle regardless of its chances of success. Due to the traditions of the Sheffield labour movement, however, a majority of councillors voted in line with Party policy regardless of it implications for the future of the campaign.

The exceptional nature of Liverpool's position is covered in Chapter Six and does not need to be repeated at length. When it comes to the campaign against rate-capping, the previous year's struggle for more resources constitutes an important additional factor. In particular, it meant that much of the necessary ground-work had been done in establishing mechanisms that were essential for effective mobilization.

This existing level of focus sets Liverpool apart from authorities like the GLC and Sheffield and is a difference that was reinforced by the crucial role played by activists in the authority's trade unions. Whereas the GLC relied on Party activists to mobilize support, in Liverpool the radicalism and commitment of trade unionists was pivotal in encouraging the involvement of the broader workforce, forming a bridge to the Labour

Group and persuading councillors to delay setting a rate until June 1985. From that point on the strategy of non-compliance was continued on a deficit budget basis until the alliance of Labour Group and local authority unions foundered in September.[246]

In all three authorities, radicalized activists were involved to differing degrees, but whatever role they played their participation was not enough in itself to ensure success. In the case of the GLC, for example, community based committees had little to offer in terms of concrete support. Similarly, in Sheffield and elsewhere the existence of mechanisms by which pressure and support could be expressed helped to create and maintain campaigning activity, but they were not enough to guarantee non-compliance.

At the end of the day, individual episodes of trade union action, such as occupying council chambers and lobbying meetings, were unable to prevent Southwark Labour Group from voting to set a rate. The same was true in Hackney where a mass lobby was arranged for the council meeting held on 22 May following a court instruction to set a rate by the end of the month.[247] Of course, these limitations had been identified as part of the discussions that had taken place around the need for sustained industrial action to make the Rates Act unworkable. In this case too, however, there was no assurance that this could be implemented effectively.

Industrial Action

In addition to supporting councillors and Labour groups that were seeking to resist the Rates Act, sustained industrial action was conceived as a means of continuing opposition if they complied and as a way of penalizing authorities that were making cuts.[248] Understood in this way, the tactic was designed to overcome the focus on a small group of people and move away from the preoccupation with constitutional democracy.

For this to become a reality, however, a number of obstacles had to be negotiated, including many that had impaired previous attempts at non-compliance. First and foremost this meant establishing clear procedures through which to identify the types of industrial action available and the circumstances in which each would be instigated. As part of the same process it was also necessary to differentiate between action that could be used to defend local services and that which was designed to bring about a change in central government policy.

As happened with other options relating to non-compliance, the issue was debated ad infinitum by a range of bodies and committees and the specific or general character of decisions corresponded to the level or organization at which they were approved. At the TUC in 1984, for example, delegates voted to support official industrial action that was taken to defend jobs and services. This was conditional, however, and depended on unions being affiliated to the TUC, having involved the General Council, TUCLGC and 'properly constituted' trade union bodies, as opposed to ad-hoc campaigning committees.[249]

Those bodies that would not be recognized as properly constituted, it is safe to say, were mainly activist led JSSCs and umbrella organizations like London Bridge and NLACC. Whatever the basis of their accreditation, however, it was the composition and representative nature of an organization that would determine whether any action it called would be successful. Within NALGO attempts were made to address such concerns by including both officials and activists in the union's consultation processes and it is here that the tactic received the clearest elucidation and endorsement.

From the beginning, it was clear to all those involved that there was a fundamental difference between the use of limited industrial action to publicize issues or encourage participation and the level of commitment that would be required to defeat rate-capping. In the latter case, three broad categories of action were envisaged and each was matched to a specific set of circumstances that would act as a trigger.

The first and least combative example had been approved by NALGO in 1981 and envisaged trade union members refusing to co-operate with government-appointed commissioners if they were introduced to run a local authority's affairs. Although adoption and declaration of the tactic was a way of deterring such an intervention, it was also the clearest articulation of the principle of defending constitutional democracy. In other words, non co-operation was justified as a response to: the removal of powers from elected representatives; the suspension of an elected council; transferral of powers to a non-elected body; and, attempts to take local authorities out of democratic control.[250]

This particular tactic was approved by official and activist led bodies alike and non co-operation was also agreed by the NALGO NDAM as a response to legislation requiring local government officers to set a rate or balance budgets in non-complying authorities. The practicality of this latter decision bears comparison with earlier examples, however, as a small number of senior officers could undermine the effectiveness of any action. In the main, this was because such people were unlikely to belong to a trade union, comply with an instruction if they did or be willing to damage their career prospects by acting illegally.

All the other options involved a programme of strike action that required the support and participation of the whole membership if it was to have any chance of success. NALGO, for example, identified three sets of circumstances in which such a response would be considered. The first of these anticipated one or more of its branches taking indefinite strike action in conjunction with other local unions if they had been seriously affected by cuts. An all-out strike was also expected to take place in branches where one or more of their members were affected by compulsory redundancy. Finally, a similar response was also envisaged in authorities where wages and salaries were not paid due to the government withholding RSG contributions.[251]

There was also a proposal that council workers should take industrial action in support of colleagues in other local authorities. This was considered to represent a major escalation of the campaign and, if it was to have any chance of success, it was acknowledged that it would have to be widespread and supported by all local government trade unions. On the downside, it could require unions to take industrial action in an authority that was actively pursuing a position of non-compliance and run the risk of alienating people who depended on and valued the services that were being withdrawn.[252]

Despite such concerns, NALGO's NDAM approved a motion from Camden Branch in October 1984 that called for 'wide ranging solidarity action by all NALGO members in hit-list boroughs when any one of the branches has taken all-out strike action against cuts arising from Rate-Capping'. Camden's proposals were then developed at the following month's RCLGM when it was agreed that branches should submit motions to AGMs or appropriate branch meetings for the instigation of solidarity action if strike action was called in any NALGO branch.[253]

The stance was affirmed in February 1985 with the approval of a Hackney branch proposal that solidarity action should be taken by all NALGO branches regardless of the position of their employer when any other branch took strike action due to the position of their authority. A second motion was also submitted to the same meeting by Hackney and asked for solidarity action to be instigated if the branch took industrial action as a result of the court case brought against the local authority's no rate position.[254]

These motions appear to have been self-reinforcing and a reflection of local concerns over the position unfolding in Hackney, which awaited the outcome of a judicial review on the council's obligation to set a rate. They also demonstrate the tension between the need for clear guidance and support to branches on the frontline and the dangers of deciding details too early. To this end, the TUC had argued, somewhat disingenuously, that 'bold policies backed by inadequate understanding and support are a recipe for defeat'.[255]

The preferred alternative was to wait until 'all information' was available, at which point 'all options' should be 'fully discussed' with those involved in the campaign and tactical responses decided according to the degree of support that each engendered. Leaving decisions to such a late stage in the campaign was not realistic, however, due to the length of time it would take to develop consistent participation, mobilization and support. In this instance, then, it is worth pointing out that a firmer national lead might have made a difference, but given past performances and the logic of the TUC's wait and see approach it was never likely to be forthcoming.

The adoption of prescriptive resolutions might have ignored the circumstances of individual authorities, but to some extent they were a predictable consequence of the stance adopted by national leaders. Nevertheless, there are two ways of looking at this. From a leadership perspective, the fact that industrial action failed to materialize appears to vindicate predictions of failure. In contrast, however, such forecasts can also be viewed as a self-fulfilling prophecy that was due in no small part to an absence of concerted national support and involvement.

At the rank-and-file end of the spectrum, a great deal of emphasis was placed on calls for action but, if the final collapse of the campaign is to be taken at face value, the groundwork for that action was unsuccessful or insufficient. While mobilization and participation required a lead, the passing of worthy resolutions proved to be no substitute for disciplined organization and long-term endeavour.

What this also demonstrates is that theory is no substitute for practice. In this case, an idealist dogma based on preconceived principles of what should happen was articulated in resolutions. As evidenced by NALGO's assumption about arrangements being sound and effective, this worked to mask the practical circumstances that people needed to create on the ground if their proposals were to have a chance of success. This does not absolve national leaders of their responsibility for the failure of non-compliance, but it should be recognized that flaws in the analysis of some activists was also a contributory factor.

Preparations for industrial action were also inhibited by the wrangling that accompanied council meetings called to consider budget options. In many cases, each meeting was surrounded by uncertainty over the outcome and winning the vote became the overriding concern. This precarious state of affairs is reflected by the steady stream of authorities that voted to set a rate: Thamesdown, Leicester and Manchester in March; North Tyneside, Lewisham and Haringey in April; Sheffield, Hackney, Southwark and Islington in May; and, Camden, Greenwich and Liverpool in June.

Only Lambeth held out until July and a council-wide vote on industrial action took place in Liverpool. That was in September 1985, however, long after any attempt at co-ordinated resistance had folded. The vote was also held among debates about alternative strategies and was sidetracked by the Labour Group's decision to issue redundancy notices to all employees. In the end, GMBATU voted in favour of strike action by 4,345 to 2,934 and although the TGWU and UCATT also supported action, NALGO voted against by 3,891 to 1,445.[256]

Many reasons have been put forward as explanations why the campaign of non-compliance petered out. Each of them contains a grain of truth in so far as they are all factors that contributed to the eventual outcome. These include relying on the resolve of councillors, the mathematics of the council chamber and the inability to organize and channel appropriate levels of support. Likewise, the diversion of the campaign into the issue of legality; the absence of a national party lead; the concealed reality of budget positions; or, a concentration on opposing the Rates Act, rather than defending jobs and services, can all be cited.

The observation that opposing particular pieces of legislation focuses resistance on the parliamentary process is also relevant for two reasons. First of all, it points to the parliamentarism of the labour movement and, in so doing, affords new meaning to the focus on councillors. In other words, it was the uncritical acceptance of constitutional democratic practice that explains why, in spite of the talk about encouraging participation and mobilization, a gap existed between the statements, aims and actions of councillors and activists and those of the people they sought or claimed to represent.

Another reason for the failure to mobilize sustained popular or labour movement support lies in the fact that labour movement representatives emulated the abstracted nature of constitutional democracy. Decisions were taken by activists and councillors and a reliance on the commitment and resolve of those groups reflect the parliamentary and council practice whereby votes are cast independently of the wishes of constituents.

As the TUC had done before it, the Labour Party's NEC resolution dated 13 May 1985 displayed an unconscionable degree of arrogance and hypocrisy when it advised that:

> no council should be expected to continue with a particular tactic unless it … has identifiable and specific commitments from party members, trade unionists and community groups, to ensure that financial and personal risks are shared with those calling for or supporting such decisions.[257]

What this fails to acknowledge is how far the Labour Party's preoccupation with electoral respectability and parliamentary process conspired to inhibit the development of local hegemony through which the mobilization of support could be built and maintained. Indeed, in places like Clay Cross, Derbyshire and Liverpool national Party leaders went out of their way to dismantle mechanisms that guaranteed the accountability of councillors to the local party and ensured the implementation of mandated policy.

The answer, then, is not that non-compliance failed simply because it attempted to defend local government and mobilize support for councillors, as some have suggested.[258] On the contrary, it was the uncritical acceptance and unconscious imitation of the processes of bourgeois liberal democracy by leaders and activists alike that proved to be too much of an obstacle to overcome.

CONCLUSION

> Conformity may give you a quiet life; it may even bring you to a University Chair. But all change in history, all advance, comes from nonconformists.
> AJP Taylor, *The Troublemakers*, Chapter I

Taken at face value, the events recounted in the preceding chapters represent little more than fluctuations in the numbers of people employed by the local state and of the services it provided. Likewise, these developments appear to have been governed by economic circumstances that were beyond anyone's control and encompass the consensual re-organization of local government in England and Wales.

Delve a little deeper below the surface to the real social world of happenstance and struggle and it becomes clear, with the benefit of hindsight, that what we were witnessing was one part of the broader battle to replace Keynesian social democratic orthodoxy with neoliberal ideology. What is more, the process that was played out in society as a whole was mirrored in the microcosm of the labour movement.

Almost half a century later it might seem like a futile endeavour to ask after the success or failure of these early attempts to resist the rise of neoliberalism. Indeed such a limited undertaking would be just another academic exercise, but the importance of the period lies not in the immediate outcomes. Both the issues themselves and the manner in which they were contested point to what has happened since, what the present government is doing and what hope there is for an alternative programme that goes beyond piecemeal resistance.

During the years that have passed since rate-capping, neoliberal orthodoxy has been able to lay down deep roots in Britain. First, under successive Conservative governments the experiment was continued and then, in keeping with the Party's pragmatist tradition, the Labour administrations that followed attempted to accommodate their uncritical acceptance of fundamentalist economic prescriptions with demands for redistribution.

For the conservatives, this involved the privatization of British Rail under the Railways Act 1993 and the ideological shibboleth of denationalizing what remained of the mining industry when the Coal Industry Act came into force in 1994. Once labour local authorities had been brought to heel, existing initiatives in housing and privatization were also extended and new fronts opened up in education. Building on earlier legislation that promoted the sale of council houses, for example, the Housing Act 1985 offered local authorities the option of abandoning their responsibility for providing affordable housing.

As was always the case when supposedly voluntary initiatives failed to have the desired effect, an element of compulsion was considered to be the answer. In this vein, Conservative governments in the 1990s sought and exercised new powers over the transfer of housing stock and, as an added bonus, this provided central government with a source of income from the capital receipts that such transfers generated.

First introduced under the auspices of the LGPLA, the privatization of local government services was also extended under the euphemism of 'compulsory competitive tendering'. The 1988 Local Government Act added seven areas to the original categories of construction and maintenance work that had to be offered to the private sector. These were the cleaning of buildings, street and other cleaning work, refuse collection, education and welfare catering, other forms of catering, grounds maintenance, and vehicle maintenance. To this list was added the management of sports and leisure services in 1989 and the Local Government Act 1992 cast the net even wider to include housing management, legal services, construction and property services, information technology, finance and personnel.

Now confident that their plans were unlikely to face any serious challenge, the architects of the neoliberal project moved their attention to education. In what proved to be a first step, the Education Reform Act 1988 allowed primary and secondary schools to withdraw from their local education authority and become funded by central government; otherwise known as 'grant maintained' status. School finance could also be removed from local authority control and made the responsibility of the head teacher and school governors as part of the Local Management of Schools initiative.

The Further and Higher Education Act 1992 built on this platform by removing further education and sixth form colleges from the control of local education authorities and introducing competition for funding between institutions. Not content with its achievements, however, the government used the Education Act 1993 to encourage more schools to apply for grant-maintained status. Two further pieces of legislation were introduced in 1996, the Education (Student Loans) Act and the Nursery Education and Grant-Maintained Schools Act. Both of these were overtly neoliberal in their intent to extend student loans and introduce a version of the long touted voucher scheme into nursery education.[259]

As their forebears had done in the 1970s, the individuals that participated in the Labour administrations after 1997, showed little compunction in their willingness to accommodate the assumptions of neoliberal political economy. In what were essentially cosmetic concessions, the new governments concluded a Faustian pact with the broader labour movement that was premised on: renaming compulsory competitive tendering as 'best value'; introducing a minimum wage; and an acceptance of the European Union's Social Chapter.

In contrast to such progressive achievements, the Learning and Skills Act 2000 and Education Act 2002 re-conceptualized grant-maintained status and local management of schools under the guise of academies. Likewise, the neoliberal requirement for balanced budgets was accommodated in the form of the Private Finance Initiative which, in striking similarity to the creative accountancy techniques adopted by local authorities in the 1980s, served to exclude infrastructure projects from the calculation of central spending.[260] More fundamentally, the redistributive elements of the social wage and welfare state were recast in the guise of pension and tax credits. Previously advocated in the Conservative policy document 'The Right Approach' and the Party's 1979 election manifesto, such initiatives were adopted wholeheartedly by the Labour governments of the early twenty-first century.

Returning to earlier events, it is possible to trace the roots of this modern day neoliberal hegemony in the struggles for improved service provision in the 1960s and the areas that were the subject of retrenchment and defence in the 1970s and 1980s. A link is evident, for example, between the expansion of housing and transport under Labour governments in the 1960s, the campaign against the Housing Finance Act 1972 and South Yorkshire's dispute over the funding of its transport programme. In both cases, opposition and resistance were justified in terms of local democracy and autonomy and therefore the right of local councils to decide their own levels of service provision and taxation.

The general response to central attempts to restrict local government spending during this period tended to be ameliorative. Essentially, this involved the protection of services by increasing local taxes and developing financial devices to avoid centrally devised targets and penalties. Instead of campaigns involving broad-based mobilization and participation, opposition and resistance was carried out by councillors and professionals through the structures and mechanisms of the local state.

Other examples of resistance in the early 1980s, most notably against the privatization of local service provision, tended to involve those who were directly affected. Such campaigns were mounted in Basingstoke, Gloucester and Wandsworth, for example, and in Liverpool where the campaign to oppose the privatization of cleansing services formed the central feature of the local election campaign in 1983. Perhaps inevitably, however, the specific focus of such activity meant that it was unlikely to involve broad-based, long-term campaigning activity.

Inherent difficulties in identifying reductions in service quality, as opposed to a wholesale withdrawal of services, also worked against the mobilization and participation of a broader constituency and made the mounting of sustained campaigns difficult. This problem was compounded by the subsumption of the defence of services into the campaign against rate-capping and the fact that day-to-day struggles were relegated to matters of local authority decision-making. To some extent, this can be interpreted as a consequence of the Labour Party's NEC advice that the effects of central policy should be minimized and that the government should be blamed for any harsh measures.

Service expansion and contraction was also contemporaneous with changing employment patterns in public and private sectors and within localities. In particular, the move toward mass unemployment, the scale of local regeneration schemes and labour movement demands for remedial action help to show how and why such a high level of importance was attached to local authority employment in the 1980s.

Under pressure from rising unemployment, financial restraint, deregulation and privatization, however, the labour movement focused on overall totals, as opposed to job type, working conditions and remuneration. This is reflected in the trend whereby full-time posts were replaced by part-time jobs. Similarly, attempts to avoid the threat of privatizing jobs and services involved negotiated reductions in the working conditions of local authority employees.

As with the defence of services, the struggle to protect jobs faced difficulties in mobilizing resistance. Reductions in conditions and job numbers were achieved under the threat of even greater cuts and through piecemeal tactics such as the non-filling of vacancies, early retirement and voluntary redundancy as opposed to wholesale compulsory redundancies. In similar fashion to other oppositional activity, resistance was localized and focused on those with the remit to save local authority jobs. The defence of jobs also became synonymous with the aims of the campaign against rate-capping.

Ultimately, the success or failure of both localized and broader campaigns depended on the mobilization and participation of labour movement officers, leaders, activists, members and the broader public. As the preceding chapters demonstrate, however, there was one overriding factor that governed how far this was attempted and the extent to which it was ever achievable: the labour movement's infatuation with the ideological premises of bourgeois democracy.

Opposition to the business veto, for example, was based on the principle of one person one vote, but failed to acknowledge that the abstract equality afforded by universal suffrage serves to mask the everyday experience of inequality and injustice. Similarly, the uncritical belief that judicial, legislative and executive functions were independent elements within the state apparatus was used as an argument to justify the existing role of local government.

There is also a paradox in the parallel development of campaigns to defend constitutional local democracy and autonomy, based on the ability to raise local taxes and vary local service provision, alongside the struggle for democracy and accountability within the labour movement. This latter dynamic involved a threat to established principles and processes as people radicalized by their first-hand experience of neoliberal policies joined the Labour Party and trade unions to pursue an alternative agenda.

More than anywhere else, this was apparent in the vexed relations between the parliamentary leadership and the wider party. Tensions between Labour ministers and local parties were evident in the 1960s, but these acquired a new momentum with the PLP's rejection of the 1973 Party programme and its conversion to monetary economic theory. The demand for greater accountability within the Party, particularly between MPs, councillors and local parties and between the PLP and the LPAC, was therefore an undercurrent that predated the campaign against rate-capping.

For its part, the PLP argued throughout the period that Labour groups could not be instructed to carry out particular policies. At the same time, however, disciplinary action was taken against local parties that were opposed to cuts and the PLP intervened directly in Liverpool in 1984. Viewed in this light, the PLP seems to have been more interested in protecting Labour councillors from the demands of local activists and, following the advice given as part of the law lords' ruling on Fares Fair, preventing them from honouring manifesto commitments.

This was partly a response to the growth of activism within the labour movement and the demand that elected representatives should be accountable to them. In the trade unions, for example, shop stewards sought to secure control over policy and practice, but their aims were limited. The failure to carry the policy to its logical conclusion meant that the focus fell on abstracted decision-making processes within the labour movement and failed to address the separation of activists, councillors and officers from rank-and-file members and the population at large.

Admittedly, there was an early emphasis on participation and mobilization as part of the campaign against rate-capping, but ultimate responsibility and therefore risk fell on Labour groups. This is reflected by the development of tactics and strategy through the LGCU Strategy Sub-Group and the fact that local support had a significant bearing only where councillors were selected on the basis of their commitment to carry out manifesto pledges.

Rather than attempting to transcend constitutional practices through the establishment of enduring, broad-based participatory structures, the campaign relied on publicity, parliamentary lobbying, demonstrations and days of action to connect parliamentarians, councillors, full-time officers and activists to their members and the public in general. These links and activities were inevitably transient, however, as were the structures and tactics developed in and through campaign committees and the various delegate, Labour Party and trade union conferences.

The greatest potential to overcome such restrictions was exhibited by Clay Cross in the 1970s, where the development of a local hegemony took time and effort to build and was assisted by the size of the local authority. In the 1980s, Liverpool came closest to creating similar circumstances, but this was dependent on the pivotal role played by trade union activists in encouraging mobilization and participation. Ultimately, however, the structures and practices developed in Liverpool were not embedded within the broader populace and, when it came to taking open ended industrial action, not representative of trade union members either.

For the tactic to be effective, it would have required an unprecedented level of engagement and involvement through effective and durable representative structures. Within NALGO the NDAMs and RCLGMs went some way toward addressing this precondition. If the final outcome is taken at face value, however, such bodies might have facilitated activist and officer interaction, but they could not guarantee that the necessary groundwork would be undertaken to ensure that industrial action was a feasible option. Thus, although the tactic required a lead to be taken, the passing of worthy resolutions proved to be no substitute for disciplined organization.

The evidence presented in this book is testimony to the difficulties involved in generating involvement and commitment of people with competing demands that might include them taking more than one job to make ends meet or caring for family members. In the cold light of day, when public sector pay is once again being reduced, conditions undercut and unemployment an all too real threat, activists are again met with an air of resignation that is expressed as: 'at least it's a job.'

How far activists were able or concerned to engage in dialogue with those they sought to mobilize was an important factor in the campaign against rate-capping and a question that is equally pertinent today. In the 1980s, the reliance on the determination of councillors and activists meant that the campaign was driven by people who had a clear perspective, but this was one that was not easily translated into mass participation.

This was essentially due to the fact that the concept of rate-capping and the experience of reduced service quality were not tangible enough to provoke the level of outrage that was generated by the poll tax, for example. Whereas the latter affected almost everyone and therefore had a greater potential for mass resistance, the people that used or relied on local government services were not only a minority but in many cases their vulnerability meant that they were not able to participate in a defensive campaign.

To this list of obstacles can be added the fact that the services targeted for cuts were also the areas where advances in welfare provision had been achieved through the successful struggles of earlier generations. Those gains had been won by well organized pro-active campaigning, but the zeal that had been created was no longer evident. What this meant in practice, therefore, was that the representative structures of later campaigns had to be created anew and in a very short time.

The reasons for this lie in the parliamentary leadership's refusal to offer support for the miner's case, regardless of how justified it was, and the failure to forge a united front between the miners and local government. In other words, the dread of illegality and fear of anything that smacked of a challenge to parliamentary authority is another way in which the labour movement's acceptance of liberal democracy plays out. So much so that deliberate steps are taken to inhibit the development of a class-based consciousness amongst its constituents, let alone a hegemonic agenda.

Perhaps it would be too much of a contrivance to suggest that the failure of the miners strike, the rate-capping campaign and the subsequent recriminations were part of a preconceived plan. What cannot be ignored, however, is the fact that the situation was used to marginalize social democratic, collectivist and socialist traditions within the labour movement. This was a long and complicated process that came to fruition in the form of New Labour. At its heart was the replacement of Clause IV with a perverse neoliberal doctrine that allows wealth created by the many to be appropriated by the few, but when that system inevitably fails, as it has in successive financial crises, the process is reversed and the costs of repairing the damage created by the few are socialized and recouped from the many.[261]

The Labour Party's acceptance of this dogma has been re-affirmed by its subscription to the Conservative-Liberal Democrat coalition's austerity programme. This is evident in the pronouncements of its parliamentary leaders and by the absence of any sustained resistance to the cuts agenda at the local level. Local authority trade unions have taken limited and successful industrial action over proposed changes to pension arrangements, but elsewhere their main aim has been to avoid compulsory redundancies. Partly a reflection of earlier approaches that concentrated on job totals at the expense of the quality of work, this response is also due to the overwhelming and brutal nature of the funding cuts that are being faced.

The current situation is also a product of the neoliberal restructuring of the local state whereby privatization and other measures have effectively removed decisions about service standards from the democratic arena. This has been part of a deliberate strategy to depoliticize related issues in the eyes of the local electorate and ensure that the local state is no longer a means through which socio-economic interests can be advanced. A by-product of this process has also been to produce voter apathy and an increasing level of pessimism over the prospects for any alternative agenda.

From what in historical terms is a low starting point, any future struggle is likely to be long and hard. Steps in the right direction are already being taken by groups like Defend Council Housing, the Coalition of Resistance and a myriad of local campaigns. If the lessons of the past are to be learned, however, it is important to focus on building broad-based, representative grassroots networks that include local trade unions, service users and the public.

The achievement of immediate gains can help to encourage wider participation and, while social media can assist organization and in getting the message out, it is concrete achievements that afford credibility to wider political analyses. As the campaigns discussed in the book demonstrate, there are no right or wrong answers. Outcomes are the product of actions taken in the circumstances that prevail at any given time. Regardless of the fate of individual struggles, the overall objective of achieving a society that meets people's needs and allows them to realize their true potential is part of a much bigger struggle, and one that is perpetual.

While the Labour Party might have been more effective at suppressing the cause of socialism within its ranks, it is worth remembering that the situation that prevails today is the product of a small and committed group of dissenters within the Conservative Party of the 1970s. Everyone must make their own decisions about how best to achieve their objectives, but all can rest assured that change is achievable so long as people are prepared to make it happen.

POSTSCRIPT

The Introduction was prefaced by a quotation from fiction and although John Ball was a real person, it is fitting that the book closes with the real words of a later revolutionary. That both characters lived in earlier centuries merely serves to demonstrate the validity of the opening citation and the fact that 'the struggle for human weal' is an age old process.[262] For this reason the following words provide a pertinent reminder to all of us who enjoy reading or writing books about socio-economic struggle.

> I was made to write a little book ... yet my mind was not at rest, because nothing was acted, and thoughts run in me, that words and writings were all nothing, and must die, for action is the life of all, and if though dost not act, thou dost nothing.
> Gerrard Winstanley, *A Watchword to the City of London and the Armie*

APPENDIX
TARGETS AND PENALTIES

The reduction of grant allocation as a way of penalizing local authorities deemed to be high-spenders formed an integral part of the block grant system that was introduced under the LGPLA. As part of this scheme, each individual authority was given a GREA and target by the government. Whether or not they were then selected for grant 'hold back' depended on the amount they planned to spend and how this compared to the limits set in Whitehall. Those penalized lost funding according to the percentage of their calculated overspend and, because authorities could budget to absorb previous penalties, the system was changed each year and grew in severity.[263]

In 1981-82, for example, the first targets were allocated to local authorities in England and were set at a level that was 5.6 per cent below the amount of current expenditure identified in the 1978–79 budget. Those councils that exceeded their target *and* their GREA faced a deduction of grant that increased according to how much they planned to spend. This meant that if the planned spend was 2 per cent over target, two pence in the pound was deducted. If the excess rose to between 3 and 4 per cent, an authority lost six pence and this increased to nine pence where spending over target was 5 per cent or more. If a council stayed within its GREA, however, it could avoid any penalties at all.

For the year 1982–83, the target covered total expenditure and was based on the lower of the authority's 1981-82 budgets. In other words, if the council had budgeted for an amount that was lower than that predicted by government formulae, this figure became the basis for its target and was adjusted in line with 1982-83 prices. The rate at which penalties were incurred was also changed so that for each percentage point over target, three pence in the pound was now deducted. This applied to the first 5 per cent of overspend and translated into penalties that increased from three pence for a 1 per cent overspend up to a maximum of 15 pence for spending that was deemed to be 5 per cent or more above the authority's target.

The process was made more complicated and more severe from 1983–84, when the upper penalty limit was removed and the concession for authorities spending above target but below GREA was withdrawn. For this year, individual targets were calculated on the basis of 1982–83 targets. Thus, if an authority intended to spend less than 1 per cent over its 1982-83 target, their new target would be the 1982–83 figure plus 4 per cent. If they planned to exceed this 1 per cent threshold, the target would be as above, but 5 per cent was used as the adjustment figure.

There was also a change in the rate at which penalties were applied. For the first 2 per cent of overspend authorities lost one and two pence respectively. For every percentage point thereafter an authority lost five pence, so that between 3 and 5 per cent, the penalty increased from seven pence to 17 pence. At 10 per cent, 15per cent and 20 per cent the tariff was therefore 42, 67 and 92 pence and so on.

Targets for 1984–85 were also based on data taken from the previous year. Now, however, the figure reflected the highest of an authority's 1983-84 budget, GREA or Target. An additional proviso was also introduced to prevent any target exceeding the previous year's figure by 3 per cent or reducing it by more than 6 per cent. Penalties were now deducted at the rate of two pence for the first 1 per cent of overspend, four pence for the next and eight pence for the third. For every additional percentage point thereafter, the penalty was increased by nine pence.

Finally, 1985–86 targets were based on either the previous year's GREA or target and became yet more convoluted. So much so that an authority which had budgeted to spend at or below its GREA in 1984–85 was given a target that consisted of its GREA for that year plus 3.75 per cent. Those that spent above target in 1984–85, had their new target based on the previous year's figure, but again this was increased by 3.75 per cent. The amount of penalty was also increased for the smaller amounts of overspend, so that for a 1 per cent excess an authority would be penalised seven pence and for 2 per cent the penalty would be eight pence. From 3 per cent onward the hold back was nine pence and although this was the highest rate used in the previous year it now started one percentage point sooner.

BIBLIOGRAPHY

Abel Smith, Brian and Townsend, Peter, *The Poor and the Poorest*, London: G Bell & Sons, 1965.

Achur, James, Trade Union Membership 2010, Department for Business Innovation and Skills, 2011. Available at: http://www.bis.gov.uk/assets/biscore/employment-matters/docs/t/11-p77-trade-union-membership-2010.pdf Accessed 3 March 2012.

ALA/AMA, Background Paper, undated.

ALA/AMA, Letter sent to Patrick Jenkin Secretary of State for the Environment, 10 April 1985.

Alexander, Alan, *The Politics of Local Government in the United Kingdom*, London: Longman, 1982.

Altvater, Elmar, 'Financial Crises on the Threshold of the 21st Century' in *Socialist Register*, 33, 1997.

Ascher, Kate, 'The Politics of Administrative Opposition - Council House Sales and the Right to Buy' in *Local Government Studies*, 9, 2, 1983.

Ascher, Kate, *The Politics of Privatisation*, Basingstoke: Macmillan, 1987.

Ashford, Douglas, 'The Effects of Central Finance on the British Local Government System' in *British Journal of Political Science*, 4, 1974.

Bacon, Robert and Eltis, Walter, *Britain's Economic Problem: Too Few Producers*, Basingstoke: Macmillan, 1976.

Bassett, Keith, 'Labour, Socialism and Local Democracy' in Martin Boddy and Colin Fudge (eds.), *Local Socialism?* Basingstoke: Macmillan, 1984.

Becker, Gary and Elias, Julio, 'Incentives in the Market for Live and Cadaveric Organ Donations', Working Paper, 2007. Available at: http://home.uchicago.edu/~gbecker/MarketforLiveandCadavericOrganDonations_Becker_Elias.pdf Accessed 12 March 2012.

Benn, Tony, 'The Real Choices Facing the Cabinet', National Archive CAB/129/193/7, 1976. Available at: http://filestore.nationalarchives.gov.uk/pdfs/small/cab-129-193-cp-76-117-7.pdf Accessed 4 March 2012.

Blunkett, David, Letter sent as Chairperson of LGCU to Patrick Jenkin, Secretary of State for the Environment, 5 February 1985.

Blunkett, David, 'Possible Deficit Budgeting', Paper Prepared for LGCU, 16 April 1985.
Blunkett, David, 'No Rate Tactic Prospects and Problems', Paper Prepared for LGCU, 19 April 1985.
Blunkett, David, Letter to author, 23 November 1994.
Blunkett, David and Jackson, Keith, *Democracy in Crisis: The Town Halls Respond*, London: Hogarth, 1987.
Boddy, Martin, 'Local Economic and Employment Strategies' in Martin Boddy and Colin Fudge (eds.), *Local Socialism?* Basingstoke: Macmillan, 1984a.
Boddy, Martin, 'Local Councils and the Financial Squeeze' in Martin Boddy and Colin Fudge (eds.), *Local Socialism?* Basingstoke: Macmillan, 1984b.
Brittan, Samuel, 'The Economic Contradictions of Democracy' in *British Journal of Political Science*, 5, 1975.
Burgess, Graham, Interview with ex Branch Chairperson of Liverpool NALGO, 1994.
Byrne, Tony, (Third Edition), *Local Government in Britain*, London: Penguin, 1985.
Byrne, Tony, Interview with ex Chair of Liverpool City Council Finance Committee, 1994.
Cartwright, John and Hughes, Simon, Amendment to proposed Motion (Resistance to Rate-capping (No. 2)), Notices of Notes and Motions, 26 March 1985.
Castells, Manuel, *City, Class and Power*, Basingstoke: Macmillan Press, 1980.
Caulcott, Tom, 'Responding to the Challenge - The Public sector in Recession' in *Local Government Studies*, 9, 6, 1983.
CBI, 'Keeping the Wheels Turning: Modernising the Legal Framework of Industrial Relations', 2010. Available at: www.cbi.org.uk/media/878203/F83C60652C990D95802577BB004B289A__Keeping-the-wheels-turning.pdf Accessed 3 March 2012
Chandler, Jim and Lawless, Paul, *Local Authorities and the Creation of Employment*, Aldershot: Gower, 1985.
Chomsky, Noam, *Profit over People: Neoliberalism and Global Order*, New York: Seven Stories Press, 1999.
Clarke, Alan and Cochrane, Allan, 'Inside the Machine: The Left and Finance Professionals in Local Government' in *Capital and Class*, 37, 1989.
Coates, David, *The Labour Party and the Struggle for Socialism*, Cambridge: Cambridge University Press, 1975.

Cockburn, Cynthia, *The Local State: Management of Cities and People*, London: Pluto, 1977.
Collard, David, *The New Right: a Critique*, Fabian Tract 387, London: Fabian Society, 1968.
Conservative Party, *The Right Approach: a Statement of Conservative Aims*, London: Conservative Central Office, 1976.
Conservative Party, *Conservative Manifesto*, 1979, London: Conservative Central Office, 1979.
Conservative and Unionist Party, *The Right Road for Britain: the Conservative Party's Statement of Policy*, London: Conservative and Unionist Central Office, 1949.
Conservative and Unionist Party, *A Better Tomorrow: The Conservative Programme for the Next 5 Years*, London: Conservative Central Office, 1970.
Conservative Research Department, Report of the Nationalised Industries Policy Group, Thatcher Archive, MSS 2/6/1/37, 1977. Available at: www.margaretthatcher.org/archive/displaydocument.asp?docid=110795 Accessed 3 March 2012.
Conservative Research Department, Politics Today series, 3, London: Conservative Central Office, 21 February 1983.
Conservative Research Department, Politics Today series, 2, London: Conservative Central Office, 13 February 1984.
Coombes, Keva, Discussion Document for the Merseyside County Labour Party, 27 February 1985.
Corby, Susan, Public Sector Disputes and Third Party Intervention, ACAS, 2003.
Available at: www.acas.org.uk/media/pdf/p/1/pubsectordisputesjun03_1.pdf Accessed 3 March 2012.
Cresswell, Peter, Interview with ex Branch Secretary of Liverpool NALGO, 1994.
Crewe, Ivor, 'How to Win a Landslide Without Really Trying: Why the Conservatives Won in 1983' in Austin Ranney (Ed.), *Britain at the Polls, 1983*, Durham N C: Duke University Press, 1985.
Crick, Michael, *The March of Militant*, London: Faber and Faber, 1986.
Crosland, Anthony, Economic Strategy – The IMF, National Archive CAB/129/193/8, 1976. Available at: http://filestore.nationalarchives.gov.uk/pdfs/small/cab-129-193-cp-76-118-8.pdf Accessed 4 March 2012.
Cunningham, John, Letters sent as Shadow Secretary of State for the Environment, 14 January 1985-12 April 1985.

Davies, John, 'Transformations in the Political Culture of Liverpool, 1920s-1980s', unpublished MPhil Thesis, Lancaster, 1987.

Dearlove, John, *The Reorganisation of British Local Government*, Cambridge: Cambridge University Press, 1979.

Dobb, Maurice, *Political Economy and Capitalism; some Essays in Economic Tradition*, London: Routledge, 1937.

Drain, Geoffrey, Letter sent as NALGO General Secretary to the Secretaries of Local Government Branches, District Councils, Sectional and Professional Societies, 15 September 1981.

Duncan, Simon and Goodwin, Mark, *The Local State and Uneven Development*, Cambridge: Polity, 1988.

Dunleavy, Patrick, *Urban Political Analysis*, Basingstoke: Macmillan, 1980.

Dunleavy, Patrick, 'The Limits of Local Government' in Martin Boddy and Colin Fudge (eds.), *Local Socialism?* Basingstoke: Macmillan, 1984.

Elcock, Howard, *Local Government: Policy and Management in Local Authorities*, London: Routledge, 1982.

Evans, Colin, 'Privatisation of Local Services' in *Local Government Studies*, 11, 6, 1985.

Fellows, Roger and Grimes, Keith, 'Towards the unitary state: Tory attacks on local government – The Metropolitan County Councils' in *Critical Social Policy*, 10, 1984.

Flynn, Rob, 'Co-optation and Strategic Planning in the Local State' in Roger King (Ed.), *Capital and Politics*, London: Routledge and Kegan Paul, 1983.

Foucault, Michel, *The Birth of Biopolitics: Lectures at the Collège de France, 1978-1979*, Basingstoke: Palgrave Macmillan, 2008.

Fryer, Bob, 'British Trade Unions and the Cuts' in *Capital and Class*, 8, 1979.

Fryer, Bob, Manson, Tom and Fairclough, Andy, 'Employment and Trade Unionism in the Public Services: Background Notes to the Struggle Against the Cuts' in *Capital and Class*, 4, 1978.

Gamble, Andrew, *Britain in Decline: Economic Policy, Political Strategy and the British State*, Basingstoke: Macmillan, 1985.

Garnett, Mark and Hickson, Kevin, *Conservative thinkers*, Manchester: Manchester University Press, 2009.

Gibson, John and Travers, Tony, 'Block Grant: the Story of a Failure' in *Public Money*, 5, 2, 1985.

Glasgow NALGO, District Branch Letter to Liverpool Branch, February 1984.

Goldsmith, Mike, 'The Conservatives and Local Government, 1979 and After' in David Bell (Ed.), *The Conservative Government 1979-84: An Interim*

Report, London: Croom Helm, 1985.

Goss, Sue, *Local Labour and Local Government*, Edinburgh: Edinburgh University Press, 1988.

Gough, Ian, *The Political Economy of the Welfare State*, Basingstoke: Macmillan, 1985.

Green, David, *The New Right: the Counter Revolution in Political, Economic and Social Thought*, Brighton: Wheatsheaf, 1988.

Gyford, John, *The Politics of Local Socialism*, London: Allen and Unwin, 1985.

Gyford, John and James, Mari, *National Parties and Local Politics*, London: Allen and Unwin, 1983.

Habermas, Jurgen, *Legitimation Crisis*, Cambridge: Polity, 1997.

Halford, Roger, 'Local Authority Contracting-Out - The Implications for Employees' Pay and Conditions' in *Local Government Studies*, 8, 5, 1982.

Hampton, William, *Local Government and Urban Politics*, London: Longman, 1987.

Hayes, Mark, *The New Right in Britain: An Introduction to Theory and Practice*, London: Pluto, 1994.

Healey, Denis, *Hansard*, HC Deb 26 March 1974 vol 871 cc277-8, 1974. Available at: http://hansard.millbanksystems.com/commons/1974/mar/26/introduction Accessed 4 March 2012

Healey, Denis, Memorandum of the Chancellor of the Exchequer, National Archive CAB/129/193/1, 1976. Available at: http://filestore.nationalarchives.gov.uk/pdfs/small/cab-129-193-cp-76-111-1.pdf Accessed 4 March 2012.

Henney, Alex, *Inside Local Government: A Case for Radical Reform*, London: Sinclair Browne, 1984.

Horkheimer, Max, 'Materialism and Metaphysics' in *Critical Theory: selected essays*, New York: Herder and Herder, 1972.

House of Lords, Bromley London Borough Council -v- Greater London Council, 17 December 1981. Available at: http://www.swarb.co.uk/lisc/LocGv19801984.php Accessed 12 March 2012.

Howe, Geoffrey, *Hansard*, HC Deb 09 March 1976 vol 907 cc251-383, 1976. Available at: http://hansard.millbanksystems.com/commons/1976/mar/09/public-expenditure Accessed 4 March 2012.

Howell, David, *Hansard*, HC Deb 01 February 1983 vol 36 cc228-71, 1983. Available at: http://hansard.millbanksystems.com/commons/1983/feb/01/approval-of-financial-plans-and#S6CV0036P0_19830201_HOC_488 Accessed 12 March 2012.

Howell, David, *Hansard*, HC Deb 28 March 1984 vol 57 cc309-84, 1984. Available at: http://hansard.millbanksystems.com/commons/1984/mar/28/rates-bill Accessed 12 March 2012.

Howells, Chris, 'The Politics of Local Authority Finance' in *Critical Social Policy*, 2, 2, 1982.

Institute of Directors, Freebie Growth Plan, 2011. Available at: http://www.iod.com/mainwebsite/resources/document/policy_publications_freebies_1102.pdf Accessed 3 March 2012.

Islington NALGO, Letter to Liverpool NALGO Branch, 23 June 1984.

Jenkin, Patrick, Letters sent as Secretary of State for the Environment, 21 February 1985-24 April 1985.

Jinkinson, Alan, Letter sent as NALGO Assistant General Secretary to Liverpool City Branch, 3 April 1984.

Jones, George and Stewart, John, (Second Edition), *The Case for Local Government*, London: Allen and Unwin, 1985.

Keating, Michael, 'Size, Efficiency and Democracy: Consolidation, Fragmentation and Public Choice' in David Judge, Gerry Stoker and Harold Wolman (eds.), *Theories of Urban Politics*, London: Sage, 1995.

King, Anthony, 'Overload: Problems of Governing in the 1970s' in *Political Studies*, 23, 1975.

King, Peter, *Twentieth-Century British History*, London: W. H. Allen, 1980.

Kline, Roger, 'Privatising local government: the special case of Birmingham' in *Critical Social Policy*, 8, 1983.

Kogan, David and Kogan, Maurice, (Second Edition), *The Battle for the Labour Party*, London: Fontana, (1983).

Labour Party, Annual Conference Reports 1966-1987.

Labour Party, NEC Statement on Local Government Cuts, LPAC, 1981.

Labour Party, NEC Statement on Rate Controls, LPAC, 1984.

Lansley, Stewart, Goss, Sue, and Wolmar, Christian, *Councils in Conflict: the Rise and Fall of the Municipal Left*, Basingstoke: Macmillan, 1989.

Lawless, Paul, *Urban Deprivation and Government Initiative*, London: Faber and Faber, 1979.

Leopold, John and Beaumont, Phil, 'The Local Government Committee of the TUC: A Decade of Activity' in *Local Government Studies*, 8, 6, 1982.

Leys, Colin, 'The British Labour Party's Transition from Socialism to Capitalism' in *Socialist Register*, 32, 1996.

Leys, Colin, *Market-Driven Politics: Neoliberal Democracy and the Public Interest*, London: Verso, 2003.

LGCU, Rate Support Grant - 1985/ 86, undated.

LGCU, Groupwork Report, January 1985.

LGCU, Programme of Work, Management Committee Report, 16 January 1985.
LGCU, Notes of Meeting with the Secretary of State for the Environment, 4 February 1985.
LGCU, The Local Authority Case, Meeting with the Secretary of State for the Environment, 4 February 1985.
LGCU, Press Release, 4 February 1985.
LGCU, The Way Forward, Strategy Sub-Group Report, 12 April 1985.
LGCU, Government Returns, Management Committee Report, 15 April 1985.
LGCU, Briefings, Bulletins and Local Links, February 1984-April 1985.
LGCU, Management Committee Minutes, 4 June 1984-15 April 1985.
LGCU, Management Group Minutes, 18 December 1984-12 March 1985.
LGCU, Strategy Sub-Group Minutes, 3 April 1985-18 April 1985.
Liverpool City Council, Campaigning for Jobs and Services, undated(a).
Liverpool City Council, Campaign Working Party Terms of Reference, undated(b).
Liverpool City Council, Rates Services and Jobs: The Campaign in Liverpool, 1983.
Liverpool NALGO, No Redundancy Agreement 1980-81, Branch Organizer Report to District Organization Officer, undated(a).
Liverpool NALGO, The Liverpool Crisis - an Explanation for other NALGO Branches, Branch Report, undated(b).
Liverpool NALGO, The Rate, the Cuts and the Government, Report to SGM, 11 February, 1980.
Liverpool NALGO, The Fight Against Cuts and Redundancies in Liverpool, Branch Negotiators Report, 17 June, 1980.
Liverpool NALGO, Local Government in Crisis: National Labour and Trade Union Conference, Branch Delegate Report, 20 November 1980.
Liverpool NALGO, Letter to District Organization Officer, 8 March 1984.
Liverpool NALGO, Letter to councillors opposing the Labour Group Budget, 29 March 1984.
Liverpool NALGO, Branch Executive Council Minutes, 14 February 1979-21 October 1987.
Liverpool NALGO, Service Conditions Committee Minutes, 21 June 1979-1 October 1987.
Liverpool NALGO, Finance and General Purposes Committee Minutes, 11 October 1979-22 May 1986.
Liverpool NALGO, Campaign Committee Minutes, 14 December 1983-16 September 1985.

Liverpool NALGO, Our City Our Fight, Campaign Bulletin, 15 December 1983-13 July 1984.
Liverpool NALGO, Minutes of meetings between Liverpool City councillors, full-time and lay Trade Union officials: 28 February 1984-24 January 1985.
Livingstone, K en, 'Interview' in Martin Boddy and Colin Fudge (eds.), *Local Socialism?* Basingstoke: Macmillan, 1984.
Livingstone, Ken, *If Voting Changed Anything, They'd Abolish It*, London: Fontana, 1988.
Livingstone, Ken, Letter to author, December 1994.
London NALGO, Hit List Branches Meeting Minutes, 10 August 1983.
Loughlin, Martin, *Local Government in the Modern State*, London: Sweet and Maxwell, 1986
Lowes, David, In Defence of Local Government: an Immanent Critique of Labour Movement Campaigns to Defend Local Democracy, Jobs and Services in the 1980s, unpublished PhD Thesis, Liverpool JMU, 1998.
Lowes, David, *The Anti-capitalist Dictionary: Movements, Histories and Motivations*, London: Zed, 2006.
Lowes, Ian, Interview with ex Convenor of Liverpool GMBATU Branch 5, 1994.
Machin, Andrew, 'Comparisons between Unemployment and the Claimant Count' in *Labour Market Trends*, February 2004.
Mackintosh, Maureen and Wainwright, Hilary (eds.), *A Taste of Power*, London: Verso, 1987.
McLaverty, Peter, Trade Unions and Political Change in Local Government: A Comparison of Sheffield and Doncaster, unpublished PhD Thesis, Sheffield, 1989.
McNally, David, 'From Financial Crisis to World-Slump: Accumulation, Financialization, and the Global Slowdown' in *Historical Materialism*, 17,2, 2009.
Marchington, Mick and Armstrong, Roger, 'A Comparison Between Shop Steward Activity in Local Government and the Private Sector' in *Local Government Studies*, 8, 6, 1982.
Marsh, David and Locksley, Gareth, 'Trade Union Power in Britain' in *West European Politics*, 4, 1, 1981.
Marsh, David, *The New Politics of British Trade Unionism*, Basingstoke: Macmillan, 1992.
Marx, Karl, *Capital: a Critique of Political Economy* (Volume One), London: Lawrence and Wishart, 1954.
Marx, Karl, *A Contribution to the Critique of Political Economy*, Moscow: Progress Publishers, 1977.

Mason, Charlie, 'Labour Market Policy' in Ken Young and Charlie Mason (eds.), *Urban Economic Development*, Basingstoke: MacMillan, 1983.

Maud, John Redcliffe and Wood, Bruce, *English Local Government Reformed*, Oxford: Oxford University Press, 1974.

McChesney, Robert, 'Introduction' in Noam Chomsky, *Profit over People: Neoliberalism and Global Order*, New York: Seven Stories Press, 1999.

Merseyside Trade Union and Labour Movement Campaign Committee, Leaflets, Letters and Minutes, November 1983-March 1985.

Middlemas, Keith, *Politics in Industrial Society*, London: Andre Deutsch, 1979.

Miliband, Ralph, *The State in Capitalist Society: The Analysis of the Western System of Power*, London: Quartet, 1969.

Miliband, Ralph, (Second Edition), *Parliamentary Socialism*, London: Merlin Press, 1972.

Milton, John, *Paradise Lost*, Project Gutenberg, 1991. Available at:http://www.gutenberg.org/cache/epub/20/pg20.html Accessed 12 March 2012.

Minogue, Martin and O'Grady, Jeremy, 'Contracting Out Local Authority Services in Britain' in *Local Government Studies*, 11, 3, 1985.

Mirowski, Philip and Plehwe, Dieter (eds.), *The Road from Mont Pèlerin: The making of the Neoliberal Thought Collective*, Cambridge MA: Harvard University Press, 2009.

Mitchell, Austin, 'Clay Cross' in *The Political Quarterly*, 45, 1974.

Morris, Margaret, *The General Strike*, Harmondsworth: Penguin, 1976.

Morris, William, *A Dream of John Ball and a King's Lesson*, Walking, Available at: http://www.marxists.org/archive/morris/works/1886/johnball/johnball.htm#ch ap-4 Accessed 12 March 2012.

NALGO, 'Public Expenditure Cuts - National Strategy for Reconvened Group Meeting, National Local Government Committee Report, 15 September 1981.

NALGO, Campaign in Defence of Local Government, National Local Government Committee Report, 20 March 1984.

NALGO, Campaign in Defence of Local Government: Rate-Capping and Penalties Industrial Action, National Local Government Committee Report, 7 December 1984.

NALGO, Fight to Defend Local Democracy Bulletin, 8 November 1983-13 March 1985.

NALGO, National Delegate Advisory Meeting Minutes, 30 November 1983-16 October 1984.

NALGO, Rate-Capping Liaison Group Meeting Minutes, 20 November 1984-3 March 1985.

National Archive, Public Expenditure to 1978–79, CAB/129/178/5, 1974. Available at: http://filestore.nationalarchives.gov.uk/pdfs/small/cab-129-178-c-74-80-5.pdf Accessed 4 March 2012.

National Archive, Draft White Paper on Inflation, CAB/129/184/C/76, 1975. Available at: http://filestore.nationalarchives.gov.uk/pdfs/small/cab-129-184-c-76.pdf Accessed 4 March 2012.

National Archive, Conclusions of a Meeting of the Cabinet held at Chequers on Friday 20 June 1975, CAB/128/56/29. Available at: http://filestore.nationalarchives.gov.uk/pdfs/small/cab-128-56-cc-75-29.pdf Accessed 4 March 2012.

National Archive, Conclusions of a Meeting of the Cabinet 10 July 1975, CAB/128/57/3. Available at: http://filestore.nationalarchives.gov.uk/pdfs/small/cab-128-57-cc-75-33.pdf Accessed 4 March 2012.

National Archive, Conclusions of Meeting of the Cabinet 6 July 1976, CAB/128/59/13. Available at: http://filestore.nationalarchives.gov.uk/pdfs/small/cab-128-59-cm-76-13.pdf Accessed 4 March 2012.

National Archive, Conclusions of a Meeting of the Cabinet 23 November 1976, CAB/128/60/11. Available at: http://filestore.nationalarchives.gov.uk/pdfs/small/cab-128-60-cm-76-33.pdf Accessed 4 March 2012.

National Archive, Conclusions of a Meeting of the Cabinet held 1 December 1976, CAB/128/60/13. Available at: http://filestore.nationalarchives.gov.uk/pdfs/small/cab-128-60-cm-76-35.pdf Accessed 4 March 2012.

National Archive, Housing Act 1980. Available at: www.legislation.gov.uk/ukpga/1980/51/pdfs/ukpga_19800051_en.pdf Accessed 4 March 2012.

National Archive, Operational Selection Policy OSP9, Fiscal Policy 1971-1979, 2005. Available at: http://www.nationalarchives.gov.uk/documents/information-management/osp9.pdf Accessed 4 March 2012.

National Union of Conservative and Unionist Associations, 'The industrial charter: A Statement of Conservative Industrial Policy', Conservative and Unionist Central Office, 1946.

Newman, George, *Path to Maturity: NALGO 1965-1980*, London: National and Local Government Officers' Association, 1982.

Newton, Kenneth and Karran, Terence, *The Politics of Local Expenditure*, Basingstoke: Macmillan, 1985.

Niskanen, William, *Bureaucracy: Servant or Master?* London: Institute for Economic Affairs, 1973.

NLACC, National Local Authority Co-ordinating Committee Minutes, 23

February 1985-2 May 1985.
Norfolk NALGO, Letter to Liverpool NALGO Branch, April 1984.
North East NALGO, District Council Letter to Liverpool NALGO Branch, undated.
Norton, Philip, *Conservative Dissidents: Dissent within the Parliamentary Conservative Party, 1970-74*, London: Temple Smith, 1978.
Painter, Joe, 'Regulation Theory, Post-Fordism and Urban Politics' in David Judge, Gerry Stoker and Harold Wolman (eds.), *Theories of Urban Politics*, London: Sage, 1995.
Panitch, Leo, *Social Democracy and Industrial Militancy:The Labour Party, the Trade Unions and Incomes Policy 1945-1974*, Cambridge: Cambridge University Press, 1976.
Panitch, Leo, 'Recent theories of Corporatism' in *British Journal of Sociology*, 30, 1980.
Parkinson, Michael, Liverpool on the Brink, Hermitage: Policy Journals, 1985.
Pickard, Jim, 'Johnson Calls for Tougher Strike Legislation' in *The Financial Times* 4 October 2010.
Pirie, Madsen, *The Logic of Economics: and its implications for the Public Sector*, London: Adam Smith Institute, 1982.
Rayner, Geof and Conway, Jean, 'Wandsworth - the Cuts and the Fightback' in *Critical Social Policy*, 1, 1, 1981.
Reginae Elizabethae, An Act for the Relief of the Poor, Anno 43 Chapter 2 Available at: www.sochealth.co.uk/history/poorlaw.htm Accessed 3 March 2012.
Reid, Jimmy, 'Speech to a Glasgow demonstration soon after the start of the UCS work-in' in Tony Benn (Ed.), *Writings on the Wall: a Radical and Socialist Anthology 1215–1984*, London: Faber and Faber, 1984.
Renshaw, Patrick, *The General Strike*, London: Methuen, 1975.
Rhodes, Rod, 'Some Myths in Central local relations', in *Town Planning Review*, 51, 1980.
Ridley, Nicholas, The Local Right: enabling not providing, Policy Study 92, London: Centre for Policy Studies, 1988.
Ridley, Nicholas, The Selsdon Group Manifesto 1973, 25th Anniversary Reprint, 1998. Available at: www.selsdongroup.co.uk/manifesto.pdf Accessed 12 March 2012.
Rogers, Chris, 'The Politics of Economic Policy Making in Britain: a Re-Assessment of the 1976 IMF Crisis' in *Politics & Policy*, 37, 5, 2009.
Rose, Richard, 'On the Priorities of Government: A Developmental Analysis of Public Policies' in *European Journal of Political Research*, 4, 1976.

Saunders, Peter, 'Rethinking Local Politics' in Martin Boddy and Colin Fudge (eds.), *Local Socialism?* Basingstoke: Macmillan, 1984.

Seyd, Patricia, *The Rise and Fall of the Labour Left*, Basingstoke: Macmillan, 1987.

Shelley, Mary Wollstonecraft (Ed.), *Shelley's Poems and Essays and Letters from Abroad*, London: Ward, Lock & Co, 1889.

Shutt, John, 'Tory enterprise zones and the labour movement' in *Capital and Class*, 23, 1984.

Sissons, Andrew and Brown, Chris, Do Enterprise Zones Work? an Ideopolis policy paper, London: The Work Foundation, 2011.

Skelcher, Chris, 'Transportation' in Stewart Ranson, George Jones and Kieron Walsh (eds.), *Between Centre and Locality*, London: Allen and Unwin, 1985.

Skinner, David and Langdon, Julia, *The Story of Clay Cross*, Nottingham: Spokesman, 1974.

Sklair, Leslie 'The Struggle Against the Housing Finance Act' in *Socialist Register*, 12, 1975.

Sonnet, Keith, Letter sent as NALGO Local Government Service Conditions Officer to Liverpool City Branch, 31 May 1984.

South West NALGO, South West District Letter to Liverpool NALGO Branch, 14 March 1984.

Stewart, Murray and Underwood, Jacky, 'New Relations in the Inner City' in Ken Young and Charlie Mason (eds.), *Urban Economic Development*, Basingstoke: Macmillan, 1983.

Stoker, Gerry, *The Politics of Local Government*, Basingstoke: Macmillan, 1988.

Storey, David, 'Local Employment Initiatives in North East England: Evaluation and Assessment Problems' in Ken Young and Charlie Mason (eds.), *Urban Economic Development*, Basingstoke: Macmillan, 1983.

Stott, Roger, *Hansard* HC Deb 01 February 1983 vol 36 cc228-71, 1983. Available at: http://hansard.millbanksystems.com/commons/1983/feb/01/approval-of-financial-plans-and#S6CV0036P0_19830201_HOC_488 Accessed 12 March 2012.

Suddaby, John, 'The Public sector Strike in Camden '79' in *New Left Review*, 116, 1979.

Taaffe, Peter and Mulhearn, Tony, *Liverpool: A City that Dared to Fight*, London: Fortress, 1988.

Taylor, AJP, *The Troublemakers: Dissent Over Foreign Policy 1729–1939*, Harmondsworth: Penguin, 1985.

Taylor, John, 'The CCLGF - A Critical Analysis of its Origins and Development' in *Local Government Studies*, 5, 3, 1979.
Taylor, Robert, *The Fifth Estate: Britain's Unions in the 1970s*, London: Routledge, 1978.
Thomson, Andrew, 'Local Government as an Employer' in Richard Rose and Edward Page (eds.), *Fiscal Stress in the Cities*, Cambridge: Cambridge University Press, 1982.
Thompson, Paul and Allen, Mike, 'Labour and the Local State in Liverpool' in *Capital and Class*, 29, 1986.
Tiebout, Charles, 'A Pure Theory of Local Expenditures' in *The Journal of Political Economy*, 64, 5, 1956.
Travers, Tony, 'Local Government De-Manning' in *Public Money*, 3, 1, 1983.
Travers, Tony, *The Politics of Local Government Finance*, London: Allen and Unwin, 1986.
TUC, Annual Reports 1960-1987.
TUC, Local Government Committee Minutes, 5 December 1983.
TUC, National Consultative Conference on the Rates Act and the Defence of Local Government, 4 December 1984.
Tullock, Gordon, *The Vote Motive*, London: Insitute for Economic Affairs, 1976.
Tullock, Gordon and Buchanan, James, *The Calculus of Consent: Logical Foundations of Constitutional Democracy*, Ann Arbor: University of Michigan Press, 1962.
Wainwright, Hilary, *Labour: A Tale of Two Parties*, London: Hogarth, 1987.
Walsh, Kieron, 'Workforce', in Stewart Ranson, George Jones and Kieron Walsh (eds.), *Between Centre and Locality*, London: Allen and Unwin, 1985.
Willis, Norman, Letter sent as TUC General Secretary to Patrick Jenkin, Secretary of State for the Environment, 1 April 1985.
Winstanley, Gerrard, 'A Watchword to the City of London and the Armie' in George Sabine (Ed.), *The Works of Gerrard Winstanley*, New York: Russell and Russell, 1965.
Young, Ken and Mason, Charlie, 'The Significance of Urban Economic Development Programmes' in Ken Young and Charlie Mason (eds.), *Urban Economic Development*, Basingstoke: Macmillan, 1983.
Young, Ken and Mills, Liz, 'The Decline of Urban Economies' in Richard Rose and Edward Page (eds.), *Fiscal Stress in the Cities*, Cambridge: Cambridge University Press, 1982.

Notes

1. Reginae Elizabethae Anno 43, Chapter Two.
2. The term Liberal is used here instead of Liberal-Democrat Party to emphasize the neoliberal agenda and underline the fact that it is the liberal wing of that Party that underpins the coalition.
3. Measures include: the decontrol of exchange rates, deregulation of the financial sector and of labour markets, using interest rates to control inflation, liberalization of trade, privatization, reductions in public services due to budget cuts and wage cuts. For more see David Lowes, *The Anti-capitalist Dictionary*, London: Zed, 2006, p. 231. It is also worth noting that these same nostrums were imposed on the supposedly sovereigns states of Greece and Italy in late 2011 and early 2012.
4. See Patrick Renshaw, *The General Strike*, London: Methuen, 1975, Margaret Morris, *The General Strike*, Harmondsworth: Penguin, 1976 and Conservative Research Department, Report of the Nationalised Industries Policy Group, Thatcher MSS (2/6/1/37), 1977. In an uncannily similar fashion, the Conservative-Liberal coalition appeared to be hell-bent on provoking a dispute over public sector pensions in 2011-12.
5. Susan Corby, Public Sector Disputes and Third Party Intervention, ACAS, 2003, p. 9.
6. These were the employment acts of 1980, 1982, 1988 and 1989, the Trade Union Act 1984 and the Public Order Act 1986.
7. Andrew Machin, 'Comparisons between Unemployment and the Claimant Count' in *Labour Market Trends*, February 2004, p. 2.
8. The first such calls were reported by Jim Pickard, 'Johnson Calls for Tougher Strike Legislation' in *The Financial Times*, 4 October 2010.
9. James Achur, Trade Union Membership 2010, Department for Business Innovation and Skills, 2011, p. 5.
10. This call was made in the Freebie Growth Plan, Insitute of Directors, 2011 and was contemporaneous with Republican attempts to remove the collective bargaining rights of state workers in Wisconsin, USA.
11. Figures from James Achur, (2011), p. 23 and p. 1, except the 1978 TUC figure which is from David Marsh, *The New Politics of British Trade Unionism*, Basingstoke: Macmillan, 1992, p. 152.
12. Andrew Gamble, *Britain in Decline*, Basingstoke: Macmillan, 1985, p.253 notes that on each of these occasions the Conservative government declared a state of emergency as it also did with the power station strike in 1970.
13. Hilary Wainwright, Labour: *A Tale of Two Parties*, London: Hogarth, 1987, p.

36.

14 For a more detailed explanation of this process, see Maurice Dobb, *Political Economy and Capitalism*, London: Routledge, 1937.

15 Accounts which fit this description include: David Blunkett and Keith Jackson, *Democracy in Crisis*, London: Hogarth, 1987 and Ken Livingstone, *If Voting Changed Anything They'd Abolish it*, London: Fontana, 1988.

16 Although further investigation would be a digression from the present remit, it is worth noting that there are parallels between such measures and the consequences of the 2010 Government Spending Review for local government.

17 Figures taken from Kenneth Newton and Terence Karran, *The Politics of Local Expenditure*, Basingstoke: Macmillan, 1985, pp. 53 – 4. Unless otherwise, stated the data cited throughout this chapter is drawn from this source, Howard Elcock, *Local Government*, London: Routledge, 1982 and William Hampton, *Local Government and Urban Politics*, London: Longman, 1987.

18 Peter Townsend and Brian Abel Smith, *The Poor and the Poorest*, London: G Bell and Sons, 1965.

19 For an overview of this process see Keith Middlemass, *Politics in Industrial Society*, London: Andre Deutsch, 1979 chapters 14-15 and Leo Panitch, *Social Democracy and Industrial Militancy*, Cambridge: Cambridge University Press, 1976 for its vicissitudes.

20 TUC, Annual Reports, 1976, p. 412. Issues relating to health and welfare services appear in TUC, (1963), (1964) and (1966), expenditure and employment for personal services TUC, (1970) and services for the disabled TUC, (1972) and in Labour Party, Annual Conference Reports, 1972.

21 Joe Painter, 'Regulation Theory, Post-Fordism and Urban Politics' in David Judge, Gerry Stoker and Harry Wolman, *Theories of Urban Politics*, London: Sage, 1995, p. 284 defines the 'social wage' as goods and services provided collectively to all or those unable to afford them privately.

22 According to Ian Gough, *The Political Economy of the Welfare State*, Basingstoke: Macmillan, 1985, pp. 95-6 this indirect subsidy involved a further slight of hand whereby the bulk of the welfare state was financed by the working population through income tax, national insurance, VAT and sales taxes on alcohol, petrol and tobacco. A similar point was made by Pierre Laroque, *La Sécurité sociale dans l'économie française*, 1948, cited in Michel Foucault, *The Birth of Biopolitics*, Basingstoke: Macmillan, 2008, p. 211.

23 26 out of 30 proposed institutions had been designated by 1971 and served 162,914 students; Labour Party, (1971), p. 87.

24 Tony Byrne, *Local Government in Britain*, London: Penguin, 1985, p. 78.

25 See Manuel Castells, *City, Class and Power*, Basingstoke: Macmillan, 1980, especially Chapter Two.

26 This argument is heard again today, but was originally articulated by: Samuel Brittan, 'The Economic Contradictions of Democracy' in *British Journal of Political Science*, 5, 1975, Anthony King, 'Overload' in *Political Studies*, 23, 1975, Richard Rose, 'On the Priorities of Government' in *European Journal of Political Research*, 4, 1976 and Robert Bacon and Walter Eltis, *Britain's Economic Problem*, Basingstoke: Macmillan, 1976.

27 These figures represent an amalgamation of the following estimates in millions and as a percentage of the whole worke-force: Cynthia Cockburn, *The Local State*, London: Pluto, 1977, p. 62, 1.5 in 1954, 2.5 in 1974 (11 per cent); Robert Taylor, *The Fifth Estate*, London: Routledge, 1978, p. 30, 1.82 in 1960 (7.5 per cent), 3.0 in 1974 (12.1 per cent); Kieron Walsh, 'Workforce' in Stewart Ranson, George Jones and Kieron Walsh, *Between Centre and Locality*, London: Allen and Unwin, 1985, p. 100, 1.45 in 1952 (6.2 per cent), 2.9 in 1974 (11.3 per cent). As a percentage of the public sector: Kenneth Newton and Terence Karran, (1985), p. 86, 1.66 in 1958 (25 per cent), 3.0 in 1980 (40 per cent); and, Andrew Thomson, 'Local Government as an Employer' in Richard Rose and Edward Page, *Fiscal Stress in the Cities*, Cambridge: Cambridge University Press, 1982, p. 111, 1.87 in 1961 (32 per cent), 3.0 in 1979 (41.2 per cent).

28 Figures taken from Gerry Stoker, *The Politics of Local Government*, Basingstoke: Macmillan, 1988, p. 11, Kenneth Newton and Terence Karran, (1985), p. 27 and Andrew Thomson, (1982), p. 110.

29 Peter Cresswell, Interview, 1994.

30 TUC, (1972), p. 250 and p. 51.

31 Early initiatives included acquiring land to build factories and lending up to 75 per cent of the capital value to private developers under the Local Authority Land Act 1963. Re-interpretation involved acquiring and selling land under section 112 of the Town and Country Planning Act 1971 and using sections 122, 123 and 137 of the Local Government Act 1972 in the same way. See Ken Young and Charlie Mason, *Urban Economic Development*, Basingstoke: Macmillan, 1983 and Jim Chandler and Paul Lawless, *Local Authorities and the Creation of Employment*, Aldershot: Gower, 1985.

32 This legislation was based on the Tyne and Wear Act of 1976 which was designed to address specific local problems, see David Storey, 'Local Employment Initiatives in North East England' in Ken Young and Charlie Mason, (1983). Martin Boddy, 'Local Economic and Employment Strategies' in Martin Boddy and Colin Fudge, *Local Socialism?* Basingstoke: Macmillan, 1984a, p. 162 describes the Act in these terms.

33 The earlier figure is taken from Keith Middlemass, (1979), p. 437 and the latter from Peter King, *Twentieth Century British History*, London: W H Allen, 1980, p. 368.

34 Charlie Mason, 'Labour Market Policy' in Ken Young and Charlie Mason, (1983), p. 54.

35 See Paul Lawless, *Urban Deprivation and Government Initiative*, London: Faber, 1979, pp. 154-5 for Manchester and Wandsworth and Jim Chandler and Paul Lawless, (1985) pp. 142–9 for Sheffield. It is also worth pointing out that these jobs and the commodities they produced did not simply vanish into thin air. On the contrary, they were mainly transferred overseas, mostly to Asia, to increase profit margins through the exploitation of cheaper labour-power.

36 With the exception of Ken Young and Liz Mills, 'The Decline of Urban Economies' in Richard Rose and Edward Page, (1982), p. 88 for Manchester, the sources are the same as the previous footnote.

37 Andrew Thomson, (1982), p. 110 makes the observation about absorbing jobs and the Tyne and Wear data is from David Storey, (1983), p. 205.
38 See Martin Boddy, (1984a), p. 163 – 4.
39 See David Lowes, (2006), pp. 61 – 6 on the broader concept and Cynthia Cocbkurn, (1977), on the role of elected local government.
40 See Ralph Miliband, *The State in Capitalist Society*, London: Quartet, 1969, p. 49.
41 For more on this see Simon Duncan and Mark Goodwin, *The Local State and Uneven Development*, Cambridge: Polity, 1988; Rob Flynn, 'Co-optation and Strategic Planning in the Local State' in Roger King, *Capital and Politics*, London: Routledge and Kegan Paul, 1983; and Leo Panitch, 'Recent Theories of Corporatism' in *British Journal of Sociology*, 30, 1980.
42 This case for local government is made by David Blunkett and Keith Jackson, (1987).
43 Kenneth Newton and Terence Karran, (1985), take this view and Alan Alexander, *The Politics of Local Government in the United Kingdom*, London: Longman, 1982, pp. 86 – 8, provides the figures.
44 For evidence see Douglas Ashford, 'The Effects of Central Finance on the British Local Government System' in *British Journal of Political Science*, 4, 1974 and Rod Rhodes, 'Some Myths in Central-Local Relations' in *Town Planning Review*, 51, 3, 1980.
45 These examples are from Chris Skelcher 'Transportation' in Stewart Ranson, George Jones and Kieron Walsh, (1985), p. 155 and John Redcliff-Maud and Bruce Wood, *English Local Government Reformed*, Oxford: Oxford University press, 1974, pp. 106 – 7.
46 Suggested by Alex Henney, *Inside Local Government*, London: Sinclair Browne, 1984, p.113.
47 The following discussion draws on: Cynthia Cockburn, (1977); John Dearlove, *The Re-organization of Local Government*, Cambridge: Cambridge University Press, 1979; Simon Duncan and Mark Goodwin, (1988); Patrick Dunleavy, *Urban Political Analysis*, Basingstoke: Macmillan, 1980 and 'The Limits of Local Government' in Martin Boddy and Colin Fudge, (1984); Sue Goss, *Local Labour and Local Government*, Edinburgh: Edinburgh University Press, 1988; Michael Keating, 'Size, Efficiency and Democracy' in David Judge, Gerry Stoker and Harry Wolman, (1995); John Redcliffe-Maud and Bruce Wood, (1974); Peter Saunders, 'Rethinking Local Politics' in Martin Boddy and Colin Fudge, (1984); and, Gerry Stoker, (1988).
48 Figures from Gerry Stoker, (1988), pp. 44-5.
49 Alex Henney, (1984), pp. 380–1 makes this criticism and advocates business votes and business scrutiny committees (p. 129) even though businesses are vested interests.
50 Sue Goss, (1988), p. 64.
51 The process was eventually completed by the Local Government Act 2000 which required councils governing populations greater than 85,000 to introduce an executive consisting of either: council leader and cabinet; directly elected mayor and cabinet; or, mayor and council manager.

52 In 1969, for example, a NUPE and South Dorset CLP motion welcomed the Redcliffe-Maud report and the need to combine efficiency of operation with 'effective' democracy; Labour Party, (1969), p. 150. See also Roger Fellows and Keith Grimes 'Towards the Unitary State' in *Critical Social Policy*, 10, 1984.
53 It is also worth noting that the redrawing of parliamentary constituencies proposed by the Coalition government in 2011 again appears to be designed to weaken working class representation by merging urban and rural areas.
54 For more about the influence of Fabian ideas see Keith Basset, 'Labour, Socialism and Local Democracy' in Martin Boddy and Colin Fudge, (1984) and David Coates, *The Labour Party and the Struggle for Socialism*, Cambridge: Cambridge University Press, 1975. The TUC's National Advisory Committee for Local Government Services welcomed the proposals for unitary and metropolitan areas, but called for the greater financial independence of local authorities; TUC, (1970), pp. 233-4.
55 Simon Duncan and Mark Goodwin, (1988), p. 33.
56 The United Nations Monetary and Financial Conference held at Bretton Woods in July 1944 agreed to deter short-term capital flows by restricting currency fluctuations to a value of plus or minus one percent. This became known as the Bretton Woods System and included the provision of long term assistance by the World Bank and short term loans from the IMF. Elmar Altvater, 'Financial Crises on the Threshold of the 21st Century' in *Socialist Register*, 33, 1997 and David McNally, 'From Financial Crisis to World-Slump' in *Historical Materialism*, 17, 2009, both equate the end of the Bretton Woods dollar-gold convertibility with deregulation and subsequent financial crises
57 See Philip Mirowski and Dieter Plehwe (eds.), *The Road from Mont Pèlerin*, Cambridge MA: Harvard University Press, 2009, for a history of the MPS and the development of neoliberalism and Foucault, (2008) on the latter.
58 Such machinations resemble those theists who, arrogantly or naively depending on your point of view, tell the world that while it is impossible for mortals to know the will of an omnipotent being, they themselves have a unique insight. Put another way: 'Knowledge of the infinite must itself be infinite, and a knowledge which is admittedly imperfect is not a knowledge of the absolute.' Max Horkheimer, 'Materialism and Metaphysics' in *Critical Theory*, New York: Continuum, 1972, p. 27.
59 On the fringes, the application of market principles to organ donation has been advocated by Gary Becker and Julio Elias, 'Incentives in the Market for Live and Cadaveric Organ Donations' in *Journal of Economic Perspectives*, 21, 3, 2007. David Collard, *The New Right*, Fabian Tract 387, 1968, also provides a chilling reminder of how far the then neoliberal prospectus is now accepted as normal.
60 On this see Noam Chomsky, *Profit Over People*, New York: Seven Stories, 1999 and Colin Leys, *Market Driven Politics*, London: Verso, 2003.
61 Among others this line is propounded by David Green, *The New Right*, London: Harvester, 1987.
62 Advocates of this approach include James Buchanan and Gordon Tullock, *The Calculus of Consent*, Ann Arbor: University of Michigan press, 1965 and

Gordon Tullock, *The Vote Motive*, London: Institute of Economic Affairs, 1977.

63 See William Niskanen, *Bureaucracy: Servant or Master?* London: Institute of Economic Affairs, 1973; Madsen Pirie, *The Logic of Economics*, London: Institute of Economic Affairs, 1982; and, Charles Tiebout, 'A Pure Theory of Local Expenditures', *Journal of Political Economy*, 64, 5, 1956. As a precursor of Norman Tebbit's 'on your bike' dictum, citizens are expected to migrate rather than demonstrate over local issues.

64 Mark Garnett and Kevin Hickson, *Conservative Thinkers*, Manchester: Manchester University Press, 2009 and Mark Hayes, *The New Right in Britain*, London: Pluto, 1994 provide more details about these different tendencies and form the basis of the following discussion.

65 See Philip Norton, *Conservative Dissidents*, London: Temple Smith, 1978 who identifies John Biffen, Richard Body, Jock Bruce-Gardyne, Piers Dixon, Hugh Fraser, Enoch Powell and Nicholas Ridley as stalwarts.

66 See National Archive, Public Expenditure to 1978 – 79, CAB/129/178/5, 1974, p. 9 and Denis Healey, *Hansard*, HC Deb 26 March 1974 vol 871 cc277-8, 1974.

67 For details of the re-organization see National Archive, Operational Selection Policy OSP9, 2005.

68 Barnett cited by John Taylor, 'The CCLGF' in *Local Government Studies*, 5, 3, 1979, p. 9. Williams in George Newman, *Path to Maturity*, London: National and Local Government Officers' Association, 1982, p. 400 and National Archive, Conclusions of a Meeting of the Cabinet held at Chequers on Friday 20 June 1975, CAB/128/56/29.

69 See page 61 below for the impact of cash limits and Geoffrey Howe, *Hansard*, HC Deb 09 March 1976 vol 907 cc251-383, 1976 for his remarks.

70 National Archive, Draft White Paper on Inflation, CAB/129/184/C/76, 1975, p. 16.

71 Denis Healey, Memorandum of the Chancellor of the Exchequer, National Archive CAB 129/193/1, 1976. Also see Chris Rogers 'The Politics of Economic Policy Making in Britain' in *Politics & Policy*, 37, 5, 2009 for a broader discussion of this and other points summarized here

72 See National Archive, (2005).

73 Based on an historical analysis of past performances David Coates, (1975), predicted the course that would be taken by the Wilson and Callaghan governments.

74 The focus is again on developments that had a bearing on the policy and practice of the campaigns of the 1980s and is not intended to be a comprehensive account.

75 Figures from James Achur, 2011, p. 23.

76 Membership details from David Marsh, (1992), p. 152 and Kenneth Newton and Terence Karran, (1985), p. 86 for employment.

77 See David Lowes, 'In Defence of Local Government', unpublished PhD Thesis, Liverpool JMU, 1998, Chapter 2 for a fuller account of the changes in Labour Party membership and associated sources.

78 See David Marsh and Gareth Locksley, 'Trade Union Power in Britain' in *West European Politics*, 4, 1, 1981, Mick Marchington and Roger Armstrong, 'A Comparison Between Shop Steward Activity in Local Government and the Private Sector' in *Local Government Studies*, 8, 6, 1982; and Robert Taylor, (1978).
79 John Suddaby, 'The Public sector Strike in Camden '79' in *New Left Review*, 116, 1979.
80 For more about internal Labour Party developments see David Kogan and Maurice Kogan, *The Battle for the Labour Party*, London: Fontana, 1983, Sue Goss, (1988), Patricia Seyd, *The Rise and Fall of the Labour Left*, Basingstoke: Macmillan, 1987, and Hilary Wainwright, (1987).
81 David Skinner and Julia Langdon, *The Story of Clay Cross*, Nottingham: Spokesman, 1974; Austin Mitchell, 'Clay Cross' in *Political Quarterly*, 45, 2, 1974 and Leslie Sklair, 'The Struggle Against the Housing Finance Act' in *Socialist Register*, 12, 1975 form the basis of the following account.
82 Labour Party, (1972), pp. 355-6
83 The sources that inform this account are David Blunkett and Keith Jackson, (1987), John Gyford and Mari James, *National Parties and Local Politics*, London: Allen and Unwin, 1983 and Chris Skelcher, (1985).
84 John Gyford and Mari James, (1983), p. 139.
85 At the launch of the Selsdon Group Manifesto, 1973, for example, Nicholas Ridley declared in typically utilitarian fashion that: 'inflation is more damaging than unemployment, to a larger section of the population', p. 3.
86 See David Blunkett and Keith Jackson, (1987) and George Jones and John Stewart, *The Case for Local Government*, London: Allen and Unwin, 1985.
87 Figures from Gerry Stoker, (1988), p. 13 – 14 and Simon Duncan and Mark Goodwin, (1988), p. 99.
88 George Newman, (1982), p. 459.
89 TUC, (1976), pp. 412-3, (1977) pp. 136–7 and (1976), p. 309.
90 For more details see Bob Fryer, 'British Trade Unions and the Cuts' in *Capital and Class*, 8, 1979, Bob Fryer, Tom Manson and Andy Fairclough, 'Employment and Trade Unionism in the Public Services' in *Capital and Class*, 4, 1978 and George Newman, (1982).
91 Bob Fryer, (1979), p. 98 gives the sources of these arguments as NUPE's 1976 documents: Inflation: Attack or Retreat and Time to Change Course and a SCPS/ CPSA 1975 pamphlet Cuts that Puzzle.
92 John Leopold and Phil Beaumont, 'The Local Government Committee of the TUC' in *Local Government Studies*, 8, 6, 1982; and, comments made during separate interviews in 1994 with Graham Burgess, Peter Cresswell and Ian Lowes.
93 See Bob Fryer, (1979) and George Newman, (1982) for further examples of activity.
94 Local sections of the AUEW, TGWU, GMBATU and EETPU also supported the NSC's lobby of Parliament in November 1976. See Bob Fryer, (1979), p. 101.
95 See George Newman, (1982), p. 402f.

96 See John Gyford, *The Politics of Local Socialism*, London: Allen and Unwin, 1985; David Kogan and Maurice Kogan, (1983); Ken Livingstone, (1988) and Patricia Seyd, (1987).
97 Labour Party, (1976), pp. 158–61.
98 National Archive, Conclusions of a Meeting of the Cabinet 10 July 1975, CAB/128/57/3 and National Archive, Conclusions of a Meeting of the Cabinet 6 July 1976, CAB/128/59/13.
99 National Archive, Conclusions of a Meeting of the Cabinet 23rd November 1976, CAB/128/60/11; Tony Benn, The Real Choices Facing the Cabinet, National Archive CAB/129/193/7, 1976; Anthony Crosland, Economic Strategy - The IMF, National Archive CAB/129/193/8, 1976; and, National Archive, Conclusions of a Meeting of the Cabinet held 1 December 1976, CAB/128/60/13.
100 For a broader discussion of the issues covered and figures used in this section see: Martin Boddy, 'Local Councils and the Financial Squeeze' in Martin Boddy and Colin Fudge, *Local Socialism?* Basingstoke: Macmillan, 1984b; Tom Caulcott, 'Responding to the Challenge' in *Local Government Studies*, 9, 6, 1983; Simon Duncan and Mark Goodwin, (1988); Mike Goldsmith, 'The Conservatives and Local Government, 1979 and After' in David Bell (Ed.), *The Conservative Government 1979-84*, London: Croom Helm, 1985; Chris Howells, 'The Politics of Local Authority Finance' in *Critical Social Policy*, 2, 2, 1982; and, Tony Travers, *The Politics of Local Government Finance*, London Allen and Unwin, 1986.
101 See Conservative Research Department, *Politics Today*, 3, Conservative Central Office, 21 February 1983, p. 46.
102 Average weekly rents for local authority housing in England rose from £8.18 in 1980-1, to £13.59 in 1982-3.Gerry Stoker, (1988), p. 178.
103 Current expenditure, for example, rose from £22,291 million in 1979-80 to £23,958 million in 1982-83, see Tom Caulcott, (1983), p. 74.
104 Overspend figures taken from Simon Duncan and Mark Goodwin, (1988), p. 112 and NALGO, Campaign in Defence of Local Government, 20 March 1984, p. 3 respectively and those relating to current expenditure from Tony Travers, (1986), p. 211.
105 Figures from NALGO, (20 March 1984), p. 2.
106 Underspend figures are from Martin Boddy, (1984b), p. 218 and Tom Caulcott, (1983), p. 80 and Tom Caulcott, (1983), p. 72 for capital expenditure totals.
107 For details about Sheffield see David Blunket and Keith Jackson (1987), p. 154, Michael Parkinson, *Liverpool on the Brink*, 1985, pp. 29–31 for Liverpool and for Lambeth and the GLC Ken Livingstone, (1988), p. 130 and pp. 217–8.
108 Liverpool NALGO, *Local Government in Crisis*, Branch Delegate Report, 20 November 1980.
109 See Roger Kline, 'Privatising local government' in *Critical Social Policy*, 8, 1983.
110 Conservative Party, *Conservative Manifesto*, London: Conservative Central Office, 1979, p. 8.
111 See Colin Evans, 'Privatisation of Local Services' in *Local Government Studies*,

11, 6, 1985, for a fuller account.
112 House of Lords, Bromley London Borough Council-v-Greater London Council, 1981, cited at http://www.swarb.co.uk/lisc/LocGv19801984.php last visited 30 January 2012. See Ken Livingstone, (1988) for a fuller account of the GLC's transport policy.
113 Cited by Roger Stott, *Hansard*, HC Deb 01 February 1983 vol 36 cc228-71, 1983.
114 David Howell, *Hansard*, HC Deb 01 February 1983 vol 36 cc228-71, 1983.
115 Figures taken from Gerry Stoker, (1988), p. 186 and Tony Travers, 'Local Government De-Manning' in *Public Money*, 3, 1, 1983, p. 64.
116 For these and other examples see: Colin Evans, (1985), Roger Halford, 'Local Authority Contracting-Out' in *Local Government Studies*, 8, 5, 1982, Roger Kline, (1983) and Geof Rayner and Jean Conway, 'Wandsworth - the Cuts and the Fightback' in *Critical Social Policy*, 1, 1, 1981.
117 See Kate Ascher, *The Politics of Privatisation*, Basingstoke: Macmillan, 1987, p. 222 and p. 115.
118 For more on Wandsworth see Martin Minogue and Jeremy O'Grady, 'Contracting Out Local Authority Services in Britain' in *Local Government Studies*, 11, 3, 1985.
119 See National Archive, Housing Act 1980, p.21.
120 Liverpool NALGO, (20 November 1980).
121 See Kate Ascher, 'The Politics of Administrative Opposition' in *Local Government Studies*, 9, 2, 1983 for a fuller account.
122 For coverage of the broader developments in this area see: Jim Chandler and Paul Lawless, (1985), Simon Duncan and Mark Goodwin, (1988), John Shutt, 'Tory enterprise zones and the labour movement' in *Capital and Class*, 23, 1984 and Murray Stewart and Jacky Underwood, 'New Relations in the Inner City' in Ken Young and Charlie Mason (eds.), *Urban Economic Development*, Basingstoke: Macmillan, 1983.
123 Figures cited by Andrew Sissons and Chris Brown, *Do Enterprise Zones Work? An Ideopolis policy paper*, London: The Work Foundation, 2011, p. 7.
124 Figures from Simon Duncan and Mark Goodwin, (1988), p. 142.
125 For more details see Martin Boddy (1984a), Peter McLaverty, 'Trade Unions and Political Change in Local Government', unpublished PhD Thesis, Sheffield, 1989 and Patricia Seyd, (1987).
126 Figures taken from Murray Stewart and Jacky Underwood, (1983), p. 229.
127 Figures from Travers, (1983), p. 65 and Maureen Mackintosh and Hilary Wainwright (eds.), *A Taste of Power*, London: Verso, 1987, p. 15.
128 Labour Party, (1980) pp. 111-112 and (1981) pp. 30-31
129 Labour Party, (1983) p. 80
130 Liverpool NALGO, Finance and General Purposes Committee Minutes, 12 November 1981.
131 TUC, (1981), pp. 504–6.
132 NALGO, Public Expenditure Cuts, National Local Government Committee Report, 15 September 1981, p. 4
133 The NALGO conference motion was submitted by the Scottish District

Council and the consultative process is evidenced in Liverpool NALGO, Branch Executive Council Minutes 1979–1987.
134 Conference details are sourced from Liverpool NALGO, (20 November 1980).
135 See John Gyford and Mari James, (1983), p. 179.
136 Figures from Liverpool NALGO, (20 November 1980).
137 See Chapter 10 in Martin Boddy and Colin Fudge, *Local Socialism?* Basingstoke: Macmillan, 1984.
138 Liverpool NALGO, Service Conditions Committee Minutes, 22 May 1980 and 3 February 1983. Also Liverpool NALGO, Finance and General Purposes Committee Minutes, 16 October 1980 and 26 May 1983.
139 See TUC, (1980), p. 308.
140 NALGO, (15 September 1981), p. 1.
141 NALGO, (15 September 1981), p. 5.
142 David Blunkett, Letter to the author, 1994
143 Cited in NALGO, (20 March 1984).
144 See page 84 above regarding Composite 30.
145 For more details see John Gyford and Mari James, (1983), p. 179 and TUC, (1981), p. 331.
146 On the General Council see: TUC, (1980), p. 264 and on the TUCLGC see: TUC, (1980), p. 309 and p. 307, TUC, (1981), p. 329 and TUC, (1982), p. 312.
147 This inconsistency is identified by John Gyford and Mari James, (1983), pp. 167 - 9.
148 My italics.
149 Examples from John Gyford and Mari James, (1983) and John Gyford, (1985), p. 28.
150 For examples see John Gyford and Mari James, (1983) and Hilary, Wainwright, (1987).
151 Observation made by Ian Lowes, Interview, (1994).
152 The focus here is on factors that helped shape the way the campaign was conducted and not the financial arguments that are explored in Liverpool City Council, *Rates Services and Jobs*, 1983 and Michael Parkinson, (1985).
153 For more on Sheffield see David Blunkett and Keith Jackson, (1987), Patricia Seyd, (1987) and Hilary Wainwright, (1987) and on Liverpool see John Davies, 'Transformations in the Political Culture of Liverpool 1920s-1980s', unpublished MPhil Thesis, Lancaster, 1987, Michael Parkinson, (1985) and Peter Taaffe and Tony Mulhearn, *Liverpool*, London: Fortress, 1988.
154 Figures taken from John Davies, (1987), p. 80 and Michael Parkinson, (1985), p. 13.
155 Liverpool City Council, (1983).
156 Points made by Michael Parkinson, (1985) and Ian Lowes, (1994).
157 Michael Crick, *The March of Militant*, London: Faber and Faber, 1986 and Stewart Lansley, Sue Goss and Christian Wolmar, *Councils in Conflict*, Basingstoke: Macmillan, 1989.
158 Details about councillors and policy sub-committees from Tony Byrne, Interview, 1994.
159 For more on Sheffield see Simon Duncan and Mark Goodwin, (1988), Patricia

Seyd (1987) and Hilary Wainwright, (1987). For Southwark see Sue Goss, (1988) and Ken Livingstone, 'Interview' in Martin Boddy and Colin Fudge (eds.), *Local Socialism?* Basingstoke: Macmillan, 1984 for London.
160 Observations made by Graham Burgess, (1994) and Peter Cresswell, (1994).
161 These include but are not restricted to Michael Crick, (1986), John Davies, (1987) and Peter McLaverty, (1989).
162 This is recorded in NALGO, National Delegate Advisory Meeting Minutes, 16 October 1984 and confirmed by Tony Byrne, (1994).
163 Michael Crick, (1986), p. 254.
164 Suggestion by Paul Thompson and Mike Allen, 'Labour and the Local State in Liverpool' in *Capital and Class*, 29, 1986; details of branch delegations and disputes provided by Ian Lowes, (1994).
165 Graham Burgess, (1994) and Peter Cresswell, (1994).
166 Points made by Graham Burgess, (1994), Peter Cresswell, (1994) and Ian Lowes, (1994).
167 Liverpool NALGO, 'The Rate, the Cuts and the Government', Report to SGM, 11 February 1980.
168 Liverpool NALGO, Service Conditions Committee Minutes, 3 November 1983.
169 Events recounted in Liverpool NALGO, Branch Executive Council Minutes, 20 August 1980 and Liverpool NALGO, No Redundancy Agreement 1980-81, Branch Organizer Report to District Organization Officer, undated.
170 Liverpool NALGO, 'The Liverpool Crisis', Branch Report, undated.
171 Comments made by Graham Burgess, (1994), Peter Cresswell, (1994) and Ian Lowes, (1994).
172 Ian Lowes, (1994).
173 Details of JTUCs and Trades Councils from Bob Fryer, (1979), David Blunkett and Keith Jackson, (1987), Roger Kline, (1983), Kate Ascher, (1987), London NALGO, Hit List Branches Meeting Minutes, 10 August 1983, Liverpool NALGO, Branch Executive Council Minutes, 23 January 1980 and Liverpool City Council, Campaigning for Jobs and Services, undated(a).
174 John Davies, (1987), Graham Burgess, (1994), Peter Cresswell, (1994) and Ian Lowes, (1994).
175 Liverpool NALGO, 'The Fight Against Cuts and Redundancies in Liverpool', Branch Negotiators Report, 17 June, 1980 and Liverpool NALGO, Letter to District Organization Officer, 8 March 1984.
176 Liverpool City Council, (undated(a)
177 MTULMCC, Leaflets, Letters and Minutes, 1983–1985.
178 Liverpool NALGO, Minutes of meetings between Liverpool City councillors, full-time and lay Trade Union officials, 28 February 1984.
179 Liverpool City Council, Campaign Working Party Terms of Reference, undated(b).
180 Liverpool NALGO, 'Our City Our Fight', 15 December 1983.
181 MTULMCC, Letter to Shop Stewards committees and leaflet promoting conference, February 1984.
182 MTULMCC, Minutes of Organizing Meeting, 4 November 1983 and Islington

NALGO, Letter to Liverpool NALGO Branch, 23 June 1984.
183 See Michael Parkinson, (1985), p. 42 for details of petition.
184 Sources: Norfolk NALGO, Letter to Liverpool NALGO Branch, April 1984; North East NALGO, Letter to Liverpool NALGO Branch, undated; South West NALGO, Letter to Liverpool NALGO Branch, 14 March 1984; Liverpool NALGO, Branch Executive Council Minutes, 26 October 1983 and 23 February 1984 and Glasgow NALGO, Letter to Liverpool NALGO Branch, February 1984.
185 Details from Liverpool NALGO, Our City Our Fight, 5 February 1984 and 18 April 1984.
186 Details from: Liverpool NALGO, Our City Our Fight, 18 April 1984 and Liverpool NALGO, Letter to councillors opposing the Labour Group budget, 29 March 1984.
187 Michael Parkinson, (1985), pp. 59 – 60.
188 Quoted from Alan Jinkinson, Letter sent as NALGO Assistant General Secretary to Liverpool City Branch, 3 April 1984. This and Keith Sonnet, letter sent as NALGO Local Government Service Conditions Officer to Liverpool City Branch, 31 May 1984, provide accounts of the meetings referred to.
189 Michael Parkinson, (1985), pp. 53 – 4.
190 Quote comes from David Blunkett, (1994).
191 This view is outlined by David Blunkett, 'Possible Deficit Budgeting', Paper prepared for the LGCU, 16 April 1985 and reiterated by Ken Livingstone, (1988) and David Blunkett and Keith Jackson, (1987).
192 NALGO, (15 September 1981) and (20 March 1984) provides details of these threats and of the experiences in Scotland. The capping bill was accompanied by: the London Regional Transport Bill; a Paving Bill for the cancellation of Metropolitan County Council elections prior to abolition; and, the Education (Grant and Awards) Bill.
193 See Conservative Research Department, Politics Today, 2, Conservative Central Office, 13 February 1984, Martin Boddy, (1984b) and Simon Duncan and Mark Goodwin, (1988) for the respective points.
194 Conservative Research Department, (13 February 1984), p.20.
195 Cited in David Blunkett and Keith Jackson, (1987) p. 166.
196 TUC, National Consultative Conference, 4 December 1984 p.4 and LGCU, Rate Support Grant - 1985/ 86, undated, p. 3.
197 Example taken from: Keva Coombes, Discussion Document for Merseyside County Labour Party, 27 February 1985.
198 Inconsistency described by David Blunkett and Keith Jackson, (1987) p. 158 and TUC, (4 December 1984) makes the point about spending being masked.
199 NALGO, (20 March 1984), p. 7 – 8 is the source of details on transport, education and abolition.
200 See page 36 above.
201 See for example contributions made by Conservative MPs to the debate relating to amendment 31, including David Howell, Hansard, HC Deb 28 March 1984 vol 57 cc309-84, 1984.
202 NALGO, (20 March 1984).

203 TUC, Local Government Committee Minutes, 5 December 1983, p. 17.
204 See Nicholas Ridley, *The Local Right*, Policy Study 92, London: Centre for Policy Studies, 1988 for an exposition of the neoliberal view and John Cartwright and Simon Hughes, Amendment to proposed Motion (Resitance to Rate-capping (No. 2)), Notices of Notes and Motions, 26 March 1985 for the Liberal Party's approval.
205 LGCU, (undated) gives details of the joint statement, TUC, (4 December 1984) identifies the services at risk and Keva Coombes, (27 February 1985) describes Merseyside's predicament.
206 LGCU, The Local Authority Case, Meeting with the Secretary of State for the Environment, 4 February 1985 is the document referred to and the demands are consistent with those articulated by the LGCU's strategy conference 13 November 1984 - as recorded by NALGO, Campaign in Defence of Local Government, 7 December 1984, the Association of London Authorities (ALA) and AMA in their Background Paper, undated, and by motions and amendments for NALGO's annual conference outlined in Liverpool NALGO, Branch Executive Council Minutes, 27 March 1985.
207 The Unit changed its name to the Local Government Information Unit in March 1985, but for clarity and consistency all references are to the LGCU.
208 NALGO, (20 March 1984) and Fight to Defend Local Democracy, Bulletin, 4 May 1984.
209 Details of both bodies from NALGO, National Delegate Advisory Meeting Minutes, November 1983 – October 1984 and Rate-Capping Liaison Group Meeting Minutes, November 1984 – March 1985.
210 NALGO, (20 March 1984), pp. 9 – 11.
211 NALGO, (20 March 1984), p. 10 and NALGO, Fight to Defend Local Democracy, Bulletin, 22 November 1983.
212 NLACC, Record of Attendance, 30 March 1985 and Minutes, 13 April 1985.
213 Details from: David Blunkett and Keith Jackson, (1987); NALGO, Fight to Defend Local Democracy, Bulletin, 4 May 1984; LGCU, Bulletin No. 4, June 1984 and NALGO, (20 March 1984).
214 Sources: LGCU, Management Committee Minutes, 4 June 1984-15 April 1985, NALGO, Rate-Capping Liaison Group Meeting Minutes, 13 March 1985 and NALGO, Fight to Defend Local Democracy, Bulletin, 4 March 1985.
215 Details of these and other initiatives are recorded in TUC, (1985) and (1986), LGCU, Briefing No. 1, December 1984 and NALGO, (20 March 1984).
216 Preceding examples are from: NALGO, (20 March 1984), p. 11, LGCU (June 1984), LGCU (December 1984), LGCU Briefing No. 3, February 1985, LGCU, Local Link, February 1985, LGCU, Groupwork Report, 1985 and David Blunkett and Keith Jackson, (1987), p. 177.
217 LGCU, Bulletin No. 2, February 1984 and LGCU, (December 1984).
218 Sources: London NALGO, (10 August 1983); LGCU, Management Group Minutes, 4 June 1984; and, NALGO, Rate-Capping Liaison Group Meeting Minutes, 14 December 1984.
219 See David Blunkett and Keith Jackson, (1987) and John Gyford, (1985) for accounts of the event.

220 Figures from LGCU, (December 1984).
221 Examples from: LGCU, Briefing No. 2, January 1985.
222 Sources: NALGO, (20 March 1984) and Fight to Defend Local Democracy, Bulletin, 1 February 1984.
223 Figures are from Ivor Crewe, 'How to Win a Landslide without Really Trying' in Austin Ranney (Ed.), *Britain at the Polls*, 1983, Durham N C: Duke University Press, 1985 and Fight to Defend Local Democracy Bulletin, 8 November 1983 for the NALGO view.
224 Details are from NALGO, (1 February 1984), Fight to Defend Local Democracy, Bulletin, 2 February 1984 and Liverpool NALGO, Service Conditions Committee Minutes, 26 July 1984.
225 Quote from: NALGO, (20 March 1984) p. 13.
226 NALGO, (20 March 1984), p. 10 for NLGC assumption and Tony Byrne, (1994) and Ian Lowes (1994) make the point about the role of representatives in general.
227 NALGO, (20 March 1984); NALGO, (16 October 1984) and NALGO, (7 December 1984).
228 This preference is recorded by David Blunkett, No Rate Tactic Prospects and Problems, Paper Prepared for the LGCU, 19 April 1985.
229 LGCU, Strategy Sub-Group Minutes, 3 April 1985 and 18 April 1985, LGCU, The Way Forward, Strategy Sub-Group Report, 12 April 1985 and LGCU, Government Returns, Management Committee Report, 15 April 1985.
230 LGCU, Management Group Minutes, 18 December 1984 and 1 February 1985.
231 LGCU, (15 April 1985).
232 Cited by David Blunkett, (16 April 1985).
233 See David Blunkett and Keith Jackson, (1987) and Ken Livingstone, (1988). Unless otherwise stated this discussion of no rate and deficit budgeting draws on David Blunkett, (16 April 1985) and (19 April 1985) and Keva Coombes, (27 February 1985)
234 Quote from: David Blunkett, (19 April 1985). LGCU, (18 December 1984) and LGCU, Programme of Work, Management Committee Report, 16 January 1985 provide the other points.
235 Identified in LGCU, (4 February 1985) and Notes of Meeting with the Secretary of State for the Environment, 4 February 1985.
236 LGCU, Press Release, 4 February 1985 and David Blunkett, Letter sent as Chairman of the LGCU to Patrick Jenkin, Secretary of State for the Environment, 5 February 1985.
237 Patrick Jenkin, Letter sent as Secretary of State for the Environment to the LGCU, 21 February 1985 and 14 March 1985.
238 Norman Willis, Letter sent as TUC General Secretary to Patrick Jenkin, Secretary of State for the Environment, 1 April 1985 and Patrick Jenkin, Letter sent as Secretary of State for the Environment to the TUC, 3 April 1985.
239 John Cunningham, Letter sent as Shadow Secretary of State for the Environment to Patrick Jenkin, 14 January 1985 and Patrick Jenkin, Letter sent as Secretary of State for the Environment to John Cunningham, 30 January 1985.

240 ALA/AMA, Letter sent to Patrick Jenkin Secretary of State for the Environment, 10 April 1985; John Cunningham, Letter sent as Shadow Secretary of State for the Environment to Patrick Jenkin, 12 April 1985; and, Patrick Jenkin Letter sent as Secretary of State for the Environment to John Cunningham, 24 April 1985.
241 See Simon Duncan and Mark Goodwin, (1987), pp. 233-4 and Gerry Stoker, (1988), p. 165.
242 Details of district auditor from: Stewart Lansley, Sue Goss and Christian Wolmar, (1989), p. 38 and David Blunkett and Keith Jackson, (1987), p. 182.
243 This account draws on Ken Livingstone, (1984), (1988), Letter to the author, December 1994 and on Hilary Wainwright, (1987).
244 This account draws on David Blunkett, (1994), David Blunkett and Keith Jackson, (1987) and Peter McLaverty, (1989).
245 Cited by David Blunkett and Keith Jackson, (1987), p. 180.
246 The various explanations for the acrimonious breakdown of the Liverpool campaign are discussed by David Blunkett and Keith Jackson, (1987), Simon Duncan and Mark Goodwin, (1988), Peter Taaffe and Tony Mulhearn, (1988) and Hilary Wainwright, (1987) among others. Suffice it to say here, however, that the concerns aired at the LGCU about deficit budgeting being a recipe for distrust proved to be a self-fulfilling prophecy.
247 NLACC, Minutes, 2 May 1985.
248 NALGO, (7 December 1984).
249 The NALGO conference of 1984 also pledged 'unqualified support to whatever industrial action proves necessary (subject to the industrial action regulations) in the course of an escalating campaign'. The wording of this and the TUC motion are cited in NALGO, (7 December 1984), Annex A and the caveats in TUC, (4 December 1984), p.10.
250 NALGO (15 September 1981), (20 March 1984), (7 December 1984) and TUC, (4 December 1984).
251 NALGO, (20 March 1984) and (7 December 1984).
252 NALGO, (7 December 1984), TUC, (4 December 1984) and David Blunkett, (1994).
253 NALGO: (16 October 1984) and Rate-Capping Liaison Group Meeting Minutes, 20 November 1984.
254 NALGO, Rate-Capping Liaison Group Meeting Minutes, 27 February 1985.
255 NALGO, (7 December 1984) and TUC, (4 December 1984), p. 9.
256 Figures from Parkinson, (1985), p. 170. Taafe and Mulhearn, (1988), p. 292 give the overall result as 7,284 in favour and 8,152 against.
257 Cited by David Blunkett and Keith Jackson, (1987), p. 182.
258 Peter McLaverty, (1989), p. 4.
259 See David Collard, (1968), pp. 9 – 10.
260 To this list can be added the raising of the retirement age, which was justified in terms of the need to balance future budgets, but it also has the unacknowledged effect of increasing the reserve army of labour.
261 For a fuller account of this process see Colin Leys, 'The British Labour Party's Transition from Socialism to Capitalism' in *Socialist Register*, 32, 1996.

262 The phrase is used by Mary Shelley to describe a characteristic of her late husband's poetry, Shelley's *Poems and Essays and Letters from Abroad*, London: Ward, Lock & Co, 1889, p. vi.
263 This summary is based on John Gibson and Tony Travers, 'Block Grant' in *Public Money*, 5, 2, 1985, pp. 17-22, Martin Loughlin, *Local Government in the Modern State*, London: Sweet and Maxwell, 1986 and Tony Travers, (1986).

INDEX

Adam Smith Institute, 45
Aims of Industry, 45
Allaun, Frank, 94
Alternative Economic Strategy (AES), 65
Amalgamated Union of Engineering Workers (AUEW), 61, 85
Association of London Authorities (ALA), 120, 121, 129, 132
Association of Metropolitan Authorities (AMA), 59, 92, 120, 121, 129, 132

Baker, Kenneth, 113
Barking, 56, 78
Barnett, Joel, 48
Benn, Tony, 65
Beveridge, William, 22, 45
Biffen, John, 47
Birmingham, 63, 72, 76, 81, 103; Labour group, 73
Block Grant, 35-6, 70, 93, 132, 151
Body, Richard, 47
Boyson, Rhodes, 47
Bretton Woods, 16, 40, 43
Byrne, Tony, 102

Camden, 54, 57, 64, 72, 73, 78 122, 137, 138
Campaign for Labour Party Democracy (CLPD), 54, 91
Cardiff Corporation Act (1930), 74
cash limits, 47, 49, 61, 71

Centre for Policy Studies (CPS), 45, 47
Children's Act (1948), 24
Children and Young Persons Act (1969), 24
Chronically Sick and Disabled Persons Act (1970), 24
Civil and Public Servants Association (CPSA), 62, 120,
Clay Cross, 57–8, 122, 146
Coal Industry Act (1994), 142
Confederation of Health Service Employees (COHSE) 62, 120
Community Land Act (1975), 31
Confederation of British Industry (CBI), 15
Conservative governments, 1970–1974, 35, 46–7, 56; 1979–1997, 14, 68, 113f, 142-3; parliamentary majority, 124
Conservative Party, 45f, 68 passim, 113 passim; and local democracy, 76, 113; and Labour councils, 69–71; opposition to rate-capping, 115
Consultative Council on Local Government Finance (CCLGF), 61, 132
Coventry, 63, 87, 94
creative accountancy, 60, 72, 79, 114, 143
Crosland, Anthony, 65
council house sales, 70, 78-9
Cunningham, John, 108-9, 115, 132

deregulation, financial, 43; of

transport, 73-4
Direct Labour Organizations (DLO), 47, 73; jobs lost, 76
Dixon, Piers, 172n
Dobson, Frank, 64

Economic Theory of Regulation, 44
Edmonds, John, 108
Education Act (1993), 142; (2002); 143
Education (Grants and Awards) Bill, 114, 121
Education Reform Act (1988), 142
Education (Student Loans) Act (1996), 143
Electrical, Electronic, Telecommunication and Plumbing Union (EETPU), 61, 173n
Employment and Training Act (1973), 26
Enterprise Zones (EZ), 79-80, 81
European Economic Community, 50
extra-parliamentary politics, 51, 54, 125, 127

Fire Brigades Union (FBU), 117, 120
Fraser, Hugh, 172n
Further and Higher Education Act (1992), 142

Gardyne, Jock Bruce, 172n
General Municipal Boiler-makers and Allied Trade Union (GMBATU), 61, 117, 120; in Liverpool, 100, 105, 108, 109, 110, 139
General Strike, 14, 127
Grant Related Expenditure Assessments (GREA), 70, 72, 123, 151-2
Greater London Council (GLC), 38, 55, 64, 72, 81, 82, 123, 131; and non-compliance, 133-4, 135; Fares Fair, 74-5; Labour Group, 64; trade unions, 75, 133
Greater London Labour Party (GLLP), 54, 64, 75, 99, 133
Greenwich, 72, 122, 123, 138

Hackney, 78, 132, 135, 137, 138
Hamilton, John, 102
Haringey, 122, 132, 138
Hattersley, Roy, 94
Hatton, Derek, 102
Hayek, Friedrich von, 45
Healey, Denis, 49
Hodge, Margaret, 132
Housing Act (1969), 27; (1980), 70, 73, 77; (1985), 142
Housing Finance Act (1972), 46, 53, 70, 98; Labour Party leaders, 58, 91, 94; opposition to, 56-7, 143
Howe, Geoffrey, 49

Industrial Relations Act (1971), 16, 46, 53
inflation, 28, 29, 47, 59, 60; control of, 43, 47, 48-9; effect on cuts, 61, 71, 114
Inner London Education Authority (ILEA), 81, 131, 132
Inner Urban Areas Act (1978), 31, 80
Institute of Directors, 15
Institute of Economic Affairs (IEA), 45, 46
International Monetary Fund (IMF), 14, 16, 19, 41, 49-50, 65, 171n
Islington, 122, 132, 138

Jenkin, Patrick, 109, 117, 131–2
Jinkinson, Alan, 109
Joint Shop Stewards Committee (JSSC), 63, 101, 133, 136; in Liverpool, 103-5
Joint Trade Union Committee (JTUC), 63, 88, 90, 103, 120, 124
Joseph, Keith, 47

Keynes, John Maynard, 22, 45
Keating, Ron, 87
Kinnock, Neil, 94, 108
Knight, Ted, 87

Labour Co-ordinating Committee, 54
Labour governments, 24; 1945–1951,

25; 1964–1970, 25, 39; 1974–1979, 48-9, 54, 80; accepts Conservative government cuts, 48; advocates cuts, 49, 59 passim; and IMF, 49–50, 61, 65; and inflation, 48-9, 54; 1997-2010, 143

Labour Party, 38, 48f, 64, 92, 108-9, 120, 140; annual conference (LPAC), 25, 54, 58, 64-5, 84, 90, 93; internal organization, 54–5, 94; local government conferences, 94, 109, 128; membership, 52–3; National Executive Committee (NEC), 23, 58, 65, 81, 91, 93, 95, 128, 129, 139, 144

Lambeth, 78, 86; Labour group, 72, 87; local authority, 122, 139

Layden, Jack, 132

Learning and Skills Act (2000), 143

Leeds, 82, 87, 122

Leicester, 123, 132, 138

Lewisham, 73, 122, 132, 138

Liverpool, 56, 77, 84, 96f, 121, 130, 138, 146; Labour group, 55, 72, 98, 100, 102, 108–9; local authority, 63, 82; local economy, 97-8; and non-compliance; 134-5, 139; trade unions, 100f

Liverpool NALGO, 85, 104, 110, 122; and 1983–84 campaign, 106-7; and local Labour Party, 101-2

Livingstone, Ken, 88

Local Authority Land Act (1963), 169n

Local Authority Social Services Act (1970), 24

local government, 25, 33, 115; elections, 37; employment, 28f, 52; funding, 35–6, 61, 69f; part-time workers, 29; regeneration, 30-33, 79-81; re-organization, 36, 37-9, 54, 55, 59

Local Government Act (1972), 169n; (1988), 142; (1992), 142; (2000), 170n

Local Government and Planning (Scotland) Act (1982), 112

Local Government Campaign Unit (LGCU), 119, 120 passim, 128-9, 130, 131, 146

Local Government Finance Act (1982), 71, 72

Local Government Planning and Land Act (1980) (LGPLA), 70 passim, 76, 79, 80, 92 passim, 151

local spending, 34 passim, 59, 61; determinants of, 69, 72; targets and penalties, 71, 112, 114, 151-2

London, 32, 38, 63, 64, 74, 80, 81, 88, 99, 121, 124, 133

London Labour Briefing, 54

London Regional Transport Bill, 114, 178n

Manchester, 31, 32, 63, 80; Labour Party, 55, 94, 99; local authority, 81-2, 122, 138

Merseyside, 80, 88, 98; county council, 74, 75, 104, 114, 117, 124-5, 131

Merseyside Trade Union and Labour Movement Campaign Committee (MTULMCC), 103, 104-5, 120

Metropolitan county councils, abolition of, 114

Militant Tendency, 99

money supply, 43, 47, 48, 49, 69

Mont Pèlerin Society (MPS), 41, 45

Municipal Corporations Act (1835), 33

National and Local Government Officers Association (NALGO), 52 passim, 56, 61 passim, 77, 86, 88, 115, 117, 118, 120, 124, 129, 136-7; annual conference, 49, 64, 78, 85; industrial action against rate-capping, 125, 143-5; National Delegate Advisory meetings (NDAM), 119, 125, 136, 137, 146; National Executive Council (NEC), 84, 90; National Local Government Committee (NLGC), 89, 90, 119, 125; National Local Government Group meeting (NLGGM), 88 passim, 119; national strategy, 90; publicity, 63, 121-2;

Rate-Capping Liaison Group meetings (RCLGM), 119-20, 125, 137, 146; relations with Labour Party, 108–9; shop steward system, 53
National Association of Teachers in Further and Higher Education (NATFHE), 62, 117, 120
National Local Authorities Co-ordinating Committee (NLACC), 120, 136
National Steering Committee Against the Cuts (NSC), 62-3, 120
National Union of Mineworkers (NUM), 56, 57
National Union of Public Employees (NUPE), 57, 61, 77, 87, 99, 117, 120, 124; and cuts, 62 passim; growth of, 52; in Liverpool, 105, 108, 109, 110; National Executive Committee (NEC), 86; shop stewards system, 53-4
National Union of Teachers (NUT), 62, 117, 120; in Liverpool, 108, 109, 110
neoliberal era, 16
neoliberalism, 40f; accepted by the Treasury, 48; centres of, 41, 45; in Conservative Party, 46–7; as government policy, 35, 48-9, 56, 59, 69f, 141-3; implications for democracy, 44, 113, 114-15, 148; and international political economy, 16, 40–1; and Labour Party, 48f, 64, 65, 93, 116, 143, 145, 148; main themes, 41f, 116; organizations, 41, 45
North-East Derbyshire, 58, 94
Norwich, 70, 78, 95
Nursery Education and Grant Maintained Schools Act (1996), 143

Parliamentary Labour Party (PLP), 54, 58, 65, 83, 91, 92-3, 94, 116, 119, 123, 132, 145; and Liverpool, 108–9
Plant, Arnold, 45
Poor Law, 13
Powell, Enoch, 46, 172n

Prentis, Dave, 108-9
privatization, 14, 44, 73f, 84, 85, 90, 102, 116, 142, 143, 144, 148
Public Choice, 44, 113
Public Expenditure Survey Committee, 35, 48
Public Sector Borrowing Requirement (PSBR), 49, 62, 69, 113

quangos, replace elected bodies, 114
Quantitative Theory of Money, 43

Railways Act (1993), 142
Rank and File Mobilizing Committee, 54
rate-capping, 109, 112f; campaign against, 118f; arguments for, 113; arguments against, 115; non-compliance with, 123, 127f; opponent's demands, 117, 123, 131
Rate Support Grant (RSG), 59, 92, 114, 123, 131; calculation, 36, 59, 70; reductions in 61, 81
Rates Act (1984), 112, 117, 123, 129, 131, 135, 139; provisions, 113-14
regeneration, 26, 30-3, 79-81
Relative Price Effect (RPE), 29
Report of the Committee on Local Authority and Allied Personal Social Services (Seebohm Report), 25
Report of the Inter-Departmental Committee on Social Insurance and Allied Services (Beveridge Report), 22
Representation of the People Act (1832), 33
Ridley, Nicholas, 47, 172n
Robbins, Lionel, 45
Royal Commission on Local Government, 37, 39; in London, 38

Salford, 81
Sedgemore, Brian, 65
Selsdon Group, 47
Sheffield, 31, 63, 78, 107, 120, 121; Labour group, 55, 56, 72; Labour Party, 84, 97; local authority, 70, 81,

82, 122, 123; and non-compliance, 134, 138; trade unions, 99, 103
shop stewards, 52, 55, 63, 146; Movement, 53–4; role in Liverpool, 85, 101, 104, 106-7
Shore, Peter, 65
Short, Edward, 58
social wage, 25, 60, 63, 116, 143
socialism, 51, 149; practice of, 25
Socialist Campaign for a Labour Victory, 54
Socialist Charter, 54
South Yorkshire County Council, 34, 131, 143; Transport Policy, 58-60, 75
Southwark, 78, 99, 122, 123, 135, 138
Straw, Jack, 108

Thatcher, Margaret, 47, 68
Town and Country Planning Act (1971), 169n
Trade Disputes and Trade Unions Act (1927), 97
Trade Union (Amalgamations) Act (1964), 52
Trade Union Congress (TUC), 16, 25, 30, 32, 39, 62, 83, 85, 91, 92, 104, 117, 121, 129, 135, 137; Local Government Campaign Co-ordinating Committee (LGCCC), 119, 124; National Consultative Conference on the Rates Act, 123; Local Government Committee, (TUCLGC), 63, 88, 92, 115, 119, 120, 124, 132, 136
trade unions, 15-16, 30, 38; in Clay Cross, 57-8; and cuts, 61-4; national officers in Liverpool, 108-9; membership changes, 52, 53; and rate-capping, 135f
trades council, 30, 53, 63, 77, 92, 105; Liverpool, 97, 98, 103-4; Sheffield, 56, 99
Transport Act (1980), 73-4
Transport Act (1983), 73, 75-6
Transport and General Workers Union (TGWU), 54, 61, 74, 77, 99, 117, 120;
in Liverpool, 97, 100, 108, 139
Transport Supplementary Grant (TSG), 59-60
Treaty of Maastricht (1992), 16
Tyne and Wear Act (1976), 169n

unemployment, 15, 28, 30 passim, 62, 63, 64, 70, 81, 144, 147; uses of, 14, 43, 60, 85
Union of Construction Allied Trades and Technicians (UCATT), 54, 61, 139
United States of America, 16, 40, 42, 45
Upper Clyde Shipyard, 16, 47
Urban Development Corporation (UDC), 79-80

Wandsworth, 31, 76, 77, 103, 144
welfare state, 15, 17, 25, 41, 46, 143
Williams, Shirley, 48-9
Willis, Norman, 132
World Bank, 16

Young Chartists, 54
Aa

ABOUT THE AUTHOR

David Lowes has been active in labour movement politics for over thirty years. He has first-hand experience of the events described and draws on privileged access to trade union and private records.
He is currently engaged in daily struggles with a local authority in the north-west of England to resist the government's austerity measures.
He is the author of *The Anti-Capitalist Dictionary* (2006) and is a member of the Socialist History Society.